rh

# Transparent

# Lives

## Surveillance

## in Canada

**AU** PRESS
Athabasca University

*Editors:*

COLIN J. BENNETT,

KEVIN D. HAGGERTY,

DAVID LYON,

VALERIE STEEVES

Copyright © 2014

Colin J. Bennett, Kevin D. Haggerty, David Lyon, and Valerie Steeves

Published by AU Press, Athabasca University
1200, 10011 – 109 Street, Edmonton, AB T5J 3S8

ISBN 978-1-927356-77-7 (print)  978-1-927356-78-4 (PDF)  978-1-927356-79-1 (epub)
doi:10.15215/aupress/9781927356777.01

Cover and interior design by Marvin Harder, marvinharder.com
Printed and bound in Canada by Friesens

Library and Archives Canada Cataloguing in Publication

Transparent lives : surveillance in Canada / editors, Colin J. Bennett,
Kevin D. Haggerty, David Lyon, Valerie Steeves.

"The New Transparency Project."
Includes bibliographical references and index.
Issued in print and electronic formats.
ISBN 978-1-927356-77-7 (pbk.).—ISBN 978-1-927356-78-4 (pdf).—ISBN 978-1-927356-79-1 (epub)

1. Electronic surveillance—Canada. 2. Privacy, Right of—Canada. 3. Social control—
Canada. I. Bennett, Colin J. (Colin John), 1955-, editor of compilation II. Haggerty, Kevin D.,
editor of compilation III. Lyon, David, 1948-, editor of compilation IV. Steeves, Valerie M., 1959-,
editor of compilation

JC599.C3T73 2014          323.44'820971          C2013-908668-4
                                                                                  C2013-908669-2

This book has been published with the help of a grant from the Federation for the Humanities and
Social Sciences, through the Awards to Scholarly Publications Program, using funds provided by the
Social Sciences and Humanities Research Council of Canada. We acknowledge the financial support
of the Government of Canada through the Canada Book Fund (CBF) for our publishing activities.

Canadian    Patrimoine
Heritage    canadien

Assistance provided by the Government of Alberta, Alberta Multimedia Development Fund.

Alberta
Government

# Contents

# Preface

*Transparent Lives: Surveillance in Canada* details nine key trends in the processing of personal information, trends that are evident throughout the world. They affect all Canadians, but few citizens are aware of how, when, for what purpose, or with what consequences their personal data are used by large organizations. Hence the title: *Transparent Lives*. This book demonstrates that our lives are open and visible to organizations as never before and that in every area of life—as citizens, consumers, workers, and travellers—this makes a difference.

That difference is summed up in the subtitle of this book: *Surveillance in Canada*. By "surveillance," we mean *any systematic focus on personal information in order to influence, manage, entitle, or control those persons whose information is collected.* Whether we are claiming health benefits in the clinic, using our loyalty cards in the store, performing our daily duties in the workplace, checking our messages on a smartphone, or waiting in the security line to board a plane, our data are collected, stored, classified, revealed, or even sold to others in ways that may variously guide our purchases, channel our choices, delay our departure, ensure that we are fairly or unfairly treated, or reward or punish our behaviour.

As organizations become more digital, they seek more personal data in order to increase efficiency, productivity, oversight, and control. As organizations find that they save money or increase their appeal to clients through their digital efforts, they intensify their use of new technologies and techniques to identify specific categories of people so that different groups can be treated differently. For instance, loyalty cards reward repeat customers, welfare payments are tightly targeted, street cameras "see" minorities and youth disproportionately in urban areas, and customers seeking coffee can quickly learn where the nearest Starbucks is located.

In these examples, as in those used throughout this book, surveillance is understood as an organizational tool that has ambiguous consequences. It is not simply good or bad, helpful or harmful. At the same time, neither is it ever neutral. This volume shines a light on how key surveillance trends produce outcomes that call for care in using personal data, especially by those who process sensitive information but also by those whose data are disclosed on a daily—even moment-by-moment—basis. The book draws attention to urgent questions of privacy, fairness, and justice.

## What Are the Key Trends?

Trend 1: **Surveillance is expanding rapidly**. Our newly digital existence has dramatically multiplied possibilities for surveillance. This expansion is readily visible in the everyday lives of our children. Seeing how profoundly a young child is touched by surveillance makes it clear that the processing of personal data influences many routine aspects of life.

Trend 2: **The accelerating demand for greater security drives much surveillance.** This is obvious in, say, an airport, but it is also visible in policing and even in workplace monitoring. It is not clear, however, that such surveillance makes us safer.

Trend 3: **Public and private agencies are increasingly intertwined**. Where surveillance was once conducted mainly by government or policing agencies, outsourcing has brought for-profit organizations into the surveillance arena. Corporate gathering of personal data now outstrips that done by police and intelligence agencies. Personal data from commercial databases are now sought and processed by government, significantly increasing the amount of information that governments collect about their citizens.

Trend 4: **It is more difficult to decide what information is private and what is not**. Your name or social insurance number clearly identify you as an individual, but what about a group photo in which you appear that is later posted on Facebook or a picture taken by a traffic camera of your car licence plate number? Each can be used to identify or track you. And such identification can also be made through the combination of different forms of data.

Trend 5: **Mobile and location-based surveillance is expanding**. A growing number of organizations, from police to marketers, are interested in not only who you are (identification) and what you are doing (behaviour) but also *where* you are at any given moment. Our mobile devices make us more visible.

Trend 6: **Surveillance practices and processes are becoming globalized**. Canada is far from unique in experiencing rapid surveillance growth. In fact, much surveillance originates in broader international policy changes. Airlines, for example, operate with similar routines worldwide. How we deal with this depends on specifically Canadian traditions, laws, and cultures.

Trend 7:  **Surveillance is now embedded in everyday environments** such as cars, buildings, and homes. Increasingly, each of these basic elements of daily life features devices that recognize owners or users through technologies like voice activation or card swiping. Surveillance is thus becoming more pervasive and less perceptible.

Trend 8:  **The human body is increasingly a source of surveillance.** Fingerprinting, iris scanning, facial recognition, and DNA records are now commonly used to identify individuals. Our bodies become passwords, and delicate tracings of our body are sometimes seen as more reliable than our statements and stories.

Trend 9:  **Social surveillance is growing**. Social media have facilitated an explosion of digitally enabled people watching. This somewhat different trend raises troubling questions about privacy while making surveillance seem more normal and less exceptional.

## What Can Be Done?

We do not live in a police state. Canada has a fairly good track record of limiting unnecessary surveillance and promoting privacy, although in recent years, events such as the advent of no-fly lists and police access to personal data online have dented our reputation. Our privacy commissions (federal and provincial) are the envy of many countries, and individuals and agencies routinely question apparently egregious lapses in care with personal data in Canada.

*Transparent Lives* is concerned, above all, with unnecessary, excessive, and sometimes illegal processing of personal data. To oppose the growth of surveillance is to raise questions about abuses that often arise from the thoughtless extension of some legitimate surveillance to other areas. This is often referred to as "function creep" or even "mission creep." Although some general protections exist, the main forms of resistance to unwanted or unwarranted surveillance happen when a specific issue comes into the public spotlight. At that time, several different responses typically occur, each of which is valuable. Together, they can be formidable.

We have a number of assets to draw upon in meeting the challenges we face. Canadians have some strong protections under the Canadian Charter of Rights and Freedoms (1982); the federal Privacy Act (1982), which pertains to government; the Personal Information Protection and Electronic Documents Act (PIPEDA, 2004), which relates to commerce; and several provincial laws. The privacy commissioners at federal and provincial levels have been vigilant in their efforts to ensure that privacy laws are observed in spirit as well as letter. Privacy professionals and NGOs have buttressed the available protections and may also act as whistleblowers on specific issues. However, such protections can only be effective when supported by an informed and active citizenry. Ordinary citizens, along with educational initiatives, have a vital role to play in exposing and questioning surveillance and in pressing for privacy.

*Transparent Lives* demonstrates dramatically just how visible we have all become to myriad organizations and what this means—for better or for worse—for how we conduct our everyday lives. The irony is that as we have become more transparent to organizations, they have become less transparent to us. The politics of personal data involves making surveillance processes more visible to us so that we can engage democratically to seek fairness for all. Our hope is that this book will stimulate action toward greater accountability within organizations. In a digital age, data, especially personal data, are profoundly political.

# Acknowledgements

This book is the work of many people, each of whom is committed to its message and has agreed to trust the editors and their assistant with the final product. It is collaboratively written to maximize its reliability and collectively edited to ensure its readability. The main authors are Colin J. Bennett, Andrew Clement, Aaron Doyle, Kevin D. Haggerty, Stéphane Leman-Langlois, David Lyon, David Murakami Wood, Benjamin J. Muller, Laureen Snider, and Valerie Steeves. In addition, other professors, postdoctoral fellows, and graduate students contributed to some sections of the text, including the appendixes, and also suggested possible illustrations. These are Ciara Bracken-Roche, Art Cockfield, Alexander Cybulski, Ian McCuaig, Jeffrey Monaghan, Jonathan Obar, Caroline Pelletier, Sachil Singh, and Dan Trottier. A number of privacy and surveillance experts kindly ran their critical eyes over the manuscript: Robin Bayley, Jay Handelman, Peter Hope-Tindall, Philippa Lawson, Pierrot Péladeau, Blaine Price, Chris Prince, Roch Tassé, Micheal Vonn, and Yijun Yu. At Athabasca University Press, we were ably assisted by Pamela MacFarland Holway, Kathy Killoh, Morgan Tunzelmann, and Megan Hall. And the project simply would not have been possible without the editorial assistance of Anne Linscott and Emily Smith and the administrative help of Joan Sharpe in the Surveillance Studies Centre at Queen's University.

The New Transparency: Surveillance and Social Sorting, a multidisciplinary research program, is a Major Collaborative Research Initiative involving several Canadian universities as well as the Open University in the United Kingdom and is fully funded by the Social Sciences and Humanities Research Council of Canada (SSHRC). The research team examines a variety of different aspects of processing personal information in today's digital world (see www.sscqueens.org/projects/the-new-transparency/about/), but we have been committed from the start to offering back to Canadians the outcome of our investigations in an accessible format. We are grateful for the ongoing support of SSHRC, as well as for that of the entire "NewT" team and our partners, particularly the Office of the Privacy Commissioner and the International Civil Liberties Monitoring Group.

# Introduction

## How Canadian Lives Became Transparent to Watching Eyes

Today, our lives are transparent to others in unprecedented ways. In Canada, as elsewhere, many kinds of organizations watch what we do, keep tabs on us, check our details, and track our movements. Almost everything we do generates an electronic record: we cannot go online, walk downtown, attend a university class, pay with a credit card, hop on an airplane, or make a phone call without data being captured. Personal information is picked up, processed, stored, retrieved, bought, sold, exchanged. Our lives—or rather, those traces and trails of data, those fragments of reality to which our lives can be reduced—are visible as never before, to other individuals, to public and private organizations, to machines.

Do we care? Some shrug off this loss of privacy as an inevitable consequence of living in a digital world. Some say, "So what? In the days when people lived in villages and small towns, their lives were forever open to personal scrutiny. What we have today is just a new electronic form of the same kind of public knowledge of private lives." Others—in particular, those who use personal data to make money—dismiss any worries as misplaced. For example, as early as 1999, Scott McNealy of the giant computer company Sun Microsystems claimed, "You have zero privacy anyway. Get over it."[1] In 2010, Facebook's Mark Zuckerberg memorably declared: "People have really gotten comfortable not only sharing more information and different kinds, but more openly and with more people. That social norm is just something that has evolved over time."[2]

In what follows, we will see that such responses range from inadequate to wrong. Surveillance does matter. It confronts us with questions that will not go away and that cannot simply be shrugged off. Yes, surveillance has exploded in a digital world, but what are its actual effects? Do we know? Yes, people in villages knew that details of their lives were open to public scrutiny, but now it is large government and business organizations, not only our neighbours, that probe our lives, and they do so on a massive scale. Yes, systems like Sun Microsystems work to diminish privacy in some settings, but "zero privacy"? This assumes that systems are all-knowing and that people cannot resist, which is clearly not the case. Yes, social media help to push the privacy envelope, but the "social norm" is much more complex and consequential than Zuckerberg cares to think. These simplistic (not to mention self-serving) responses to a complex situation fail to grasp the personal, social, and political consequences of surveillance. As Canadian Internet guru Don Tapscott says, "With radical transparency, all of our identities and behaviours become flattened and observable by others—and we lose control."[3]

"The New Transparency," the title of the seven-year research project that prompted this book, was chosen to drive home the point that *we are visible to others as never before*.[4] The extent to which personal information is gathered, processed, and retained is unparalleled in human history—a fact that may produce feelings of discomfort or uncertainty about our own lives. I did not intend that photo to be seen by a potential employer, we may realize in hindsight. Why is this store asking for my phone number yet again? But the subtitle of the research project is "Surveillance and Social Sorting." This phrase is meant to spotlight not only our discomfort at being exposed—surveilled—but also a second issue: *What happens to us when our personal information is collected and used by others?* Having a sense of control over our public persona is vitally important, as are the ways in which we are profiled and categorized, because such processes have an impact on our life chances and choices. We are treated differently depending on our profiles, and such treatment, in turn, changes our present and our future. This is social sorting.

The "we" here refers to Canadians. Surveillance, of course, knows no national boundaries. But while similar processes occur in other countries, this book spotlights how surveillance is being augmented and intensified in Canada. And Canadians do care. For instance, more than half (55 percent) of Canadians polled in 2012 said that they object to police and intelligence services, even with a court order, obtaining information from content posted on social media sites. Two-thirds of Canadians polled in the same year disagreed with the statement that the "police and intelligence agencies should have more powers to ensure security even if it means Canadians have to give up some personal privacy safeguards."[5] And 90 percent object to companies like Google selling their information to others.[6] As surveillance spreads, Canadians need to know not just about specific and spectacular cases of privacy invasion or security breaches but also about the key trends in surveillance. We badly need a way to put our experiences, our anxieties, and our hopes about the treatment of personal data in context. And we need to communicate these trends to policy makers, technical experts, information officers, educators, and the like so that we all have a voice in shaping the future of digitally dependent Canada.

## What Is Surveillance?

Not long ago, the word *surveillance* conjured up a mental image of agents in trench coats with raised collars shadowing suspects through dingy streets or placing hidden bugs in the homes of their targets. Today, all that has changed. Not that such things no longer happen; they do. But surveillance is much, much broader than that. Bureaucracies have always, for the sake of efficiency and enlarged capacity, kept files and stored information on individuals. Now, computer and communication technologies take this much further. For instance, whereas yesterday's filing cabinets for paper documents created single silos of information that only a few could access, with today's searchable networked databases, information now grows and flows in ways that would have been unimaginable to the office clerks of yesteryear. And, today, information is easy to access: a few keywords and clicks, and—voilà!—entire biographies can be made to appear.

It does not stop there. It is not just that more personal information is circulating and is being used in new ways to promote today's political and economic priorities and to manage risk. In Canada, for example, novel ways of thinking about our border with the United States as a "security perimeter" have had concrete consequences: personal information now flows more freely south, the security of international trade is now a key purpose of security efforts, and risk-management criteria help to determine who is—and who is not—allowed to travel freely based on the radio frequency identification (RFID) tags embedded in passports or on the images collected from full-body scanners.

What happens to personal information is crucial, then. People with certain kinds of profiles "pass" with greater ease than others. And this is true not only at the border but also in the marketplace. Your frequent flyer card at the airport and your loyalty card in the supermarket are the visible tip of a hidden iceberg. If that iceberg were exposed, it would show a series of systems constantly busy collecting and sorting troves of data. At the airport, some Canadians discover that they are on a no-fly list (called "Passenger Protect" in Canada), while others can daydream their way through security checks.[7] On the phone to a customer service agent, some consumers discover that they are unexpectedly rewarded, while others cannot get past the "Your call is important to us . . ." holding position. Surveillance underlies all of these processes.

Surveillance today is not just a matter of tracking "bad" or "dangerous" people. Statistics and software together turn surveillance into a way of classifying people based on whatever personal data are available. Yesterday's target was a person; today's target is a profile. Yet, as we have seen, that profile packs a punch. You soon know if the profile associated with you is categorized as risky or reliable, one to be rewarded or rebuffed. But how did it happen? What information pushes your profile in one direction, not another? Surveillance was once literally "watching"; now, it is also "seeing with data." How those data are collected, manipulated, and acted on is pivotal.

So what exactly is surveillance? We define it as *any systematic focus on personal information in order to influence, manage, entitle, or control those whose information is collected*. Put this way, it is clear that surveillance can be good or bad, acceptable or not. But it is also clear that surveillance is more than peeping at, snooping, or eavesdropping on others. Surveillance is a dominant organizational practice that often results in people being categorized in ways that facilitate different forms of treatment for different individuals. From Google to Homeland Security, from Revenue Canada to the RCMP, this sort of surveillance is central. Perhaps we should say, this *sorting* of surveillance, because the big question is how we are socially sorted by surveillance today.

At the same time, the rapid expansion of many kinds of surveillance has prompted or facilitated its further growth in new directions.[8] Most of this volume is about surveillance by *organizations* that gather data on individuals and populations, profiling them for various purposes. However, ordinary individuals are engaging in an increasing amount of small-scale surveillance. They may set up home security systems, or install nanny cams (video cameras hidden in such things as teddy bears or clocks), or track others using social media (see Trend 9). Still others may try to "return the gaze" of organizations as they watch for abusive or illegal organizational practices. The decisive difference between individuals and organizations is the kind of power available to each. Even though ordinary Facebook users have access to the largest facial-recognition system in the world (Facebook's "tag sugges-tion"), they do not control the algorithms that classify people into groups for differential treatment. This is why the social sorting dimension, available primarily to large organizations, is vital for understanding contemporary surveillance.

Surveillance is now a ubiquitous and complex phenomenon. On the one hand, it is the routine way in which many organizations work, often with benign consequences. On the other hand, surveillance is a form of power that affects everyone, sometimes as identifiable individuals and sometimes as whole populations. Some groups are touched by surveillance more than others, but in all cases the balance of power between individuals and orga-nizations shifts with the growth of new surveillance practices and processes. So while surveillance may produce good or bad outcomes, it is never neutral. And the issues are far too important to leave to bureaucrats, politicians, or technical experts. In what follows, much of the focus is on the questionable aspects of surveillance, and we conclude with how we might rise to the new challenges before us.

### Surveillance in Canada: The Context

As in any country in the world, surveillance is vital to government and com-merce in Canada. Indeed, with its early commitment in the 1960s to high tech-nology and to the growth of an information infrastructure, as seen in the country's use of mainframe computers and its pan-Canadian telephone grid, Canada was a leader in processing personal information. Operational effi-ciency was seen as a key goal. From the beginning, however, it was also clear that socio-political values influenced how computerization occurred and thus how different groups were affected.[9] As early as 1940, the Dominion Bureau of Statistics (predecessor to Statistics Canada) used punch cards and sorting and tabulating machines for the National Registration process to determine who was "available" for conscription into the armed forces. Germans, Italians, Japanese, and Doukhobors were "ineligible," as were Chinese and Indian resi-dents.[10] Social sorting has increased and intensified since that time. Today, information technology (IT) enables more precise classification of groups, increases reliance on private sector companies, and facilitates and fosters the sharing of information within and between organizations.[11]

It must be said, too, that the need for regulation—for legal limits on data processing—was acknowledged from the start. Indeed, for many around the world, Canada is seen as a beacon when considering how personal data are protected and privacy is upheld. The Canadian network of privacy commissioners, who can receive and act on complaints, is the envy of many countries. Canadians have much to be grateful for in the commitment of government to protecting ordinary citizens from the risks and hazards of circulating personal data. Much progress has been made over several decades.

For example, data-protection provisions were introduced into the Canadian Human Rights Act in 1977; the Canadian Charter of Rights and Freedoms (1982) includes freedom from "unreasonable search and seizure," which has been interpreted to include protection for privacy; and the Québec Charter of Human Rights and Freedoms (section 5, 1976) says that "every person has a right to respect for his private life." The first Canadian Privacy Act was passed in 1983, regulating how the federal government uses, collects, and discloses personal information. In 2000, another federal law, the Personal Information Protection and Electronic Documents Act (PIPEDA) was passed, regulating the use of personal data in commercial contexts. It was fully in effect by 2004.

Other countries have been slower to act or have enacted weaker protections. For example, although the United States passed its Privacy Act in 1974, earlier than Canada did, it did not establish a specific body similar to the Office of the Privacy Commissioner of Canada, which was created in 1977 to monitor and oversee compliance with privacy legislation. Americans are directed to the courts with any complaints or charges arising from their privacy laws. Ontario also scored a first, establishing in 1988 the Ontario Information Privacy Commission (IPC), a body that oversees both privacy and freedom of information. Admittedly, some believe that this apparently contradictory dual mandate dilutes the impact of the IPC. At the federal level, another important provision requiring consent appeared in the 2000 PIPEDA legislation. This provision requires organizations to obtain consent of an individual when they collect, use, or disclose his or her personal information.

Canada, however, cannot rest on its laurels. Technology changes fast, but so do commercial and government practices. If one thinks of national security or, for that matter, of social media, challenges to personal-data handling have mushroomed beyond recognition since the year 2000. Airport security currently involves data gathering and profiling procedures—finger-printing, camera surveillance, electronic devices in passports—that would have been unthinkable in the late 1990s. And as for social media, who would have guessed that personal data would be so freely—some say recklessly—shared online, or that a company such as Facebook that makes its profits from selling the personal data of its users would produce the world's young-est billionaire in just a few short years?

If we look at what ordinary Canadians say, there is cause for concern. A survey conducted by the Globalization of Personal Data (GPD) Project in 2006 showed that a majority of Canadians not only care about their personal data but also take steps to protect themselves by, for example, reading privacy policies when making a purchase from a private company (49.4%) or refus-ing to give information to businesses when they do not believe it is necessary (77.1%)—and, in follow-up survey by Vision Critical in 2012, these figures had risen to 60 percent and 79 percent, respectively.[12] Canadians clearly know that privacy issues affect them.

More than half of Canadians simply trust government to look after their personal data properly. However, the GPD Project's landmark 2006 survey reported that less than half of the population is aware that there are laws to protect personal information (and this fell by a further 8 percent in the 2012 follow-up survey).[13] Only about a third of Canadians think that they have any control over what happens to their data. And almost all Canadians are apprehensive regarding the security of government-held data, sensing the potential for it to end up in private sector hands (slightly under one-half of Canadians surveyed trust companies to protect their data) or with foreign governments—as will happen, for instance, under new "perimeter security" border provisions that increase personal-data sharing with the United States. Canadians are also leery about national security. More than half of the 2006 survey respondents said that national security measures are intrusive (this remained steady in 2012), with many believing that the government should not share personal information with law enforcement unless people are sus-pected of wrongdoing. About 37 percent of Canadians are certain that visible minorities ought not to have extra security checks (although this proportion shrank somewhat in 2012).[14]

There are, of course, subtle—and at times not so subtle—differences between Québec and the rest of Canada. According to the 2006 survey cited above, Québécois are, by and large, more optimistic about the benefits of surveillance and show less concern about the collection and use of their personal information than residents of other Canadian provinces. Fewer worry about the possibility of a national ID card, for example, and a smaller proportion think that national-security surveillance measures are intrusive. In this, they sometimes have more in common with their counterparts in European countries, many of whom tend to be comparatively unalarmed by the rise in surveillance.

However, if polling results about surveillance and privacy are in any way indicative, Canadians do care about issues such as profiling. More than half of Canadians polled in 2006 and 2012 oppose targeting visible minorities at airports, for example. But when it comes to rewards from loyalty programs or selling marketing profiles of individuals, more than half of Canadians think that these kinds of social sorting practices are acceptable.[15] The difficulty here is that it is hard for pollsters to get at the issue of how people might be *negatively* affected by profiling done by marketers. Few citizens understand how some people may be marginalized in multiple ways as disadvantages stack up disproportionately for those rejected by advertisers, marketers, and service providers.[16]

## Surveillance in Canada: The Drivers

Part of the problem is that governments and corporations continue to build surveillance infrastructures faster than the public can learn about and debate the consequences. Why is surveillance growing so quickly? What pushes it forward and enables surveillance to seep into every imaginable space of our lives (and even into some we had not imagined)? Technology, law, politics, economy, culture, and our own perceptions and practices each play a part. There is no one dominant driving force behind the rapid expansion of surveillance in Canada. The combined pressures, however, originating at many levels and from many sources, propel the quest for more and more personal information. Some of this expansion seems relatively innocuous, while other aspects are downright egregious. Some is part of deliberate policy, whereas some is an unintended consequence of a legitimate or even desirable process. We discuss these matters later, but here we provide an overview of some of the causes behind the growth of surveillance in Canada.

The first driver is *technological potential.* Many tools have been developed over the past few decades that make systemic surveillance much easier. Because of the strong cultural belief, especially in North America, that technology is a key to solving social and political problems, adopting new high-tech management tools frequently prompts surveillance-based solutions.[17] This faith in technology is demonstrable: even though nontechnological solutions may exist, and even though technological solutions do not necessarily work in the ways claimed for them, the rate at which new technologies are embraced and deployed continues unabated.

This ties in tightly with the second driver, the *personal-information economy*.[18] Personal information is a commercial gold mine (Facebook went public in 2012, valued at $104 billion) and is also highly valued in government departments and in policing, intelligence, and security services. Personal information is often called the "oil" of the twenty-first century—and it may be salutary to think of the risks associated with that![19] More than twenty years ago, consumers rebelled when Lotus Corporation launched Household Marketplace, a system that would have tracked names, addresses, income levels, and number of children for every household in the United States.[20] Today, parallel activities are commonplace. A 2006 Canadian Internet Policy and Public Interest Clinic (CIPPC) report on Canadian "data brokers" illustrates "how detailed information about you gets into the hands of organizations with whom you have no relationship," because those same brokers are able to sell that information to commercial organizations and governments alike.[21] The authors conclude that "the increasing accumulation of personal data and consolidation of databases leaves individuals vulnerable to abuses by those with access to that data."[22]

The third driver is the turn toward *neoliberalism*, that is, governmental policies that stress free trade and deregulated markets. In its current form, neoliberalism emphasizes the economic role of the private as opposed to the public sector. From this perspective, the market may be relied on to ensure prosperity for all, thus reducing the primary task of the state to military and policing functions: law and order and security. The example of Lockheed Martin's contract with the Canadian government to provide both IT support and armaments, illustrates this trend well. Free-trade agreements between the United States and Canada encourage such economic interaction, but, at the same time, support for the security function spells profit for Canadian companies. However, the neoliberal state is sometimes less than liberal in how it works to reshape people's outlooks, expectations, and choices through surveillance. For example, legitimate protest may be redefined as subversive or even terrorist activity, as the actions of environmental groups are portrayed by the Canadian Integrated Terrorism Assessment Centre.[23]

Closely related to neoliberalism is a widespread emphasis on *risk management,* the fourth driver. For decades, and especially since the 1980s, Canada has relied heavily on statistical analyses of risk to guide public policy. Because so much uncertainty surrounds normal life, from accidents and disasters to financial failure or project collapse, government and related businesses need tools to mitigate or minimize risk while maximizing opportunity. But information is required to find out what the risks are, which is where surveillance comes in. A landmark study of Canadian police, for example, shows that policing was transformed in the late twentieth century by new technologies designed to identify and track risk. To perform this function, police use surveillance to watch people and then categorize them according to the level of risk they might pose.[24] Once again, social sorting is the other side of the surveillance coin here. Proving one's "innocence" becomes less easy for individuals falling into the wrong category, because the default position is suspicion of guilt until the system proves otherwise.

Such emphases also show up in the fifth driver, *national security.* Although organizations responsible for this task were already expanding in the twentieth century, responses to the attacks of 9/11 gave them a tremendous boost. The logic of risk management holds here, too. Travellers, in particular, have become acutely aware that the demands of national security require us to remove shoes, discard liquids, and display laptops. Increasingly, however, this involves surveillance of bodies as well as baggage. Have you ever noticed the sheer number of ceiling cameras above you as you pass through the security check at the airport? The Canadian Air Transport Security Authority operates these cameras as well as the now familiar body scanners. More importantly, well before departure, passenger data are used to track our movements. But the national security driver is both more and less than "national." It relies on a network of participating countries that increasingly functions beyond the control of the Canadian government (see Trend 6). And it also justifies watchful eyes in many other areas—such as urban space, sports arenas, and schools—now deemed to have "security" dimensions.

The sixth driver is *public perceptions* that permit or proscribe new developments in surveillance. While it is clear, as noted earlier, that a large proportion of Canadians are cautious, if not negative, about the extensive reach of surveillance—recall that a steady 60 percent think that security surveillance is intrusive—others reluctantly or resignedly accept more and more monitoring. This is significant. It is easier to introduce new surveillance measures if people are inclined to accept them. The climate of fear that characterizes Canadian life, especially since 9/11, inclines many to accept more surveillance.[25] But equally important, acclimatizing ourselves to commercial surveillance online seems to make many more sanguine about surveillance in other areas.[26] Clearly, though, if citizens dislike new measures—as was shown when an unprecedented 145,000-plus signed an online petition against "lawful access" provisions in Bill C-30 that would require Internet service providers and others to pass subscriber data to police without a warrant—the powers-that-be take notice.[27]

The seventh driver is *new laws* that allow or require surveillance or relax legal limits to surveillance. Privacy laws are increasingly put under pressure to provide exemptions for law enforcement. The "lawful access" provisions that were proposed for Bill C-30, as mentioned above, are a glaring example. Ann Cavoukian, Ontario's information and privacy commissioner, called the bill "one of the most invasive threats to our privacy and freedom that I have ever encountered."[28] But similar threats arise even within the current laws. For example, if an organization can demonstrate basic compliance with privacy principles, it can legally pursue surveillance practices with impunity. For instance, since 1997, the so-called Business Transformation Project has been used to reduce "welfare fraud" in Ontario, using several surveillance tools, such as "consolidated verification procedures," that check eligibility for social assistance every twelve months. This reduces the time that caseworkers can spend with their low-income clients and increases the demands on those clients to justify their daily activities. No one suggests that Ontario welfare agencies are contravening privacy laws when they share information with other government agencies, but the negative discrimination produced through their activities—especially against single mothers—is well documented.[29]

## Surveillance in Canada: The Trends

The best way to grasp the magnitude of surveillance changes affecting Canadians is to look at the general trends. This book examines nine key trends of surveillance—all of them large-scale changes that are accelerating faster than ever. In fact, under current conditions, it is difficult to recall just how things used to be before 9/11 or social media. The surveillance story can be told largely as a before-and-after tale. Once, Lotus Corporation—the major corporation that attempted to launch the tracking system of names, addresses, income levels, and numbers of children in individual US households—was forced to reverse policy when consumers objected to its "Orwellian" data-collection project. Now, social media users disclose far more revealing details to a broad array of corporations with every click of the mouse. Once, you could cross the Canada-US border with no more than a driver's licence. Now, your scrutinized personal data make the trip ahead of you, and you need an "enhanced" licence or a passport to make it past immigration control. And so on. Each of the trends discussed in this book explains how different influences interact to magnify surveillance. Each of the trends examined has profound impacts on social life, freedom, and justice in twenty-first-century Canada.

The discussion of the first trend, *surveillance expansion,* details some dimensions of the spread of surveillance, demonstrating that practices once considered one-time novelties are now routine and taken for granted. The second trend, *securitization and surveillance*, relates to the "security" driver: more areas of life are labelled risky and thus require surveillance for security. What is less and less clear, as illustrated by the third trend, *the blurring of sectors,* is who conducts this surveillance, because public and private agencies each play a role in often complementary or interacting ways. Such blurring is also characteristic of the fourth trend, *the growing ambiguity of personal information*. But while what counts as personally identifiable data becomes less clear, what is increasingly clear is that surveillance grows despite the ambiguities.

While personal data may be more ambiguous, there is nothing uncertain about the fact that surveillance is no longer just about who you are and what you are doing but also about *where* you are. *Expanding mobile and location-based surveillance* is the fifth trend. Moreover, you will be likely to encounter similar kinds of surveillance in different parts of the world: the sixth trend is *the globalization of surveillance.* But it, too, is complex because local cultures and conditions mean that people experience surveillance differently. Surveillance in Canada is deeply affected by global trends, but it is filtered through Canadian law, traditions, and cultures. The seventh trend, *the embedding of surveillance in everyday environments,* indicates that surveillance is increasingly ubiquitous and embedded in objects such as cars, buildings, and homes. But this ubiquity is not limited to objects; there is now *increasing surveillance in the body,* the eighth trend, because of the daily ways in which our bodies are treated as data sources, from our fingerprints or DNA to the way we walk.

The ninth trend, *growing social surveillance*, is in some ways the most recent, but it is undeniably proving highly significant. Although people watching people is nothing new, it is now tremendously enhanced by social media. As a trend, it is extraordinary. From postwar worries about Big Brother, the overbearingly vigilant tyrant, through the domestication of surveillance in the consumer scrutiny of database marketing, we have come full circle and now monitor each other. Of course, in surveillance terms, this is small potatoes compared with the power of what Google or the Canadian Security Intelligence Service (CSIS) can do. Nevertheless, could carrying out such small-scale surveillance ourselves foster the further acceptance of all kinds of surveillance as "normal"?

## Where Do We Go from Here?

The trends described in *Transparent Lives: Surveillance in Canada* paint a striking picture. Together, they show that even though much surveillance has positive outcomes, overall, as surveillance increases, the balance of power between individuals and organizations tilts perilously toward organizations. So how much can we trust these authorities, government or commercial, as they watch us constantly? How accountable are they with our personal data? Beyond simply analyzing these trends, then, we set out some conclusions, together with policy responses and specific recommendations. We hope that, most importantly, this book will stimulate urgent public debate at many levels.

## Notes

1   See Polly Sprenger, "Sun on Privacy: 'Get Over It,'" *Wired,* 26 January 1999, http://www.wired.com/politics/law/news/1999/01/17538.

2   See the interview with Zuckerberg by Marshall Kirkpatrick, "Facebook's Zuckerberg Says the Age of Privacy Is Over," *ReadWrite,* 9 January 2010, http://www.readwriteweb.com/archives/facebooks_zuckerberg_says_the_age_of_privacy_is_ov.php.

3   Don Tapscott, "Is Privacy an Outmoded Idea in the Digital Age?" *Toronto Star,* 1 June 2012, http://www.thestar.com/news/insight/article/1204668--don-tapscott-on-privacy-in-a-digital-ageis-privacy-in-the-digital-age-an-outmoded-idea/.

4   For more about The New Transparency research project, see http://www.sscqueens.org/projects/the-new-transparency.

5   Frank Graves, "An Increasingly Divided Outlook: Rethinking Canada's Place in the World," presentation to the 2012 Walter Gordon Symposium in Public Policy, School of Public Policy and Governance, University of Toronto, 20 March 2012, available from EKOS Politics, http://www.ekospolitics.com/wp-content/uploads/2012_walter_gordon_symposium_presentation.pdf.

6   The Globalization of Personal Data Project, International Survey on Privacy and Surveillance, http://qspace.library.queensu.ca/handle/1974/7656. See also Elia Zureik, L. Lynda Harling Stalker, Emily Smith, David Lyon, and Yolande E. Chan, eds., *Surveillance, Privacy, and the Globalization of Personal Information: International Comparisons* (Montréal and Kingston: McGill-Queen's University Press, 2010).

7   On Public Safety Canada's Passenger Protect program, see http://www.passengerprotect.gc.ca/home.html.

8   See the discussion of the varieties of surveillance in Charles Raab and Colin J. Bennett, *The Governance of Privacy: Policy Instruments in Global Perspective* (Cambridge, MA: MIT Press, 2006), 23–26.

9   See, for example, Michael Adler and Paul Henman, "Computerizing the Welfare State," *Information, Communication and Society* 8, no. 3 (2005): 315–42.

10  See Scott Thompson, "Consequences of Categorization: National Registration, Surveillance and Social Control in Wartime Canada, 1939–1946" (PhD diss., University of Alberta, 2013).

11  Kenneth Kernaghan and Justin Gunraj, "Integrating Information Technology into Public Administration," *Canadian Public Administration / Administration publique du Canada* 47, no. 4 (2004): 525–46.

12  Vision Critical is a division of the Vancouver-based polling company Angus Reid Global. For the 2006 statistics, see "The Globalization of Personal Data Project: An International Survey on Privacy and Surveillance—Summary of Findings, November 2008," http://qspace.library.queensu.ca/bitstream/1974/7660/1/2008_Surveillance_Project_International_Survey_Findings_Summary.pdf, 14–15. See also The Globalization of Personal Data (GPD) Project, International Survey on Privacy and Surveillance, http://qspace.library.queensu.ca/handle/1974/7656; and, for an analysis of the international findings of the 2006 survey, see Zureik et al., eds., *Surveillance, Privacy, and the Globalization of Personal Information*. For the 2012 statistics, see Angus Reid Global, "Privacy and Surveillance: June 2012 Globalization of Personal Data Follow-Up" (Vancouver: Angus Reid Global, 2012), http://qspace.library.queensu.ca/handle/1974/8623, table 71. This report is distributed by the Data and Government Information Centre, Queen's University; the tables can be downloaded at the URL provided.

13  "The Globalization of Personal Data Project," 11; Angus Reid Global, "Privacy and Surveillance," table 29.

14  "The Globalization of Personal Data Project," 13, 26, and 33; Angus Reid Global, "Privacy and Surveillance," tables 33 and 44.

15  "The Globalization of Personal Data Project," 33–34; Angus Reid Global, "Privacy and Surveillance," table 44.

16  See Oscar Gandy, *Coming to Terms with Chance: Engaging Rational Discrimination and Cumulative Disadvantage* (Farnham, UK: Ashgate, 2009); and Joseph Turow, *The Daily You: How the New Advertising Industry Is Defining Your Identity and Your Worth* (Princeton: Princeton University Press, 2012).

17  Regarding the belief in the efficacy of technology, see, for example, Vincent Mosco, *The Technological Sublime* (Cambridge, MA: MIT Press, 2004); and Arthur Kroker, *Technology and the Canadian Mind* (Montréal: New World Perspectives, 1984).

18   It's not clear who coined this phrase, but it is used, for example, by Perri 6, "The Personal Information Economy: Trends and Prospects for Consumers," in *The Glass Consumer: Life in a Surveillance Society*, ed. Susanne Lace (Bristol, UK: Policy Press, 2005); and by Greg Elmer, *Profiling Machines; Mapping the Personal Information Economy* (Cambridge, MA: MIT Press, 2004).

19   See, for example, Mike Klein, "Major Trends for Enterprise IT: Information Will Be Oil of 21st Century, Gartner Says," *WTN News*, 19 October 2010, http://wtnnews.com/articles/7897/.

20   See Denise Caruso, "Digital Commerce: Personal Information Is Like Gold in the Internet Economy," *New York Times,* 1 March 1999, http://www.nytimes.com/1999/03/01/business/technology-digital-commerce-personal-information-like-gold-internet-economy-rush.html.

21   See Canadian Internet Policy and Public Interest Clinic (CIPPIC), *On the Data Trail: How Detailed Information About You Gets into the Hands of Organizations with Whom You Have No Relationship—a Report on the Canadian Data Brokerage Industry* (Ottawa: CIPPIC, 2006), www.cippic.ca/sites/default/files/May1-06/DatabrokerReport.pdf.

22   Ibid., ii.

23   See Carys Mills, "Terrorism Monitor Closely Watched Occupy Protests," *Globe and Mail*, 10 April 2012, http://www.theglobeandmail.com/news/national/terrorism-monitor-closely-watched-occupy-protests/article4098990/. For a broader analysis, see Didier Bigo, "Security, Surveillance and Democracy," in *Routledge Handbook of Surveillance Studies,* ed. Kirstie Ball, Kevin Haggerty, and David Lyon (London and New York: Routledge, 2012), 277–84; and David Garland, *The Culture of Control* (Chicago: University of Chicago Press, 2001).

24   Richard Ericson and Kevin Haggerty, *Policing the Risk Society* (Toronto: University of Toronto Press, 1997), 449.

25   See, for example, David Lyon, *Surveillance After September 11* (Cambridge, UK: Polity Press, 2003).

26   The 2012 Vision Critical survey shows that about 50 percent of those polled, whether social media users or not, agreed that employers should be able to use social media to check on employees (Angus Reid Global, "Privacy and Surveillance," table 38). Does such broad acceptance of surveillance suggest that similar attitudes would prevail in other areas, such as national security surveillance?

27   See Laura Payton, "Online Surveillance Bill Opponents Continue Campaign," *CBC News*, 24 May 2012, http://www.cbc.ca/news/politics/story/2012/05/24/pol-lawful-access-c-30-campaign.html.

28   Ann Cavoukian, *Ever Vigilant*, 2011 annual report of the Information and Privacy Commissioner of Ontario, Toronto, http://www.ipc.on.ca/english/Resources/Annual-Reports/Annual-Reports-Summary/?id=1193.

29   See, for example, Krystle Maki, "Neoliberal Deviants and Surveillance: Welfare Recipients Under the Watchful Eye of Ontario Works," *Surveillance and Society* 9, no. 1 (2011): 47–63.

# Expanding Surveillance
## From the Atypical to the Routine

Surveillance is consistently front-page news, and it raises some of the most pressing social, political, and ethical questions of our day. At the same time, surveillance is not new. Interpersonal face-to-face scrutiny is an inherent attribute of human coexistence, and organizations also have a long history of using surveillance for various purposes.[1] However, we are at a historic turning point in terms of the expansion, intensification, and integration of surveillance measures.[2] There is simply more surveillance occurring today, and the surveillance systems we now use have unprecedented abilities to see more, penetrate deeper, and forge more novel connections than has ever been the case in the past. This expansion and intensification is perhaps the most notable and unsettling development in the dynamics of surveillance and monitoring.

Two examples drawn from different institutional settings help to illustrate the scope of contemporary surveillance. The first comes from the business world and concerns the company Acxiom. An international data aggregator, Acxiom collects personal information about people, including Canadians, from different sources, which it then sells to corporations and political groups that use it for marketing and campaigning. The information that Acxiom collects is extremely diverse, including data as familiar as name, address, and telephone number. The company also amasses and sells more sensitive data, such as marital status, family status, age, ethnicity, the value of your home, what you read, the type of car you drive, what you order over the phone or Internet, where you vacation, your hobbies, any history of mental illness you might have, your patterns of alcohol consumption, and so on. Even before the advent of social media, the quantity of information held by Acxiom was immense—roughly equivalent to a stack of King James Bibles fifty thousand miles high.[3] Given the popularity of applications like Facebook, which have revolutionized the amount of personal data available to aggregators and other organizations, that amount now massively under-represents the volume of data that Acxiom processes.[4]

The second example pertains to the collection and analysis of intelligence information from electronic sources such as cellphones and the Internet for national security purposes. Since the terrorist attacks of 9/11, Canada and the United States have increased the amount of intelligence sharing between our countries. Although the process remains highly secretive, we get occasional glimpses of the almost unimaginable amount of information that is being collected. James Bamford reports that by 2015, the American National Security Agency expects to be processing information at the astounding level of the yottabyte: ten-to-the-power-of-24 bytes.[5] Translated to the print world, this equals one septillion—that is, one trillion trillion—pages of text. In 2011, the combined space *of all computer hard drives in the world* did not amount to one yottabyte.

These two illustrations involve surveillance conducted with the aid of computers, often referred to as "dataveillance." To further round out the surveillance picture, however, one would also have to include technologies such as video cameras, drones, drug testing, automated licence plate readers, smartphones, and biometrics (that is, technologies that identify individuals on the basis of a biological characteristic). The most familiar way to identify someone through biometrics is fingerprinting, but biometric systems can now identify people based on their DNA, facial structure, hand geometry, voice, way of walking, and eye retina or iris patterns. Together, all of these phenomena are producing, and will continue to produce, sweeping transformations in almost every realm of existence, including commerce, warfare, science, international security, health, child care, work, and the formal and informal mechanisms we use to encourage people to conform to societal expectations and follow societal rules (often collectively called "social control").

Not long ago, we might have believed that surveillance was confined to the world of espionage or directed primarily at criminals. Such assumptions were never particularly accurate given the long-standing use of surveillance in realms such as work and commerce, but today, it is easier to recognize that surveillance has become an inescapable reality for almost everyone. Being monitored is increasingly the trade-off for reduced prices or improved services. It is also not just a visual phenomenon, since monitoring now involves the massive use of electronic data. In fact, many of us provide some of this data willingly because doing so makes our lives more convenient. The following hypothetical vignette provides a glimpse into how surveillance has become a part of the everyday routine for both Canadians and others in industrialized societies.

## A Day in the Life of a Nine-year-old: Farah

Farah crushes the bedcovers around her head, postponing her morning march through breakfast and homework. Her eyes snap open as she remembers today's plans. Today, she will receive what is perhaps a preadolescent's most desired technology and will find herself winging her way to another country. Were she attuned to such things, she might also recognize that her day will demonstrate how visible her life and the lives of those around her have become.

She slides out of bed forty minutes before her older brother Kay's alarm clock is set to pound in the adjacent room. Gazing out the window, Farah catches the eye of her elderly neighbour, Mrs. Krupp, who returns her wave. She and Farah became acquainted at the park, where Mrs. Krupp is one of a handful of adults who watch over the kids as they tear around the play structure.

Farah's family moved to this Mississauga neighbourhood eighteen months ago. They bought this house because it is on a direct bus route to her mom's job at a small computer software company. Her father, a physics professor at the University of Toronto, has had to resign himself to battling the traffic several times a week to get downtown.

Today, her dad is already at work, but Farah does not want to wake her mom. By habit, she avoids the creaky floorboards that her parents use to note when she climbs out of bed. Recently, though, they have been less vigilant, because two months ago her mom had a new baby, Bruno. Born prematurely, Bruno had to stay in the hospital for several weeks while physicians ran tests for blood gas analysis, took chest X-rays, and conducted regular cardio-respiratory monitoring. During the pregnancy, Farah's parents became accustomed to a high degree of medical scrutiny, given that her mom is over forty, which made her pregnancy more high risk. Consequently, Farah was often left with Mrs. Krupp while her mom went to the hospital for a raft of tests to ensure that there were no genetic anomalies and that the baby was developing according to standard norms.

Shortly before the birth, her mom had come home with a three-dimensional ultrasound image of Bruno. Farah's parents had immediately posted the picture on her mom's Facebook page among hundreds of pictures of Farah and her older brother. Everyone calls it Bruno's "first picture," but Farah doesn't think it looks anything like him—or anyone else. She hasn't spent a lot of time inspecting it, since she finds it kind of creepy.

That was also around the time that her dad set up the baby things, including a crib, right in Farah's room. Clipped to the side of the crib is a new baby monitor. It allows her parents to hear Bruno, but it also has a camera connected to the Wi-Fi system, which means they can see him on their computer or smartphone from anywhere in the world. The device has night vision and zoom capability, can measure temperature and humidity, and can detect whether the baby is moving around. It even has a speaker that her parents can use to talk to Bruno remotely. Farah has wondered whether her parents use it to see and hear her as well.

Tiptoeing downstairs, she thinks how nice it is not to stumble over the clothes and computer cables that usually litter the floor. Her dad, although exhausted, has made a special effort to keep the house uncharacteristically tidy. Farah thinks he does this because of the community health nurse who has visited their home on a couple of occasions to ensure that Bruno and her mom are doing well, a visit that includes monitoring for signs of postpartum depression or psychosis. Her parents appreciate the concern but are still uncomfortable with how the nurse scans the front room and kitchen for signs that something might be awry. Hence her dad's out-of-the-ordinary cleaning efforts.

When Farah's brother Kay wakes up, he will dash off to an early soccer practice, which means that she can play on the computer undisturbed. She enjoys the free online games and does not linger over the implications of their terms of use, which include giving the manufacturers, among other things, permission to collect information on her physical location and phone number and to view the status of the family's Wi-Fi. She is completely oblivious to the fact that national security agencies use online games to capture personal information. When she logs onto her favourite game the manufacturer also records the minutiae of her online behaviour, which it uses for product development

**Highly desirable targets for corporate data collection: children** (Source: © iStockphoto.com/Brzi)

and target marketing. The company also sells the data to other corporations eager to learn as much as possible about the consumption patterns of children. The games that Farah plays include personality questionnaires and consumer surveys. By completing the surveys, kids earn extra game points or privileges.

But right now, Farah is hungry. While making breakfast, she notices that the cereal box advertises a contest for tickets to a concert by her favourite boy band. Farah makes a mental note to ask her mom to enter for her. It will require her to go to the company's website and key in a unique product code from the cereal box. The personal information that she must also provide, when combined with the product code, gives the cereal company precise data about the family's lifestyle and consumption patterns and contributes

## Video Games "See" into Players' Living Rooms

Video game manufacturers are racing to provide ever more realistic gaming experiences that allow players to perform natural physical movements—for example, dancing or jumping to control a character in a game rather than pressing a series of buttons on a video game controller. The trade-off is that while such games are more immersive because they make natural movements part of play, they are also more invasive since these seeing devices are analyzing gamers' bodies, behaviours, and environments and thus capitalizing on a rich source of personal information.

One video game system that has used this novel technology is Microsoft's Xbox 360. Microsoft's Internet-connected video game system, released in 2005, uses a service known as Xbox LIVE to let users play games with others online, purchase games from a digital marketplace, and keep track of their gaming statistics using digital trophies known as "achievements."

Although the Xbox 360 has a variety of accessories, including a microphone for voice chat and a webcam for video streaming, its most interesting attachment is the Kinect, a sensor released in 2010 that can "see" a player's body and distinguish it from furniture and even other people. The Kinect projects infrared light onto the space in front of the device. That light is reflected back by human bodies to an infrared sensitive camera on the Kinect, which tracks movement

to a form of target marketing that is becoming more focused because of the greater ability to connect this information with personal data culled from other aspects of customers' lives.

After brushing her teeth, Farah checks her Facebook account. She is officially too young to have such an account, but she and most of her friends lied about their age when registering and are now regular users. Every bit of information that Farah reveals about herself on Facebook—every event, song, or show that she "likes," every status update and every picture— becomes part of the enormous data warehouse that the company sells to third parties. In the event of an emergency, police and security officials would also have access to the information on her page. Today, however, not much is happening, except that her friend Josh is bragging about his new toy car. Because he identifies the toy manufacturer by name, his comments will be automatically culled by firms that conduct online "data scrapes," invisibly amassing and combining the comments of thousands of users about particular topics, products, or services. These firms then sell these data to companies

and translates players' bodily movements into the game world. The Kinect has proven so vital to Microsoft's business strategy in video game systems that the device will be included in successor versions of the Xbox.

This seeing capacity of the Kinect is also used to monitor emotional responses to marketing. Should Farah or her brother, or any real-world child, decide to watch a video or television program through the Xbox 360, the Kinect plays an advertisement called a "NUad" prior to the video. During this commercial, the system monitors users' reactions to see if they are paying attention to the advertisement. Microsoft then sells this data and those from millions of other users—including players' age, race, and gender gathered by the Kinect and Xbox LIVE, along with information about player behaviour during the commercial—to advertisers for market research. Microsoft has also patented the ability to use the Kinect to prevent people from breaking "terms of use" rules that govern how many people might watch a video or play a video game. For example, if the Kinect senses more people watching a video than are allowed under such rules, it will turn the video off. Does Microsoft have every right to enforce these rules, or is the increasing potential for sensing technologies to enforce digital rights management in physical space blurring the boundaries between Microsoft's corporate and marketing policies, on the one hand, and the living rooms of its customers, on the other?

---

eager to read citizens' candid comments about products or policies. These same firms also collect online comments about people's views on policies and social issues, which they sell to political strategists.

As her best friend, Ariel, is not yet allowed on Facebook, Farah uses Gmail to send Ariel a funny picture of the family's dog. Again, although the rules for Gmail say that they are too young to have an account, Farah and all of her friends just lied about their age when registering. What she does not know is that when she communicates by email, her correspondence is subjected to different levels of automated scrutiny by global security agencies that monitor the flow of email. Should she contact suspicious people or use specific words or word combinations, her correspondence could be flagged for still greater scrutiny and follow-up by security officials. Her father often observes that, as a nuclear physicist educated in Iran, it is likely that his and all other family members' messages are routinely read.

Stepping out the door, Farah contemplates how different things look on this warm spring day compared to the image of their street on Google Street

View, which was taken in January. She only learned about Street View last week when she saw a car driving downtown with a camera sticking out of its roof. Kay then showed her some of the pictures of their neighbourhood streets available on Google's mapping system. He was particularly eager to find the image of their friend Lani (with his face blocked out) playing with his dog in his front yard.

When Farah arrives at school, her image is captured by one of the video cameras that monitor each entranceway. The cameras were installed a few months ago by the school principal after a spate of graffiti appeared on the school walls.*

Farah hurries to her classroom because today is standardized-test day and she is anxious to do well. Her brother's poor test scores have restricted his ability to enrol in his preferred high school courses, and she does not want to end up in Kay's situation. Farah's test scores will become part of her official educational dossier, which will accompany her at least until adulthood. The standardized-test scores are also used to assess teacher performance, and, in an increasingly competitive schooling environment, they have become a central means by which schools promote themselves and parents assess educational options.

With the tests done, everyone rushes outside for recess, where teachers and a security-screened parent volunteer watch over them. Josh is showing off his new toy, pointing out that what makes the car particularly cool is that it contains a small video camera. When at home, he roars the car around his house and it records what it sees; he has already downloaded the video onto a computer. He has also used it to spy on his brother and to film the car stalking his apprehensive cat (which is implanted with a machine-readable microchip for identification purposes). Josh is disappointed that the girls are not particularly impressed since several own a "Video Barbie," a doll that also has a working video camera.

---

* In some American jurisdictions, children are required to wear ID cards equipped with radio frequency identification (RFID) chips that regulate access to parts of the school, produce automated attendance reports, and inform school officials exactly where every child is within the school at all times. Some schools, given concerns about childhood obesity, also require that students have their body mass documented as part of their health program. Cameras in classrooms and halls are common, and more schools are requiring children to pass through metal detectors. Several Canadian school authorities are contemplating introducing some variation of such initiatives.

Farah's brother will buy his lunch in the cafeteria today with cash, but his money may not work here for much longer. A major international trend in schooling is to require students to pay for snacks or meals using electronic vouchers verified by a biometric identifier, such as a fingerprint or an iris scan. These systems eliminate the headache of handling cash and have the added benefit of allowing parents to monitor the purchases made on their child's account. Parents can even specify items, such as candy or fried food, that the system will not let their kids buy.

Farah returns to school and chats briefly with Mrs. Krupp, who is accompanied by Constable Garza, the police officer who works out of the adjacent high school. Constable Garza serves as a role model and provides security, in part by cultivating an informal network of informants among the kids.

In class, Farah works on the school computers. As she visits different websites, her online behaviour is automatically monitored by electronic "cookies," which track return visits and help to account for the increasingly targeted web advertisements that appear on her screen. Teachers keep a close eye to ensure that the kids do not visit inappropriate sites. Their vigilance is supplemented by the school's computer software, which tracks students' surfing behaviour, blocks them from sites deemed inappropriate, and produces automated reports on their online activity.

As the day progresses, Farah can barely contain her excitement about the fact that this evening her family will fly to Tehran to visit her extended family. Farah has often been on airplanes, but this is the first time that she has paid attention to the paperwork involved in international travel. She watched her dad apply for a visa and check the expiration dates on everyone's passports. She also heard her parents complain about having to rush to get baby Bruno a passport, which involved the comic ordeal of trying to cajole a newborn into meeting Passport Canada's standardized rules for how people must look on their passport photograph.

Both parents are waiting for her with an early birthday gift when Farah gets home. She already knows that her parents have acquiesced and bought her the smartphone she has been pestering them for. Initially, they were opposed to the idea of a ten-year-old having a cellphone, but they changed their minds as they learned more about the smartphone's location-tracking abilities. They have already installed software on the phone that will allow them to pinpoint Farah's physical location and follow her movements. Her parents have also eased their minds about the online risks to kids by installing a popular software program that allows them to access all of Farah's email and text messages and to see who she has phoned and which websites she has visited.

Kay arrives home complaining that *he* was not allowed to have a phone at Farah's age. An exceptional athlete, Kay trains every day in the hope of making Canada's youth soccer team. Should he be selected, he will be subjected to random blood and urine tests.*

Everyone makes final preparations for the trip. Since the introduction of new security measures after the 9/11 terrorist attacks, Farah's dad has become obsessed about arriving at the airport extra early. Given his profession, his Iranian heritage, and the fact that he travels frequently to the Middle East, he worries that the prescreening of passengers might inadvertently place him on a no-fly list. Having the common Iranian last name of Farad compounds the possibilities for mistaken identity, so he leaves plenty of time to sort things out should there be any confusion.

The taxi arrives and Farah's mom sets the house alarm. Her parents have had an alarm all of Farah's life, but they recently upgraded to a service that monitors for intruders, fire, carbon monoxide, and flooding. There are also cameras on the entrances that can be watched from a computer or smartphone anywhere on earth provided there is an Internet connection. On a recent trip to Turkey, her dad used his phone to watch the kids leave for school while he himself was in his hotel room overlooking the Bosporus.

As Farah's family cram into the taxi, they are photographed by a tiny camera near the windshield. Images of the cab driving to the airport are also captured by overhead traffic cameras. To avoid the rush-hour congestion, the driver veers onto the electronic toll road. Elevated sensors connect with the taxi's transponder, an electronic device that allows the toll company to automatically identify each vehicle as soon as it enters the toll road so the toll fee can be calculated. Farah's dad never bothered to install a transponder on the family car, so when he drives on this road, an advanced automated number plate recognition system scans his licence plate and processes a bill.

At the terminal, Farah's dad pays for the taxi using his credit card. That transaction record then becomes one small part of his overall financial profile and also feeds into his credit rating. Everyone unloads the luggage under the gaze of police officers and the security cameras that pervade the airport.

---

* Some American schools require every child who wants to participate in extracurricular sports to be drug tested.

Some of these cameras are so sophisticated that they can read the text messages on Farah's new phone from a distance. But they will soon be replaced by cameras that contain microphones, which will enable security officials to surreptitiously listen to and record personal conversations.

Farah's dad collects their boarding passes from the automated kiosk and surrenders the family's travel documents to an agent. A sniffer dog ambles past as they heave their luggage onto the conveyor belt. Bruno is fussy in the snaking security line, prompting Farah's mom and dad to discuss whether this year they should sign up for the Nexus program, which would provide them with an express route through security. This would require a processing fee and the surrendering to border service officials of even more details about themselves—their work history, travel patterns, and any criminal records they might have.

At the front of the line, their documents are checked again as they feed their hand luggage into the X-ray machine. Everyone then strides through the metal detector, Dad carrying baby Bruno, who is not thrilled about being removed from his stroller. Kay's backpack is swabbed to check for explosives. Each family member then steps into a "stickman" scanner, which will highlight any suspicious areas of their bodies. For this trip, they do not have their fingerprints scanned, but because of an extended visit last year to California while Farah's father enjoyed a sabbatical at Stanford University, their fingerprint data are already stored on an American border security system. When they catch their connecting flight in London's Heathrow airport, the family will also be scanned by facial-recognition software. Farah's mom whispers to her dad that she is glad that this time, no one was selected for even more invasive screening.

Farah's mom returns her laptop to her briefcase. Her dad snaps Bruno into the stroller, and everyone puts their shoes and belts back on. The family then troops to the executive lounge where Mom shuffles through her deck of customer loyalty cards to find the one that will grant them entry. She has cards for gasoline, groceries, hotels, coffee, cosmetics, and other services. Each membership gives perks and discounts and is part of a new information economy built upon minutely recording the consumption patterns of individual cardholders. Such information has become central to corporate decisions regarding product development, prices, and potential branch locations.

The setting sun illuminates the airplane cabin as they walk to their seats. Unbeknownst to them, an armed undercover RCMP air marshal furtively inspects everyone from his seat near the emergency exit.

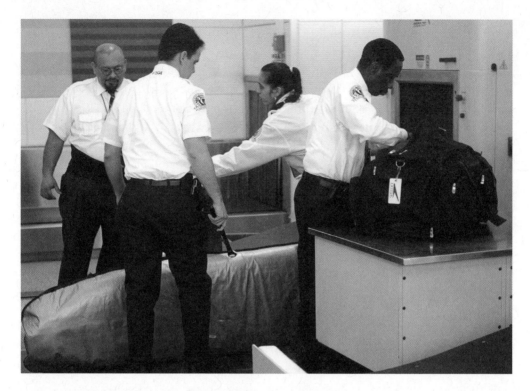

**Surveillance at the airport—now a matter of routine** (Source: © iStockphoto.com/EdStock)

Farah and her family will soon be high above Canada, but, in some respects, traces of each of them will remain behind in the form of increasingly large and refined informational profiles of text and image that have become central to how contemporary societies operate. Throughout Farah's full but not particularly remarkable day, she and her family have been monitored by different people and organizations. As a comparatively privileged family, they have a distinctive monitoring profile that is particularly focused on issues of consumption and personal security. Irrespective of one's position in society, however, all individuals can now expect to be subjected to more and different types of scrutiny than in the recent past, a trend that is poised to continue and intensify.

One might suggest that in Farah's case, much of this scrutiny can be explained by the fact that she is a child, and we expect children to be watched. However, as she matures, Farah will actually be increasingly monitored as she engages with new and different organizations. When she drives a car and becomes involved in work, finance, travel, sports, and social services, she will be monitored by new organizations. She will be subjected to additional forms of scrutiny if she has medical issues or becomes caught up in the criminal justice system. As she progresses through school, her educational dossier will become larger and more consequential. We might even anticipate that at least some of the futuristic prospects about interactive advertisements and camera-equipped security drones will become a reality in her world. Hers will be a world permeated by surveillance, something that will bring new opportunities but that also threatens to overwhelm existing privacy regimes and will challenge us all to contemplate how we should live our increasingly transparent lives.

---

### Surveillance Expansion in Context

This "day in the life" vignette gives a sense of how different forms of surveillance are becoming common and are touching ever more spheres of daily life. However, the story also sidesteps many issues that need to be contemplated in order for us to garner a fuller and more critical appreciation of the issues raised by this expansion and intensification of surveillance. The remainder of this book addresses such issues, some of which are worth flagging at the outset.

To start with, the vignette leaves unanswered whether all of this monitoring actually accomplishes what it is supposed to accomplish. This is a vital question since, too often, the public is asked to take it on faith that surveillance will perform in the ways advertised. Serious questions, however, remain about the effectiveness of such monitoring. To take an obvious example, the global expansion of antiterrorism surveillance might thwart some terrorist attacks, but it does not stand much chance of reducing this overall threat if the social, political, and economic conditions that breed terrorism are not addressed.

More prosaically, it is not clear that the ever expanding network of surveillance cameras actually reduces crime. Evidence regarding their crime-fighting effects is extremely ambiguous, and in many instances it is clear that they do not come close to producing the types of advertised crime reductions.[6] Moreover, even when cameras do manage to catch some offenders, they do not necessarily represent a wise use of resources. The most in-depth data on the subject come from the United Kingdom, which has installed more cameras than any other Western nation. For example, a report produced by London's Metropolitan Police, who have been key proponents of surveillance cameras, suggests that it takes one thousand cameras to catch a single criminal.[7] In the face of increasing evidence that surveillance cameras are poor at reducing crime, it is intriguing that security officials are now starting to justify the use of cameras on the grounds that they make people "feel safe"—again, something that is not necessarily true.

Even asking whether surveillance systems actually work can often miss the point since it ignores the factors that motivate the introduction of some surveillance systems. While officials might proclaim that surveillance is being introduced to increase security or efficiency, the greatest appeal for policy makers is often the desire to look modern or to appear to be addressing intractable problems of crime and disorder, irrespective of whether the chosen measures actually work.[8]

The expansion of surveillance also creates increased possibilities for systematic and consequential errors. Although surveillance proponents generally portray systems as working flawlessly, the reality is that all surveillance systems involve routine glitches and errors, and much organizational work can go into trying to identify and reduce these errors. Occasionally, systems contain so many endemic errors in personal data that organizations effectively abandon even the pretense that they are accurate; such is the case with both police databases on criminals and consumer credit reports, each of which tends to be rife with uncorrected, difficult-to-rectify mistakes. This is particularly disconcerting given how consequential those systems can be for shaping people's life chances.

The increased prevalence of surveillance is important not simply because of how it might track and identify suspicious people but also because it can alter everyone's behaviours. Even if the camera does not work or the locational abilities on your cellphone are turned off, living in a world permeated by surveillance subtly alters how we all act, what we say, what we post on social media—a form of self-censorship that can have a detrimental and chilling effect on political speech and action.

In addition, the vignette involving Farah and her family does not convey a sense of how surveillance might be resisted. People often find certain surveillance measures objectionable and occasionally take steps to try to eliminate or mitigate those that they see as particularly egregious or

**Camera-equipped police cars** (Source: photo © iStockphoto.com/Antonprado)

unjustified. This resistance can involve using legal measures to challenge the legality of an initiative or bringing the situation to the attention of different privacy commissioners. Such formal strategies can occasionally counter specific surveillance measures. For example, Canadian advocacy groups such as the British Columbia Civil Liberties Association and the Canadian Internet Policy and Public Interest Clinic (CIPPIC) have successfully challenged the state or transnational corporations in court and through the offices of the various information and privacy commissioners.[9] Nonetheless, serious questions remain about whether existing privacy laws in Canada can meaningfully check the general expansion of surveillance in almost all segments of society.[10]

Finally, the vignette does not explore the question of how the assorted surveillance systems originated or expanded. With the exception of a small number of high-profile surveillance initiatives, the expansion of most surveillance measures tends not to receive a full public airing. Instead, such expansion occurs through a process of "surveillance creep," the expansion

## Data Breaches and More Data Breaches . . .

The more our information is captured and communicated, the more likely it is that some of it will get lost. Data breaches, now big news in all advanced countries, occur when personal data on customers, patients, clients, or employees are stolen or, more likely, just carelessly mislaid or mistakenly disclosed. Increasingly frequent stories about lost laptops or remote storage devices bring home to ordinary people the practical consequences of living in a surveillance society.

Canadians have experienced many high-profile data breaches in recent years. In 2013, an employee of the federal Department of Human Resources and Skills Development lost an unencrypted USB flash drive containing the personal information of more than half a million Canadians, including Social Insurance Numbers and some health information. According to Public Accounts documents, in addition to USB drives, more than four hundred laptops and BlackBerries were lost or stolen from a wide variety of government departments in fiscal year 2012–13. Since 2002, 3,143 data breaches have occurred within federal agencies, affecting more than seven hundred thousand individuals. Only 13 percent of these breaches were reported to the Office of the Privacy Commissioner of Canada.[1] The ability of our federal watchdog to protect our information has thus been constrained by a lack of transparency on the part of those organizations that are responsible for safeguarding our information. We have also witnessed data breaches from provincial government agencies, hospitals, universities, and from every type of business. No type of institution is immune.

When a data breach occurs, one does not know how the information might be used or to whom it might be leaked or sold. In the hands of identity thieves, isolated pieces of personal data can be combined with others to give fraudsters access to our bank accounts or credit cards. Data

---

of existing practices to cover population groups or regions that they were not originally intended to monitor. Decisions about surveillance creep are typically opaque to the public since they are made behind the closed doors of assorted organizations. The United Kingdom, one of the most heavily surveilled places in the world, provides two iconic examples of surveillance creep. These examples could be instructive as surveillance becomes more heavily integrated in Canadian practices and policies.

The first example involves the expansion of the police DNA database. At the outset of DNA collection, British police and politicians made vociferous promises that they would only collect the DNA of the "worst of the

breaches also harm the interests and reputations of organizations, and many spend significant resources training staff and ensuring that any mobile devices used are properly password protected, and any personal data strongly encrypted. Yet breaches still occur with alarming regularity.

Some countries have strong data-breach laws that impose severe penalties for serious data breaches. Some of these laws require that letters of notification and apology be written to all individuals who might have been affected. Others require strict reporting of breaches to the relevant privacy regulator, who may then require the organization to communicate with all affected individuals if the risks are sufficiently high.

Canada's data breach–reporting requirements are still largely voluntary. Alberta is the only province that imposes a statutory obligation on private sector organizations to disclose privacy-related data breaches. And under Ontario's Personal Health Information Act, organizations must provide notice to the Ontario commissioner without reasonable delay. At the federal level, Bill C-12, which would amend PIPEDA and strengthen data breach–reporting requirements, was introduced in 2010. It has yet to be acted upon. Canada desperately needs stronger laws and penalties against data breaches. In the absence of these strong protections, some citizens have taken matters into their own hands and are suing an Ottawa hospital for $40 million for the loss, in 2012, of a memory stick containing data on twenty-five thousand patients.[2]

1. Laura Kane, "Privacy Watchdog Wants Ottawa to Force Companies to Report Release of Personal Data," *Toronto Star,* 23 May 2013, http://www.thestar.com/news/canada/2013/05/23/privacy_watchdog_wants_ottawa_to_force_companies_to_report_release_of_personal_data.html.
2. Jordan Press, "Government Data Breached Thousands of Times in Last Decade, Documents Say," *Canada.com,* 23 April 2013, http://o.canada.com/2013/04/23/government-data-breached-thousands-of-times-in-last-decade-documents-say/.

worst" criminals—typically, terrorists or pedophiles. Over time, these promises were forgotten as the police and prosecutors recognized the convenience of expanding the database to include the DNA of other categories of offenders, and then to include everyone convicted of a crime, no matter how minor. Today, the British police are empowered to collect, analyze, and store the DNA of anyone who is simply *suspected* of being involved in a crime, which, in practice, gives the police a great deal of discretion over who is included in the database and who is not.

The second example of surveillance creep involves the introduction of surveillance cameras in British municipalities. Here, a system designed and justified for one extraordinary purpose quickly found other more commonplace uses. Originally, the camera system was justified on the basis of antiterrorism legislation, but the authorities soon discovered that few terrorist activities are visibly apparent in Britain's quiet boroughs. Consequently, local authorities expanded the use of the camera system such that operators were watching for such mundane misdemeanours as urinating in public, underage smoking, garbage dumping, not picking up after your dog, and delivering papers without a licence. While such things can undeniably be daily inconveniences, it is unlikely that the public would have supported an expansive and expensive camera surveillance system as a way to ensure that people were putting their recycling on the curb on the right day.

## Conclusion

While Canadians might differ on the degree to which they support or oppose any specific surveillance measure, it is worth stressing that monitoring is a form of power—a power that operates over specifically identified individuals or through the ability to manipulate entire populations. The contemporary expansion of surveillance, such that monitoring becomes an ever more routine part of our lives, represents a tremendous shift in the balance of power between citizens and organizations. Perhaps the greatest danger in all of this is therefore not that a specific surveillance measure will be too intrusive, or that mistakes will be made in identifying or processing people, or that data will be lost. Instead, the most significant—but impossible to quantify—danger comes from the simple fact that we are creating, step by step, a society that is hard-wired for surveillance and that such devices can easily be turned to oppressive uses. From this point in history forward, our expanding surveillance infrastructure stands as a resource that will be inherited by future generations of politicians, corporate actors, or even messianic leaders. Given sufficient political will, this surveillance infrastructure can be repurposed to monitor—in remarkable detail—people whom some might see as unpalatable because of their political opinions, religious beliefs, skin colour, gender, migration status, medical history, or any number of an almost limitless list of factors that have been used throughout human history to pit people against one another. Contemplating such a scenario involves the risk of being dismissed as merely engaging in a form of "conspiracy theory," but one does not have to believe in secret forces operating behind the scenes to recognize that our ever expanding systems of transparency pose very real and alarming dangers.

## Notes

1   On the former, see John L. Locke, *Eavesdropping: An Intimate History* (Oxford: Oxford University Press, 2010); on the latter, see Kirstie Ball, "Workplace Surveillance: An Overview," *Labor History* 51, no. 1 (2010): 87–106; and Christopher Dandeker, *Surveillance, Power and Modernity: Bureaucracy and Discipline from 1700 to the Present Day* (New York: St. Martin's, 1990).

2   See, for example, Mark Andrejevic, *iSpy: Surveillance and Power in the Interactive Era* (Lawrence: University Press of Kansas, 2007); Kevin D. Haggerty and Richard V. Ericson, *The New Politics of Surveillance and Visibility* (Toronto: University of Toronto Press, 2006); Torin Monahan, *Surveillance in the Time of Insecurity* (New Brunswick, NJ: Rutgers University Press, 2010); and Daniel Solove, *The Digital Person* (New York: New York University Press, 2006).

3   Robert O'Harrow Jr., *No Place to Hide* (New York: Free Press, 2005).

4   Regarding social media and personal data, see Daniel Trottier, *Social Media as Surveillance* (London: Ashgate, 2012).

5   James Bamford, *The Shadow Factory: The Ultra-Secret NSA from 9/11 to the Eavesdropping on America* (New York: Anchor, 2009).

6   Martin Gill and Angela Spriggs, *Assessing the Impact of CCTV*, Home Office Research Study 292 (London: Home Office Research, Development and Statistics Directorate, 2005), https://www.cctvusergroup.com/downloads/file/Martin%20gill.pdf.

7   Christopher Hope, "1,000 CCTV Cameras to Solve Just One Crime, Met Police Admits," *Telegraph* (UK), 25 August 2009, http://www.telegraph.co.uk/news/uknews/crime/6082530/1000-CCTV-cameras-to-solve-just-one-crime-Met-Police-admits.html.

8   Kevin D. Haggerty and Camille Tokar, "Signifying Security: On the Institutional Appeals of Nightclub ID Scanning Systems," *Space and Culture* 15, no. 1 (2012): 124–34.

9   Colin Bennett, *The Privacy Advocates: Resisting the Spread of Surveillance* (Cambridge, MA: MIT Press, 2008).

10  James B. Rule, *Privacy in Peril: How We Are Sacrificing a Fundamental Right in Exchange for Security and Convenience* (Oxford: Oxford University Press, 2007).

# Securitization and Surveillance
## From Privacy Rights to Security Risks

One of the key forces driving the expansion of surveillance in Canada, especially in recent years, has been a collective focus on risk management and security. Ironically, although ordinary Canadians do indeed face safety, health, and financial risks, we are, on average, probably safer and better off than ever before. For example, our average life expectancy in the new millennium has climbed past age eighty.[1] Why, then, are Canadians so concerned with risk and security in the second decade of the twenty-first century? The events of 9/11 cannot fully explain our concerns. Although they provided a key impetus for increased security, the drive for risk management and security was in place before 9/11 and has expanded well beyond the antiterrorism front. Here, we discuss some of the reasons for this increased focus on risk and look at examples where it has led to new and more intensive surveillance—surveillance that itself creates new risks to privacy, fairness, and freedom.

### What We Fear, We Seek? Changing Notions of Risk and Security

Since the beginning of the 1980s, *risk* has been an important word not only in government and business but also in public discussion and academic research. That same time period has seen the rise of professional risk

**Getting to Know the Students in the Ottawa-Carleton District School Board**

In 2010, the Ottawa-Carleton District School Board informed parents that the school board would be administering a survey to all students from junior kindergarten through grade 12 to solicit detailed information about, among other things, each child's home life, religion, sexual orientation, ethnicity, and experiences of bullying and harassment.

The school board reasoned that it needed the information in order to better identify and deal with the risks faced by individual children while at school. After a public outcry against the privacy-invasive nature of the survey, the board retreated and made the survey voluntary. It also agreed to survey the parents of elementary schoolchildren rather than the children themselves because of the sensitive nature of the questions. However, although the school board promised to keep the information confidential, responses were not anonymous; each response was linked to a unique identifier so that individual children could be identified for intervention based on the analysis of the data.

Barrie Hammond, the board's director of education, defended the survey as an important tool to promote security: "The more we know about our students, the more we know about their needs, the more we can concentrate on making school a safe place."[1]

1. "School Board Survey Gets Mixed Reaction," CTV News, 4 November 2010, http://ottawa.ctvnews.ca/school-board-survey-gets-mixed-reaction-1.570748.

managers and the development of increasingly complex risk-management plans and techniques on the part of government, businesses, and other organizations. Indeed, much of contemporary life is organized around risk.[2] Part of modernization has involved the spread of systematic ways of calculating and managing risks so that we can govern ourselves through the application of scientific reason. Statistics are an essential tool in the arsenal of risk management, and they are often related to predictions about human behaviour. In a risk-oriented society, it becomes increasingly important to collect data—and more data—about our behaviour and the risks we face.

This focus on risk has brought with it a new emphasis on security as paramount. We are used to thinking of security in terms of national security against threats like terrorism, especially since 9/11, and social security as potentially provided by governments. But the notion of security has expanded

**Safety and privacy—a balance?** (Source: © iStockphoto.com/rappensuncle)

since the 1980s to cover a number of other areas, including environmental security and food security, and behaviours that were once commonplace are now considered too risky to be tolerated. For example, new parents are not allowed to take a baby home from a Canadian hospital without first providing a special infant car seat because of the statistical risk of injury should there be an accident. Laws have been passed in seven Canadian provinces requiring cyclists to wear helmets to reduce the risk of brain injury should riders fall. And parents are encouraged by health authorities and schools to ply their children with sunscreen because of the risk of skin cancer. These illustrations show that not only have our laws changed, but so have our common-sense notions of what is risky and what is not.

Greater surveillance has accompanied this increased concern about risk for two reasons. First, the hunger for data to fuel risk calculations has weakened privacy norms that traditionally required others, especially scientific researchers, to ask for permission before they collect personal information about people. For example, a number of provinces have passed health privacy legislation that allows health researchers to use personal information without consent for research purposes when obtaining consent from individual patients is impracticable. Because the information will ostensibly be used to identify health risks and promote better health, the need for surveillance is said to outweigh any countervailing interest in individual privacy. The survey of students' private lives proposed by the Ottawa-Carleton District School Board (see the inset discussion) is another example of this logic at play.

Second, once risks are identified, it becomes logical to use surveillance to monitor people both to ensure that they do not behave in a risky way and to manage the consequences when they do. The federal government, for example, tracks which Canadians leave the country in order to reduce the risk that someone who is collecting unemployment insurance benefits may be defrauding the system because he or she is on vacation and therefore not available for work. Similarly, life insurance companies now require customers to disclose whether they smoke or drink and then use that information to determine what kinds of insurance coverage customers can buy and how much it will cost them. Some individuals with certain pre-existing health conditions, like diabetes or cancer, are simply uninsurable because the risk of poor health is too high.

Again, surveillance can be used for care or for control. But the important thing to note in this context is that a society focused on risk and security easily turns to surveillance to better understand and better manage behaviours that are viewed as risky.

### Increasing Risks, Decreasing Trust

Ironically, so much focus on security can breed insecurity. Although we devote more and more attention to managing it, risk seems increasingly to be out of our control in important ways. Our society's perception that risk is everywhere has prompted ever more strenuous efforts to control it. And the more we ponder and discuss risks, the more this leads to a climate of doubt and fear. This, in turn, leads to the demand for yet more knowledge about risk, creating a vicious circle that helps to justify surveillance in the pursuit of security.

As noted above, there is something paradoxical about this heightened awareness of risk and fear: even though we are probably, on average, safer than ever, people tend to spend more energy dwelling on the risks that remain. Employment is less stable and more precarious, the governmental social safety net is fraying, and Canadians are confronted with an array of new social and technological risks. Things seem to be changing rapidly. Traditional certainties and traditional institutions, such as the family, are breaking down. Life is experienced as more individualized; there is a sense that individuals are alone to fend for themselves in a risky world. Instead of being caught up in the old ways, we are oriented toward helping individuals understand and secure the future against all manner of risks.

Our understanding of risk is also shaped by globalization and more and more interconnection between Canada and the rest of the world (see Trend 6) and this helps to fuel the increasingly rapid pace of change, again adding to the climate of uncertainty. For example, more movement of people internationally creates a drive to monitor travellers who might be potential terrorists or carriers of diseases like H1N1. Once again, risks proliferate and surveillance is needed to provide security in an increasingly uncertain world.

What does the research evidence say about public attitudes toward risk and security? Surveying the public on their views of various risks paints a complex and nuanced picture and reveals much variation among people of varying ages, gender, levels of wealth, and education.[3] An umbrella term like *fear* only begins to convey a complex cluster of diverse public understandings and emotions about risks—ways of thinking and feeling that are not easily captured in closed-ended, check-box survey questions. We must be careful not to overstate the extent of public fears: for example, in 2009, 93 percent of Canadians surveyed felt satisfied about their personal safety from crime.[4] We also do not want to imply that the public is always passive and accepting. One example of public response to issues related to risk is the Occupy movement, a direct reply to financial risks gone awry. But such public resistance itself can also become the target of surveillance, as seen with the G20 summit in Toronto in June 2010.

Despite these examples, the psychology of risk continues to shape our understanding of both the problems we face and the solutions available to us. Research in risk perception reveals the "dread factor": people tend to focus on certain risks because of their terrifying nature, even if they are improbable.[5] Likewise, psychological research also highlights the "availability heuristic," the somewhat self-evident point that risks about which we have more immediate knowledge become more salient to us.[6] For example, the American public was immersed in massive coverage of the hijacked jets crashing into the Twin Towers on 11 September 2001. Notwithstanding this horrific incident, flying is, in general, safer than driving, but the one striking case of 9/11 made such a powerful impression that air travel reduced dramatically the following year in the United States; ironically, car traffic correspondingly increased, leading to a dramatic rise in the number of deaths on the road. A German psychologist, Gerd Gigerenzer, calculated that there were 1,595 additional fatalities in the United States that year as a result.[7]

The role of experts and expert systems in our thinking about risk is particularly key. We often rely on experts to identify risks and to help us manage them. Yet people also have an increasing sense that expert knowledge is not particularly reliable. Expert knowledge is never final—always changing— and experts often disagree; all of this makes it difficult for people to trust experts and adds to the climate of doubt and anxiety. An unprecedented level of higher education leaves people less trusting and more critical, and access to more knowledge through the Internet adds to the climate of perpetual doubt. Public faith in key institutions like science, the government, and the marketplace is undermined: survey results consistently point to declining trust in government, politicians, and other major institutions.[8]

In addition, the language that experts use to discuss risks is often part of the problem. While experts make sense of risk in terms of numbers and probability, in the lives of ordinary people, in the media, and in politics, the key is often the dramatic nature of the risk rather than its likelihood. Risks, by definition, outrun certainty and control: something bad might happen to us, and, no matter how unlikely it is, we cannot rule it out.

Likewise, it generally does little good to talk to people about statistical measures of risk: research suggests that most people tend to make sense of risk in terms of their feelings and impressions, not in terms of numerical probabilities.[9] Recent risk-communication research suggests that many controversies around risks arise because lay people think about risk in different ways than do risk experts. In other words, the controversies are "rooted in the difference between the experts' quantitative language and the qualitative terminology ordinarily employed by citizens in everyday life."[10]

Thus, a number of social thinkers argue that, as criminologist David Garland put it, there is an "increasingly endemic sense of insecurity— experienced even by well-to-do individuals who are, by historical standards, healthier and more affluent than ever before. . . . Today's freed-up individuals enjoy their freedoms against a background of a newfound dependency upon expert systems and newfound uncertainty about the lives they choose."[11] People are trying to absorb and deal with more new information about risk, sometimes at an overwhelming level.

Our perceptions of risk are also influenced by the media. While the media have always amplified dramatic risks, the fragmentation of the mass media audience into more specialized and politically polarized niches splinters consensus and adds to a culture of uncertainty and distrust. In Canada, viewers of Sun-TV get a different picture of the world than viewers of CBC-TV. What's more, trust in the mainstream media has declined considerably, according to surveys.[12] Social media such as Facebook and Twitter allow for a critical political discourse challenging official views; this discourse, although empowering, adds to the sense that traditional certainties have been undermined.

The global news media often focus our attention on statistically improbable but terrifying risks, amplifying these effects. The news media have what researchers call an "event orientation": they focus on dramatic individual events rather than providing the big picture.[13] While the news media have always done this, new tendencies in the media world heighten concerns about certain risks. For example, the amount of attention given to crime, especially violent crime, has increased measurably over the decades, in one case more than doubling in two British newspapers between the 1940s and 1990s.[14] In the case of television news, this was partly due to the influence of news consultants such as Frank N. Magid Associates, who, beginning in the 1980s, counselled that crime coverage boosts ratings.[15] But no matter what the reason, the result is a picture of a world of proliferating risks, based on dramatic events that shock and disturb.

## Policy Making in a Risk Society

From this perspective, surveillance is an appropriate response to a generalized sense of insecurity. Psychological tendencies, the media, and politicians all contribute to an atmosphere in which surveillance measures are often introduced on the basis of one dramatic and horrifying but statistically improbable incident that receives a great deal of media, political, and public attention. The increase of security after 9/11 is the most striking example; a more local one is the piecemeal introduction of public video camera surveillance in different Canadian cities in response to the outcry over particular individual violent crimes.[16] Sensational individual crimes can take on huge political significance. The 2005 gang-related Boxing Day shooting of a fifteen-year-old bystander, Jane Creba, in downtown Toronto was key to Prime Minister Harper winning his first minority government. As Harper campaign organizer Tom Flanagan noted, "Our internal polling had already established criminal justice as the issue area where we had the strongest lead over the Liberals, and Jane Creba's tragic death helped to make our position more salient to voters."[17] Even though such events are extremely rare, Stephen Harper used the opportunity to campaign with great success on a tough on crime agenda.

Given our growing intolerance of risk, it appears logical to implement surveillance measures both to provide more data to help identify risks and to protect against offenders. The actual nature and level of the risks become less important than the need to appear to be in control. For example, the federal government introduced a range of sweeping and costly law-and-order measures in 2012 even though crime, including violent crime, was statistically at a forty-year low.[18] Nonetheless, there is a risk that something bad *could* happen to us, even though coming to harm may be less likely than it used to be. As Canada's Public Safety minister put it in a Senate committee meeting in early 2012, "Let's not talk about statistics. Let's talk about danger."[19]

Certainly, and perhaps more telling and much more meaningful in terms of social impact, politicians have consistently been able to use a "tough on crime" approach to win votes among strategic sectors of the electorate, leading to a spate of surveillance measures. Likewise, even though few Canadians, when surveyed, express high levels of concern about terrorism, authorities were able to use the argument of "counterterrorism" to justify a broad campaign of surveillance around the protests at the G20 meetings in Toronto in 2010.[20]

Risk is increasingly being downloaded from governments onto both individuals and businesses. Canadians have less trust in the traditional social safety net than they did in the past: for example, they are often unsure to what extent they will be able to rely on the Canada Pension Plan to fund their retirements. Thus, many feel the increased burden to manage their own life course, which entails more financial risk and uncertainty. Vulnerable groups in particular, such as the old and the poor, may become increasingly marginalized and disenfranchised. This is another way in which we are moving from rights to risks. Canadians have felt particularly financially insecure since the financial crisis of 2008. A number of researchers studying public attitudes toward crime have argued that broader concerns about economic and social insecurity may encourage people to accept crime control measures more willingly—the so-called displacement hypothesis.[21] While this is difficult to prove, if it is true, it helps us to understand the political context in which we see a range of new anticrime surveillance measures that may go unchallenged politically.

It is not only financial risk but also other forms of risk that are being downloaded to the individual in a process that sociologists call "responsibilization," in which individuals are instructed to monitor and take charge of, for example, workplace safety, crime prevention in the home, or the Internet usage patterns of their children.

As sociologist Ulrich Beck argued, in a risk society, the social hierarchy is increasingly based on the capacity to manage risk rather than on the possession of wealth. In other words, the distinction between the advantaged and the disadvantaged rests not on the distribution of "goods" but on the ability to avoid "bads."[22] Moreover, because those who are most vulnerable to risk include those whose actions contribute to risk, certain groups of people—for example, particular ethnic minorities or troubled young people—are often seen not only as at-risk but also as risky themselves. Marginalized people are exposed to more risks *and* are categorized as bad risks. Thus, people who might need our help are also, paradoxically, viewed as a threat. Emphasis is placed on the threat posed by the marginalized rather than on the help that they might need. A risk society is thus also increasingly what criminologist Jock Young calls an "exclusive society," in which marginalized groups are cut off from desirable forms of security.[23] This is where the social sorting function of surveillance is key—surveillance helps us to classify and monitor sets of people deemed risky and, sometimes, to exclude them from full participation in society.

In addition, risk management often hides moral judgments in technical assessments of risk.[24] The use of expert knowledge and statistics to lump people, especially marginalized groups, into risk categories, is growing. Although these risk categories may be presented in language that sounds neutral, often moral evaluations—judgments about who is good and who is bad—are hidden in the technical wording of experts. How riskiness is assessed may be decided and agreed upon behind the scenes—for example, in the development of risk assessment algorithms. Because these judgments are hidden, this way of assessing risk lacks accountability and is difficult for ordinary people to resist. In short, risk can thus come to trump rights.

The Smart Border program negotiated between Canada and the United States shortly after 9/11 illustrates the kind of surveillance that displays these

## Police Surveillance at Canada's G20 Summit

When Canada agreed to host the 2012 G20 meetings in Toronto, Canadian police undertook one of the largest domestic intelligence operations in Canadian history, all in the name of counterterrorism and security. The RCMP-led joint intelligence group employed five hundred people at its peak. A police Internet Monitoring Unit extensively surveilled activists' social media use in what is known as "open source investigation." They developed maps of activists' social networks and drew inferences about their behaviour based on whom they followed and were followed by on Twitter, the events they said they would attend, and other personal information disclosed on social media.[1]

A team of twelve undercover police officers infiltrated activist groups across the country. Two of the officers spent eighteen months pretending to be members of southern Ontario activist organizations. This surveillance resulted in fifty-nine criminal charges against seventeen people, most of whom were arrested pre-emptively on the first day of the summit.[2] Charges were later dropped against eleven of the seventeen activists. The remaining six pleaded guilty to a variety of minor charges such as counselling to commit mischief. Plain-clothes officers, clad in protester garb, mixed with protesters during the events, and dozens of video cameras recorded the demonstrations. Police also conducted "crowd-sourced" surveillance after the event, posting forty thousand images and five hundred pieces of video online and appealing to the public to identify suspects.

Such measures are a good example of risk management trumping rights. Police targeted activists because they believed that they posed a risk to security. Based on the undercover surveillance, these same people were excluded from participating in democratic protests that were largely peaceful. Since the majority of charges were later dropped, legal accountability for the surveillance itself and the resulting restrictions on the activists' freedom of expression was bypassed in those cases. Risk once again took priority over democratic rights.

1. Kate Milberry, "Surveillance and Security Spectacle at the Toronto G20: The Miami Model and the Ambivalence of Social Media," paper presented at the Security and Its Publics conference, Carleton University, Ottawa, ON, 20–22 September 2012.
2. Jeff Monaghan and Kevin Walby, "'They Attacked the City': Security Intelligence, the Sociology of Protest Policing, and the Anarchist Threat at the 2010 Toronto G20 Summit," *Current Sociology* 60, no. 5 (2012): 653–71.

**Photographing police officers during the protests over the G20 summit in Toronto on 26 June 2010**

(Source: © iStockphoto.com/Jen Grantham)

qualities.[25] Certain kinds of travellers are precleared while risk-scoring algo-rithms are used to flag those categories of travellers who should receive extra attention from authorities. The exact nature of the algorithms and the risk criteria used to single out certain kinds of people remain secret, producing a lack of accountability in the surveillance and social sorting process and illus-trating the move from rights to risk.

Although Canada was not directly affected by the attacks of 9/11, the attacks and subsequent international terrorist incidents have cast a long shadow. Responses to potential terrorism have a kind of self-reinforcing qual-ity: the responses themselves, by reminding the public that a threat is out there, seem to justify the need for more surveillance measures. To provide a small example, after the July 2005 attacks on commuters in London, England, the Ottawa bus service, OC Transpo, launched a poster campaign pushing for public vigilance—essentially requesting that members of the public spy on one other.[26] Posters told Ottawa commuters, "If you see something, say something," and asked them to phone a hotline "if something does not look right." A later round of OC Transpo posters, in 2006, urged: "If something looks suspicious, let us know." Such campaigns do more than just enlist the public to monitor one another: they also reinforce the message that danger is always out there, justifying the need for other surveillance measures—a good example of how striving for security in turn creates insecurity.

## Surveillance as Risk

In our risk society, some risks get hyped, but it is important to note that real new risks do exist. Modernization is a double-edged sword: it simultaneously reduces and enhances risks. Surveillance itself is a good example. Although it is supposed to help manage risks, it also creates new risks to privacy, fair-ness, and freedom. Science and technology are given a dominant role in directing human affairs, helping us to manage risk but also creating risks of, for example, climate change, computer viruses, or electromagnetic waves. The rapid pace of technological change produces new risks that we struggle to keep up with. Newly developed technologies end up having unintended consequences, some good, some bad. This is particularly true of information technologies. While information management, whether on behalf of govern-ment or business or others, is valuable in facilitating travel, entertainment, communication, industrial production, and economic transactions, it also raises issues of surveillance and privacy. Advances in areas such as surveillance cameras, biometrics, genetic science, location and tracking systems, electronic miniaturization, and convergence between computers and telecommunication systems have made the task of information gathering—as well as its storage, retrieval, and manipulation—a more central part of our lives than ever before. Legal regulation often lags far behind the deployment of such new technologies.

The massive increase in technological innovation and diffusion is particularly evident in the world of computing and the Internet, which features expansion so rapid that it boggles the mind. For example, the number of electronic devices connected to the Internet, from computers to smartphones, increased from twenty thousand to eighty thousand over a two-year period during the 1980s; a decade later, it increased from 20 million to 80 million within a similar two-year period.[27] A report published by *The Economist* states, "According to one estimate, mankind created 150 exabytes (billion gigabytes) of data in 2005. This year [2010], it will create 1,200 exabytes."[28] In 2009, according to a Canadian public opinion survey, social networking technologies were "barely on the radar" as posing privacy concerns. Two years later, around 51 percent of Canadians were quite concerned that social networking technologies like Facebook and Twitter threaten privacy.[29] Privacy risks from social media are thus a good example of the kind of rapidly emerging, technologically driven risk with which we struggle to keep pace.


## Conclusion

Grasping the "security" trend helps us to understand the broader social context in which a wide range of new surveillance measures continue to emerge in Canada. It also facilitates discussion of some of the factors that may make it easy for these measures to find support but difficult to question them. One encouraging note is that, by and large, compared to years past, the Canadian public is more educated and informed, less trusting, and more critical of various authorities and institutions in general. If this adds to a sense of uncertainty and insecurity for Canadians, it also provides fertile ground for asking questions about just how much risk management, security, and surveillance is too much and about the best ways to balance risk and rights.

# Notes

1   See Dan Gardner, *Risk: Why We Fear the Things We Shouldn't—and Put Ourselves in Greater Danger* (Toronto: McClelland and Stewart, 2008).

2   See Ulrich Beck, *World at Risk* (Cambridge, UK: Polity Press, 2009); Anthony Giddens, *Runaway World: How Globalization Is Reshaping Our Lives* (London and New York: Routledge, 2003), chap. 2; and Anthony Giddens, *Modernity and Self-Identity* (Cambridge, UK: Polity Press, 1991).

3   Peter Taylor-Gooby and Andreas Cebulla, "The Risk Society Hypotheses: An Empirical Test Using Longitudinal Survey Data," *Journal of Risk Research* 13, no. 6 (2010): 731–52.

4   Shannon Brennan, *Canadians' Perceptions of Personal Safety and Crime, 2009,* Statistics Canada (Ottawa: Minister of Industry, 2011), http://www.statcan.gc.ca/pub/85-2-x/2011001/article/11577-eng.htm, 5.

5   Paul Slovic, Baruch Fischhoff, and Sarah Lichtenstein, "Why Study Risk Perception?" *Risk Analysis* 2, no. 2 (1982): 83–93.

6   Amos Tversky and Daniel Kahneman, "Judgment Under Uncertainty: Heuristics and Biases," *Science* 185, no. 4157 (September 1974): 1124–31.

7   Cited in Gardner, *Risk,* 4.

8   See, for example, Edelman Trust Barometer, 2012 Annual Global Study, http://trust.edelman.com/trusts/trust-in-institutions-2/.

9   Brian Wynne, "May the Sheep Safely Graze? A Reflexive View of the Expert-Lay Knowledge Divide," in *Risk, Environment, Modernity: Towards a New Ecology*, ed. Scott Lash, Bronislaw Szerszynski, and Brian Wynne (London: Sage, 1996), 27–43.

10  William Leiss and Douglas Powell, *Mad Cows and Mother's Milk: The Perils of Poor Risk Communication,* 2nd ed. (Montréal and Kingston: McGill-Queen's University Press, 2004), 27–28.

11  David Garland, "The Rise of Risk," in *Risk and Morality*, ed. Richard V. Ericson and Aaron Doyle (Toronto: University of Toronto Press, 2003), 78.

12  Pew Research Centre, "Press Accuracy Rating Hits Two Decade Low," Public Evaluations of the News Media, 1985–2009, 13 September 2009, http://www.people-press.org/2009/9/13/press-accuracy-rating-hits-two-decade-low/.

13  Richard Ericson, Patricia Baranek, and Janet Chan, *Visualizing Deviance: A Study of News Organization* (Toronto: University of Toronto Press / Milton Keynes, UK: Open University Press, 1987).

14  Robert Reiner, Sonia Livingstone, and Jessica Allen, "No More Happy Endings? The Media and Popular Concern About Crime Since the Second World War," in *Crime, Risk and Insecurity: Law and Order in Everyday Life and Political Discourse,* ed. Tim Hope and Richard Sparks (London and New York: Routledge, 2001), 13–32.

15  Margalit Fox, "Frank Magid, Creator of 'Action News,' Dies at 78," *New York Times,* 9 February 2010.

16  Emily Smith, "The Piecemeal Development of Camera Surveillance in Canada," in *Eyes Everywhere: The Global Growth of Camera Surveillance,* ed. Aaron Doyle, Randy Lippert, and David Lyon (London and New York: Routledge, 2012), 122–35.

17  Tom Flanagan, *Harper's Team: Behind the Scenes in the Conservative Rise to Power,* 2nd ed. (Montréal and Kingston: McGill-Queen's University Press, 2009), 247.

18  See Shannon Brennan, *Police-Reported Crime Statistics in Canada, 2011*, Statistics Canada (Ottawa: Minister of Industry, 2012), http://www.statcan.gc.ca/pub/85-2-x/2012001/article/11692-eng.pdf, 6.

19  See Meagan Fitzpatrick, "Omnibus Crime Bill Hearings Underway in Senate," *CBC News*, 1 February 2012, http://www.cbc.ca/news/politics/omnibus-crime-bill-hearings-underway-in-senate-1.

20  Regarding Canadians' levels of concern about terrorism, see Louise Lemyre, Michelle C. Turner, Jennifer E. C. Lee, and Daniel Krewski, "Public Perception of Terrorism Threats and Related Information Sources in Canada: Implications for the Management of Terrorism Risks," *Journal of Risk Research* 9, no. 7 (2006): 755–74.

21  Stuart A. Scheingold, "Politics, Public Policy and Street Crime," *Annals of the American Academy of Political and Social Science* 539 (May 1995): 155–68.

22  See Ulrich Beck, *Risk Society: Towards a New Modernity,* trans. Mark Ritter (London: Sage Publications, 1992), and, for a critique of Beck's argument regarding class, Dean Curran, "Risk Society and the Distribution of Bads: Theorizing Class in the Risk Society," *British Journal of Sociology* 64, no. 1 (2013): 44–62.

23  Jock Stuart Young, *The Exclusive Society* (Beverly Hills, CA: Sage, 1999).

24  Richard V. Ericson and Aaron Doyle, "Risk and Morality," in Ericson and Doyle, *Risk and Morality*, 1–10.

25  Mark B. Salter, "Citizenship, Borders and Mobility: Managing Canada's Population," in *Canada in the World: Internationalism in Canadian Foreign Policy*, ed. Claire Turenne Sjolander and Heather Smith (New York: Oxford University Press, 2013), 146–63.

26  Mike Larsen and Justin Piche, "Public Vigilance Campaigns and Participatory Surveillance After 11 September 2001," in *Surveillance: Power, Problems, and Politics*, ed. Sean P. Hier and Joshua Greenberg (Vancouver: University of British Columbia Press, 2010), 187–202.

27  Ray Kurzweil, "The Law of Accelerating Returns," 7 March 2001, www.kurzweilai.net/the-law-of-accelerating-returns.

28  "The Data Deluge," *The Economist,* 25 February 2010, http://www.economist.com/node/15579717.

29  Harris/Decima, *2011 Canadians and Privacy Survey: Report Presented to the Office of the Privacy Commissioner of Canada*, Ottawa, 31 March 2011, http://www.priv.gc.ca/information/por-rop/2011/por_2011_01_e.pdf.

# The Blurring of Sectors
## From Public Versus Private
## to Public with Private

Throughout our lifetimes, we provide information about ourselves to both the public and private sectors in a variety of different contexts. When we file a tax return or get a driver's licence, we know that the information we provide will be retained by the government in some file or another. Similarly, when we use a credit card, sign a phone contract, or join a customer loyalty program, we know that the corporation we are doing business with is probably keeping a record of our encounters and what we tell them. If we have concerns about the collection and use of this information, those concerns tend to differ depending on whether we are dealing with the government or a corporation. And, in Canada, different privacy laws apply to personal information depending on whether it is held by a public agency or a private business.

For example, public sector privacy laws are intended to keep Big Brother at bay. Government surveillance can make it difficult for citizens to enjoy democratic freedoms, so we typically expect the state to get a warrant before entering our homes and invading our privacy. And we expect government agencies to collect only the personal data that are necessary to fulfill a statutory purpose and to use and disclose those data only in ways that are consistent with that purpose. Laws restricting the private sector's collection of information, however, address consumer issues like correcting mistakes in our credit-rating scores or stopping marketers from collecting information about us without our consent. For most of the twentieth century, we safely assumed that—short of a warrant—the information we gave to the government and the information we gave to corporations would be kept separate.

No more. Although there are technical, organizational, and legal limits on what may travel where, it is clear that data are now flowing freely between public and private agencies. Indeed, data from one sector so often pop up in the other sector, it can be difficult to differentiate between government and corporate surveillance. Since governments and corporations have different rationales and mandates, the implications for accountability are huge.

Let us look at an example. The Canadian Security and Intelligence Service (CSIS), the agency responsible for keeping us safe from international threats, is actively exploring partnerships with private sector owners and operators that would allow CSIS to ask companies to hand over personal information about their customers without customers' consent. The objective is to develop extensive networks of regional contacts (a surveillance net, in effect) with those who own and run institutions classified as critical infrastructure—everything from pipelines and oil sands to public transit.[1]

Once those private sector data are turned over to the government, it becomes more difficult for people to track, let alone control, their personal information. How would you know, for instance, whether CSIS had a file on you based on information gleaned from the transit company or electricity business where you work? More importantly, as technologies and security concerns facilitate the blurring of the line between the private and the public, how can you tell who is responsible for any harm you sustain because of this, and to whom do you turn for recourse?

The blurring of the public and private sectors is itself driven by two major factors. First, there is a widespread belief that government and the private sector should work in tandem to maximize efficiency and productivity. Because of this belief, many tasks that were once performed by government are now outsourced to companies. For example, the analysis of Canadian census data has been outsourced to Lockheed Martin, which uses its own software and data-processing equipment, and the BC provincial government has contracted with a US company called Maximus for the delivery of the provincial Medical Services Plan and Pharmacare services. The second crucial factor is that new technologies facilitate the breakdown of traditional institutional distinctions both across and within sectors, allowing data to flow in both directions without the traditional oversight of a judicial warrant. So the breakdown of the barriers between the public and private sectors is both a cause and a consequence of increasing surveillance.

The patterns are complex and multiple. However, to highlight these trends, we focus on three new practices that are breaking down the institutional barriers between public and private agencies: access to communications data by law enforcement; legislative changes that require more and more sharing of personal data from companies to government, and vice versa; and the contracting out of the security function to the "surveillance industry."

**What Prompted Private-Public Collaboration?**

From the 1980s on, Canada, along with many governments around the world, has been shrinking the public sector, privatizing government services, introducing or permitting the expansion of private security and policing, and cutting back health care, education, and pension programs. As publicly funded services have diminished, those who can afford it have turned to buying such services from the private sector. Thus, we have all become increasingly dependent on businesses and corporations to deliver the community services we rely on.

However, unlike governments, corporations tend to assume that the personal information they collect as they provide these services is a valuable corporate asset that can help generate more profit. There is thus a significant incentive to acquire and retain ever more data about citizens. The legal framework requires that corporations obtain individual consent for the collection of these data. However, as more commercial services become necessary to day-to-day living, we often face a choice between only two options: either we can consent to having our information bought and sold, or we can forego the benefits associated with such conveniences as having a credit card, a mortgage, or access to a physiotherapist. We make a similar deal in the security context: either we consent to having our bags and communications searched, removing our shoes, providing fingerprints, and sometimes enduring personal searches or we are barred from flying.

Once those personal data are harvested, they can flow easily between corporate and government hands. For example, commercial information about us is collected and then resold by (private) "data brokers" to (public) agencies like CSIS and the police.[2] And, of course, a body such as the (public) Canada Border Services Agency routinely has access to passenger details that (private) airlines are obliged to pass on to them before we fly. Conversely, some government information about citizens percolates through to commercial bodies. Canada Post, for instance, sells personal "change of address" information to (private) marketers. Indeed, the postal code system itself is widely used by marketers to classify consumers.

At the same time that information began to flow more freely between the public and private sectors, the infrastructures that determine organizational practices changed. Manual files stored in physical cabinets and face-to-face and telephone meetings shifted to computer databases and networked communications platforms. The mechanical metaphors that dominated the world of paper documents, storage cabinets, and telephones were replaced by the image of electronic data that move through systems at the speed of light.

Over time, gains in efficiency accredited to new technologies were accompanied by a transformation in organizational practices. Customer relationship management (CRM) and database marketing methods were developed to analyze customers whose preferences and shopping habits were tracked and stored electronically. New software transformed how companies could obtain data directly from customers' purchases; at the same time, companies using CRM started offering perks and rewards to consumers willing to trade their personal information for the benefits of "membership."

The information itself became the central item of value; it could be used not only by the company that established the system but also by others interested in the spending patterns of groups and individuals. Among these are the data brokers, mentioned above, who trade in personal data. In this way, enabled by new technologies, the sluices were opened, and personal data began to flow within and between organizations in unprecedented ways. As the following examples demonstrate, it was only a matter of time until the conventional conduits of public and private also broke down, permitting first trickles and then streams of data to flow from governments to corporations and back again.

### Access to Communications Data by Law Enforcement

One of the most compelling—and controversial—examples of the consequences of this free flow of data between the public and private sectors revolves around proposed "lawful access" provisions designed to make it easier for police to access the data generated by customers through the use of networked communications platforms.

In 2011, an Omnibus Crime Bill package, bundling together three bills, was brought before the Canadian Parliament. The relevant sections of the bill proposed that Internet service providers (ISPs), which provide access to the Internet, be required to turn over, for "security" reasons, certain subscriber data (such as the identity of a person using a particular IP address) to the state without a warrant.* The proposed law, which in effect made ISPs take on a de facto police function, elicited deeply concerned responses from both federal and provincial privacy commissioners, who combined their concerns in a letter to Canada's deputy minister of Public Safety. A media campaign on television and the Internet called "Stop Online Spying" sprang into life to raise awareness of the far-reaching negative consequences of passing such legislation, and 145,000 Canadians signed an online petition to voice their concerns. As a result, the provisions were shelved, and a number of months after the debacle the government indicated that it would not be pursuing the matter further. This does not necessarily mean that the matter is over. In fact, it is well established that most carriers already hand over personal data to police informally, without a warrant and without a law in place to mandate that they do so.[3]

The proposed law remains an excellent example of the consequences of dissolving the line between the public and private sectors and co-opting companies into the business of government. Following the logics of efficiency and privatization, the new law would have required ISPs to modify their systems for real-time surveillance. Moreover, police would have been granted new powers to obtain access to the data generated as people went about their daily lives online—shopping, working, using social media—whether or not the user was acting anonymously. There was little oversight to ensure that these powers would not be abused. One particularly problematic clause would have allowed police to force an ISP to identify an anonymous Internet user, *even where there was doubt that it would be useful to any investigation.* Categorical secrecy orders would have further obscured how the sweeping powers granted in the bill were being used, making it even more difficult to challenge future abuses of these powers in court.

Critics argued that, should the bill become law, Canadian citizens, ISPs, social networks, and even handsets and cars would be turned into spy tools for the state. Although the bill failed to become law, its introduction shows clearly how the trend toward public-private blurring alters time-honoured expectations about the kind of relationship citizens in a democracy can enjoy with their government.

* An IP address is a number given to each device (computer, printer, etc.) that is part of a computer network connected to the Internet.

These legislative conflicts also reveal the extent to which private companies can be regarded as essential tools for law enforcement. Google, for instance, regularly reports the number of law enforcement requests for information about its users by country. As Google has become more popular, the number of requests has increased significantly.[4] Google complies with such Canadian requests in roughly 24 percent of cases (contrast Twitter's 7 percent), although there are significant national variations and few details about the types of requests received. A number of online companies have been lobbying hard for clear and consistent legal standards, which would allow them to know the conditions under which these requests should be accepted or refused. Google is reasonably transparent about these processes. Most companies are not. Note, however, that Canadian companies such as Distributel and TekSavvy resist warrantless access to user data. Smaller Internet service providers without extensive legal staff might find it far more difficult to refuse requests for user data.

More worrying is the amount of data that might be shared through this back door access. This issue hit the news in a big way in 2005 when the Electronic Frontier Foundation received whistleblower evidence from the United States that AT&T had allowed the installation of a fibre optic splitter at its facility in San Francisco. The US National Security Agency (NSA) was using the splitter to monitor the email and web browsing of all of AT&T's customers in real time (see Trends 6 and 7).[5] The revelation was quickly followed by a number of lawsuits against AT&T, but these were effectively brought to a halt when Congress intervened by amending the Foreign Intelligence Security Act (FISA) to shield "electronic communication service providers" like AT&T from liability when they cooperate with intelligence agencies. The FISA amendments also created penalties for companies that fail to comply with a FISA order or that even disclose the existence of the orders served on them. The legislation was renewed in January 2013 and will stay in force until at least 2018. And, of course, in the summer of 2013, the whistleblowing of Edward Snowden reignited debate over the surveillance connections between the NSA, private corporations, and personal information gleaned from ordinary citizens both in the United States and in other countries such as Canada.

The FISA amendments also incorporated "remote computing services" or "cloud computing" into the existing definition of an "electronic communication service provider." According to a recent report to the European Parliament, this allows US agencies to access customer files and other information at various US-owned cloud data centres in the United States, Europe, or any other country, including Canada.[6] Moreover, one sweeping provision of the legislation authorizes the targeting of "a foreign-based political organization or foreign territory that relates to the conduct of the foreign affairs of the United States."[7] These provisions have not been lost on Canadian NGOs that might use the cloud-computing services of companies like Google, Microsoft, Amazon, and Apple for email and data storage facilities. And Canadian privacy law would have no jurisdiction over the intelligence operations of US federal agencies.[8]

The desire for access to communications data by law enforcement is a major factor within the trend toward public-private agency blurring. Governments in many countries other than Canada are moving in this direction, so it is anticipated that the issue will not go away soon or easily. The fact that even without explicit laws in place—and even with clear public displeasure against such data sharing—the likelihood is that these practices will continue anyway, informally and below the radar of democratic oversight. The blurring of public and private agencies with regard to personal data is also an index of increased surveillance that is ever harder to discern and check. This is also seen in the next example, which illustrates how private data are used for public purposes.

### Private Data for Public Purposes, and Vice Versa

You might imagine that security agencies such as CSIS or the RCMP Security Service are tasked with tracking activities like terrorism or money laundering. You would be correct, but this is also a task entrusted to businesses, such as banks, that employ dedicated personnel in data analytics and related fields to identify suspicious cases and to pass such findings to the conventional authorities. Increasingly, as we have shown, data collected by governments for a public purpose are shared with the private sector, and those collected by corporations in the course of commercial transactions are shared with governments. A good deal of this sharing is authorized by law and is therefore subject to some degree of oversight.

FINTRAC, the Financial Transactions and Reports Analysis Centre of Canada, is an excellent example. FINTRAC is mandated under the Proceeds of Crime (Money Laundering) and Terrorist Financing Act of 2000 to "collect and analyze financial transactions, and disseminate intelligence to assist in the detection, prevention and deterrence of money laundering and terrorist

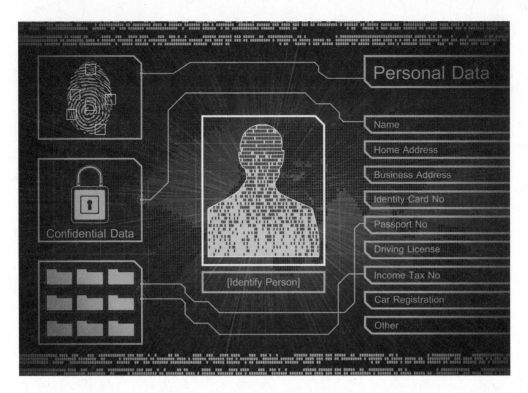

**Types of personal information** (Source: © iStockphoto.com/Danil Melekhin)

financing."[9] Under this legislation, all financial entities—all banks, credit unions, life insurance companies, security dealers, investment counsellors, foreign exchange dealers, property developers, casino operators, and even dealers in precious metals—are legally obliged to report to FINTRAC the details of all financial cash transactions of ten thousand dollars or more. The consent of the person to whom the information "belongs" is *not* required. Under a Memorandum of Understanding, the information reported to FINTRAC is then shared with the RCMP, the Canadian Police Information Centre, and similar bodies.

The FINTRAC system is possible because computing technologies have transformed the way the private sector conducts finance. Stock exchanges around the world play a pivotal role here by providing the market through which financial (and other) products are traded, and supply and demand (in theory) determine the worth and set the price. But here, too, we see the "innovative" use of masses of data: trading decisions today are "roboticized," buy- and sell-orders are made by powerful computers according to the proprietary algorithms that hedge funds and investment banks have programmed into them. Record keeping is computerized and trades are made at any time of the day or night. Because computers can respond more quickly than humans, electronic trading platforms have cut the time required to complete a trade to mere milliseconds, which, in turn, has caused trade volumes to soar.[10]

Preventing fraud in trades that occur at this speed and volume and with this level of programming sophistication and computer power can only be called a significant challenge to the government watchdogs that regulate the market. Unlike CSIS and the RCMP, these watchdogs do not have the powers, the tools, or the consent of governments to pursue lawbreakers. Instead, they require financial institutions to use real-time surveillance systems to monitor stock market trades and to signal officials when trading patterns appear abnormal. In this way, the job of policing is outsourced to the private sector conducting the business.

The passenger name records (PNRS) that are generated when we book airline tickets also provide a rich store of commercial data that can be used for government surveillance. PNRS are processed through massive global distribution systems; the main one used in Canada is Galileo, based in Colorado. PNRS can reveal a good deal of sensitive information about a traveller's preferences: meal needs, handicaps, religious practices, and allergies, for instance. Airlines also capture data on refugees or deportees. These data are used to generate no-fly lists by prescreening programs such as Secure Flight, administered by the US Transportation Security Administration, and its Canadian equivalent, Passenger Protect.[11] Sharing PNR data between countries has been a matter of continuous tension and negotiation between European data protection agencies and American authorities.

Data about Canadian citizens are also shared widely with our political parties. Under Canada's Election Act, Elections Canada is allowed to share the basic data from the electoral list. The rules for this sharing are quite stringently laid out in this act. However, each of the main federal parties has used the information they receive from the electoral list as a foundation to construct more extensive "voter management databases" that incorporate a range of other data about voters. These additional data come from a variety of private sector sources: telephone polling, traditional canvassing methods, petitions, letters, commercially available geo-demographic and marketing databases, and the analysis of online behaviour, including social media.

## Security System Requirements Can Violate Precepts of Dignity and Innocence

Although the logic behind systems like FINTRAC is that better information flow between the private and public sectors will enable the state to identify and prosecute illegal activity like money laundering or terrorism, this kind of surveillance can create real hardships for individuals who are wrongly identified as "suspicious."

For example, a Canadian student studying in the United Kingdom can trigger an investigation simply by depositing a scholarship in a British bank account. A sudden, large increase in the amount of money in an account, especially a new account, is one of the factors that may flag illegal activity and bring about a criminal investigation. In addition, since British universities with a licence to recruit international students under the points-based immigration system are required to monitor their attendance, just skipping classes can get foreign students into trouble with the law. Should they miss "ten consecutive expected contacts" without permission, the university must report them to the authorities.

---

These databases have become increasingly controversial for two reasons. First, they may have a significant impact on the democratic process, and second, they are unregulated by any of our privacy protection laws.[12]

Public data are also extensively used for private purposes. Most of these data are produced in aggregated and generic form (e.g., 64 percent of Canadians pay their credit card bills in full each month), but some are individually identified. Credit-rating companies, such as Equifax, use public information to assess your credit score in order to ascertain whether you are a "good" or "bad" credit risk. To do this, the company accesses numerous public records to determine whether you have declared bankruptcy, have liens against your property, owe outstanding fines, have a property dispute with an ex-spouse, or have any criminal convictions. Access to public data is regulated by provincial consumer credit laws.

### *Contracting Out Surveillance*

We began by showing how the idea of contracting out public services has become commonplace. In the realm of surveillance, this produces some challenges and some new grey areas. How exactly do the legal requirements to protect personal data work out when there are two sets of rules, one for

The University of East London goes one step further: foreign students who miss 25 percent of their classes are automatically deregistered. Other schools require foreign students to physically check in with staff. At Coventry University, foreign students must present their student identity cards at designated monitoring stations at least three times a week. Both the University of Greenwich and the University of the West of England require foreign students to check in once a month. The UK National Union of Students has taken a stand against this kind of monitoring, arguing that physical checks are discriminatory and violate the dignity of foreign students. The Union of Students also fears that these kinds of practices damage the relationships of trust that are at the heart of the academy.[1]

---

1. See Daniel Stevens's guest post, "Attendance Monitoring Has Gone Too Far—NUS Pulls Out the Stop Sign," Joint Council for the Welfare of Immigrants, 14 November 2012, http://www.jcwi.org.uk/blog/2012/11/14/attendance-monitoring-has-gone-too-far-%E2%80%93-nus-pulls-out-stop-sign#sthash.g1ejytLm.dpuf.

---

government and the other for the commercial sector? During 2012–13, for example, the governments of both British Columbia and Ontario considered using "common identifiers" for citizens who obtain government benefits, such as social assistance or employment insurance. Quite apart from the difficulty of handling the large databases involved, there are significant issues around accountability—who will be responsible for the personal data, the corporations supplying the equipment or the relevant government departments delivering the benefits? Will some database management be contracted out to private corporations? Will the common identifiers eventually be used in all government dealings with an individual? What rules will apply, the ones for the public sector or the ones for the private sector?

These questions have become even more difficult to resolve because partnerships between governments and private organizations in the business of surveillance are now a global phenomenon. Indeed, in most cases, the collaboration is so close that it is impossible to determine which party is dominant. In these collaborations, the public sector typically provides the money but delegates the nitty-gritty of decision making—regarding which security products should be purchased, for example—to the private sector as the acknowledged "experts" in the field. But since government contracts are worth millions of dollars to the companies involved, it is in the interests of

## Big Brother Inc.: Rights Groups Protest Export of Surveillance Products

We should not forget that, in the hands of repressive and authoritarian regimes, surveillance technologies can kill. So who is selling these technologies to such regimes, and what can be done about it?

Since 1995, the international activist group Privacy International has been engaged in an international campaign to "out" the companies that have been selling surveillance technologies to authoritarian regimes—in some cases, in violation of international law and export control restrictions. The campaign, called "Big Brother Inc.," seeks to reveal how the surveillance industry has grown in the last decade, and how, "in the hands of a repressive regime, this equipment eradicates free speech, quashes dissent and places dissidents at the mercy of ruling powers as effectively as guns and bombs, if not more so."

Repressive regimes with little respect for civil liberties have a particular interest in intercepting the communications of activists and dissidents. So they have been purchasing, mainly from Western companies, a variety of technologies for the interception of communications and the monitoring of Internet behaviour: malware (malicious software) that infects a target computer, instructing it to record every keystroke; hacking software that records communications and Internet browsing; and even systems that tap into undersea fibre-optic cables. The export of surveillance technologies is, Privacy International argues, almost indistinguishable from the export of arms.

Do such practices, therefore, violate general arms export–control regimes, requiring licences, end-user certificates, and so on? Privacy International has been pursuing litigation in several countries. In 2011, President Obama signed an executive order authorizing new sanctions and visa bans on those "digital guns for hire" who create or operate systems used to monitor, track, and target citizens in support of grave abuses of human rights.

technology companies to generate as much business as possible by selling ever more surveillance products (not to mention updates and maintenance). It is also in their interests to reinforce the security concerns that drive governments to make these purchases.

The impact of 9/11 was also economically significant. Although surveillance technologies were important before the World Trade Centre imploded, the opportunities offered by the 9/11 attacks gave a huge boost to a number of security industries.[13] Under the mantra of "connecting the dots," new systems

**Western surveillance technologies: a danger to democratic dissent?** (Source: © iStockphoto.com/EduardoLuzzatti)

Through research and investigation, public campaigning, political engagement, strategic litigation, and naming and shaming, the campaign is having some success. The names of corporations and government agencies implicated in this trade now appear in a "Surveillance Who's Who." The list is growing. Are any Canadian companies on that list? Five are mentioned.[2]

1. "Big Brother Inc.: A Global Investigation into the International Trade in Surveillance Technologies," Privacy International, 2012, https://www.privacyinternational.org/projects/big-brother-inc.
2. "Surveillance Who's Who," Privacy International, n.d., http://bigbrotherinc.org/v1/.

---

mushroomed, from data sharing and data mining to camera surveillance, full-body scanners, wider use of passenger name records by border agencies, international data-sharing, ID cards and enhanced driver's licences, behavioural observation, biometric technologies, and drones. These new priorities spread to "urban security," also reflecting 9/11 priorities with, for example, restricted access and more policing at organized events. The events of 9/11 also expanded how everyday information, such as that gleaned from social media, is appropriated for security-related surveillance.[14]

A final example comes from the world of "mega-events."[15] These globally publicized gatherings of huge numbers of people include major sports or athletic events, high-level political summit meetings, and music and cultural festivals. They attract a massive security operation, and security entrepreneurs typically travel the world, moving from event to event. Because of this, novel liaisons—and thus data sharing—among military, government, and commercial organizations are also created each time a mega-event is held. The Winter Olympics in Vancouver and the G20 meetings in Toronto provided just such occasions for data sharing, whether of video images or intelligence data relating to participants.

## Conclusion

This chapter comes to the stark conclusion that, in twenty-first-century Canada, surveillance is expanding steadily as personal data flow, in unprecedented ways, between private and public bodies. The blurring between these agencies may be illustrated in many ways, but the effect of driving more surveillance is common to each case. Public and private bodies have different mandates and different modes of accountability, and personal data become vulnerable to misuse and abuse as the data streams flow in new directions.

Data gathered for one purpose may easily be used for another when public and private organizations share data, which flies in the face of basic fair information practices. Also, accountability for personal-data handling becomes a real challenge when different legal regimes supposedly govern public and private entities. From the viewpoint of the ordinary citizen, it means that you can never know when personal information collected by government or police might become visible to commercial bodies or when data collected from a customer transaction could end up in a dispute over government benefits or could prevent you from boarding a flight. The complex and shifting network of relationships among public agencies, private corporations, and many other institutions in the vast grey area in between complicates the analysis, renders simplistic metaphors about Big Brother meaningless, challenges the ordinary citizen, and taxes our privacy laws.

# Notes

1   See Security Intelligence Review Committee, *Review of CSIS's Private Sector Relationships* SIRC Study 2010-02 (Ottawa: Canadian Security Intelligence Service, 14 February 2011).

2   See Canadian Internet Policy and Public Interest Clinic (CIPPIC), *On the Data Trail: How Detailed Information About You Gets into the Hands of Organizations with Whom You Have No Relationship—a Report on the Canadian Data Brokerage Industry* (Ottawa: CIPPIC, 2006), https://www.cippic.ca/sites/default/files/May1-06/DatabrokerReport.pdf/, 20; and "RCMP Turns to Data Brokers," *Ottawa Citizen*, 30 September 2006, http://www.canada.com/ottawacitizen/news/story.html?id=cof14734-9145-4e48-afca-cfec484aea57.

3   Leo Singer, "Unwarranted Access?" *National: Legal Insights and Practice Trends,* June 2012, http://www.nationalmagazine.ca/Articles/June-2012-Issue/Unwarranted-access.aspx.

4   Google, "Transparency Report," n.d., http://www.google.com/transparencyreport/userdatarequests/.

5   Electronic Frontier Foundation, "NSA Spying on Americans," n.d., https://www.eff.org/nsa-spying.

6   Didier Bigo, Gertjan Boulet, Caspar Bowden, Sergio Carrera, Julien Jeandesboz, and Amandine Scherrer, *Fighting Cyber Crime and Protecting Privacy in the Cloud*, European Parliament Study, 2012, http://www.europarl.europa.eu/RegData/etudes/etudes/join/2012/462509/IPOL-LIBE_ET(2012)462509_EN.pdf.

7   Ibid., 34.

8   "Cloud Computing Law Puts Canadians at Risk of Snooping by US Spies," *Ottawa Citizen*, 2 February 2013.

9   Office of the Privacy Commissioner of Canada, *Audit of the Financial Transactions and Reports Analysis Centre of Canada,* (Ottawa: Minister of Public Works and Government Services Canada, 2009), http://www.priv.gc.ca/information/pub/ar-vr/ar-vr_fintrac_200910_e.asp, 1.

10  High-speed trading platforms have cut the time it takes to complete a trading order down to 300 microseconds. In other words, the machines can process 100,000 orders per second, or 500 million per day. In this technological arms race, predatory traders labour constantly to discover and "game" the algorithms of opposing firms. (The shelf life of an algorithm is now down to fourteen days.) See Laureen Snider, "The Technological Advantages of Stock Market Traders," in *How They Got Away with It: White-Collar Crime and the Financial Meltdown,* ed. Susan Will, Stephen Handelman, and David C. Brotherton (New York: Columbia University Press, 2013), 151–70.

11  Public Safety Canada, "Safeguarding Canadians with Passenger Protect," last modified 12 September 2013, http://www.publicsafety.gc.ca/cnt/ntnl-scrt/cntr-trrrsm/pssngr-prtct/.

12  Colin J. Bennett and Robin M. Bayley, "Canadian Federal Political Parties and Personal Privacy Protection: A Comparative Analysis," Report to the Office of the Privacy Commissioner of Canada, March 2012, http://www.priv.gc.ca/information/pub/pp_201203_e.asp.

13  See, for example, Robert O'Harrow, *No Place to Hide* (Toronto: Free Press, 2005).

14  Daniel Trottier, "Policing Social Media," *Canadian Review of Sociology/Revue canadienne de sociologie* 49, no. 4 (2012): 411–25.

15  Colin J. Bennett and Kevin D. Haggerty, eds., *Security Games: Surveillance and Control at Mega-events* (London and New York: Routledge, 2011). See also http://www.security-games.com.

# The Growing Ambiguity of Personal Information

## From Personally Identified to Personally Identifiable

If the librarian asks, "Show me some ID, please," we assume that the basic address details usually written on an envelope will suffice. Some might ask for a driver's licence in addition, but what about your vehicle licence or even your face? Are they personal information? The answer is not so obvious, and this is just the point: the meaning of personal information is changing.

There was a time when it was relatively clear what "personal information" was. It was your name, your street address, perhaps also an official government-issued ID, such as your Social Insurance Number. By and large, we also knew how and when others were using this information to identify us. No doubt, confusion and misidentification occurred from time to time, but we were typically identified in ways that were familiar—and transparent—to us.

To a large extent, we also expected, or trusted, organizations we knew to protect our privacy, which they did by protecting other information linked to our personal identifiers—our bank records, our census returns, our consumer credit histories, our library borrowing record, and so on. If we did not want to be contacted by someone we did not know, we could get an unlisted telephone number.

Times have changed.

Canada's Public Safety minister recently defended attempts to update and extend the ability of law enforcement agencies to access the information that identifies us online by saying that the various ways in which we are

## Is Your Licence Plate Personal Information?

In 2011, the Alberta Court of Appeal concluded that for information to be about an "identifiable individual" under the Alberta Freedom of Information and Protection of Privacy Act, the person must be identifiable; in other words, the information must have a precise connection to an individual.[1] Such information must be *about* the individual—that is, directly related to the individual—and not about property that the individual might own (such as a car). Some information is not inherently personal but becomes so because it is associated indirectly with an individual through ownership. Thus, in Alberta, a driver's licence number is personal information but a licence plate number is not, even though, in Alberta at least, a licence plate is connected to the vehicle and linked through a database to an individual.

What happens, then, when licence plate numbers are automatically photographed and identified by automatic licence plate recognition (ALPR) cameras? These devices use optical character recognition technology to automatically read licence plates and then search that information through assorted databases. The information and privacy commissioner of British Columbia released a finding on this subject in late 2012. She found that people do have privacy expectations associated with their licence plates because while the number, on its own, is non-identifying, the common linkage between the number and identifiable information means the numbers should be protected.

Authorities seem to vacillate on whether licence plate information is private or public. For example, some police organizations have taken the position that the photos taken of plates are not personal, which justifies collecting them. They argue, however, that the public should not be able to access the records that have been generated on the basis of these photos because they contain personal information. Even after the RCMP sent out a letter formally recognizing that the data collected by authorities' scanning practices *are* personal information, the head of the RCMP's scanning program and other Canadian police officers have continued to assert that because vehicle licence plates are shown in public, there is no reasonable expectation of privacy regarding that information.[2]

---

identified online are no different from "phonebook data" that link a phone number to a name and a residential address. Just as the police can find out who the subscriber of a particular telephone number is, they should be able to find out who is behind the multiple identifiers that allow each of us to

**Your licence plate: personal data?** (Source: © iStockphoto.com/tomeng)

This confusion obfuscates the political nature of wide-scale surveillance. When data collected are "nonpersonal," it is relatively easy to convince the public and government oversight bodies of the appropriateness of the data collection. But when surveillance captures "personal" information, then legal protections and normative concerns arise, which could delay the deployment of such surveillance equipment. Whether a licence plate is, or is not, personal data has become an inherently political question.

1. *Leon's Furniture Limited v. Alberta (Information and Privacy Commissioner)*, 2011 ABCA 94 (CanLII), http://canlii.ca/en/ab/abca/doc/2011/2011abca94/2011abca94.html.
2. Christopher A. Parsons, Joseph Savirimuthu, Rob Wipond, and Kevin McArthur, "ANPR: Code and Rhetorics of Compliance," SSRN: Social Science Research Network, 4 September 2012, http://papers.ssrn.com/sol3/papers.cfm?abstract_id=2141127, 12.

communicate and network online. Here, the government is making a convenient but dubious distinction between this "subscriber data," which police would not need a warrant to access (just as they do not need a warrant to look you up in the phonebook), and the content of your communications, which would require prior judicial authorization (a warrant) on a standard of reasonable and probable cause that a crime has been, or will be, committed.

Our subscriber information is not, however, the same as our phonebook listing.[1] How we are identified online is complex and dynamic. Online communications involves many more identifiers than our name, phone number, and address. How many of us know about, let alone can decode, the following: the Internet Protocol (IP) address, the mobile identification number (MIN), the media access control (MAC) number, the Service Provider Identification Number (SPIN), the electronic serial number (ESN), the International Mobile Equipment Identity (IMEI) number, the International Mobile Subscriber Identity (EMSI) number, and the subscriber identity module (SIM)? Each of these identifiers can potentially be traced back to a unique user. So that is the first point. We are now identified in ways that are highly technical and largely mysterious. Most of us have no clue how we are identified online.

The second point is that using the Internet is not like using a telephone. It is not just a communications medium but the basic platform through which many of us engage in essential professional, personal, and political tasks: booking hotels and flights, social networking with friends and colleagues, shopping for books and music, organizing our lives through calendars, and conducting research. This information can be far more revealing about our lives than what we may say during telephone conversations. How we are identified through digital networks, therefore, provides important insights into who we are, what we do, whom we do it with, and when and where we do it.

Thus, the scrutiny of identifiers by organizations can reveal enormous amounts about our daily lives. If you want to test who might have access to your browsing habits, install a free download program like Collusion or Ghostery. Within seconds of browsing, you will see a list of ad networks or Web analysis and reporting tools that are tracking and sharing information about your online activities. Browse around further, and the list multiplies and spreads like a spider web. In the online world, we have become "identifiable" even if we are not "identified."

### Are IP and MAC Addresses Personal Information?

Every device connected to the public Internet is assigned a unique number known as an Internet Protocol (IP) address that allows applications to send information—like browsing results and email—to the correct recipient. IP addresses consist of four groups of numbers separated by periods. Since these numbers are usually assigned to Internet service providers within region-based blocks, an IP address can often be used to identify the user's general location. But the issue gets complicated because some IP addresses are dynamic, changing frequently.

The privacy commissioner of Canada has said that an IP address is personal information:

> An Internet Protocol (IP) address can be considered personal information if it can be associated with an identifiable individual. For example, in one complaint finding, we determined that some of the IP addresses that an internet service provider (ISP) was collecting were personal information because the ISP had the ability to link the IP addresses to its customers through their subscriber IDs.[2]

In spite of such decisions, there is a significant and long-running battle over whether the IP address is, or is not, personal information for the purposes of privacy law. The answer to this question is crucial for determining whether the average Internet user has any personal privacy rights over his or her searches, browsing habits, blog posts, or social networking activities. Google's official position is that an IP address is not personal information because it identifies a machine and not a person.[3] Many users may share one computer with a single IP address—members of the same family, for instance, or employees within a business, or students who share a library computer terminal. An Internet service provider will be able to associate the IP address with a home or business account but not (at least not ordinarily) to any particular person using a device linked to the Internet.

The mobility of our devices means that we are continually connecting to the Internet at coffee shops, airports, and other public places through a number of IP addresses. The privacy concerns are amplified with the growing use of media access control (MAC) addresses. MAC addresses are numbers that uniquely identify mobile devices—like cellphones, iPods, laptops, or tablets—on a network.

Just because devices and addresses are not stable does not mean that the addressing protocols are not personal information. If I change my home phone number every week, is it any less personal data? Is there really no threat to privacy because specific search queries supposedly cannot be narrowed down to a single individual? Knowing what a small group is seeking online can allow a third party to associate that behaviour with each individual member of that group, spreading the privacy risk and potential harm.

Although a MAC address or an IP address is rarely going to be directly related to one identifiable individual, it is how the MAC address or IP address is combined with other information (or could reasonably be combined with other information) about tastes, behaviours, and interests that has privacy advocates concerned.[4] If you knew and combined enough online and offline information, you might have enough data to make a highly probable (sometimes almost perfect) guess about who was doing what, when, and where.

### Identification and Re-identification

A related point is that individuals can be positively identified even when none of their personally identified information, like their name or address, is available. This is accomplished simply by combining other basic and non-identifiable information about them. A recent study of a random sample of people living in Montréal shows that almost 98 percent could be positively re-identified by name if one knew three variables: date of birth, gender, and postal code.[5] The researchers point out that these findings have especially troubling implications for health research, because people are demonstrably more comfortable about sharing their health data if there is a low risk of re-identification.

Re-identification science works to identify unique individuals despite efforts that have been made to strip obvious identifiers from existing data sets (called "de-identification"). The sophistication with which such re-identification science is pursued in some quarters has led some researchers to conclude that the goal of de-identification can give a false sense that anonymity has been achieved. Common anonymization practices no longer protect privacy. Re-identification science disrupts basic assumptions about what is, and is not, personal data and has forced regulators and analysts to rethink essential principles about information privacy. Personal identification is not a binary choice between data being either identifiable or not identifiable. Rather, the process of identification resides on a complicated and dynamic continuum and depends on what other information may later be combined with that already collected. Risks to individuals do not disappear when personal identifiers are removed. And this is not just a scientific

## Is Your Facial Image Personal Information?

As Ayan strolls down Montréal's Sherbrooke Street, her friends and acquaintances recognize her face, and if they know her reasonably well, they can associate her face with her name. This situation has led some to assert that she, like anyone else in a public place, has no reasonable expectation of privacy. As soon as Ayan chooses to be out "in public," she immediately surrenders her privacy rights.

But things are not so simple. If the clothing store that Ayan enters captures her image on its surveillance cameras, does that mean that she has surrendered any rights to control how that image might be used, or who might access it? Our laws say no. Even if her image cannot be immediately associated with Ayan herself as "an identifiable individual," organizations must, by law, protect those data and only use them for legitimate purposes. The fact that Ayan, and most of the people she knows, use social media further complicates this situation. Social media sites use facial-imaging software that allows her and her friends to tag images with identifiers and share them widely.

Such software uses algorithms to measure facial features such as the relative position, size, and/or shape of the eyes, nose, cheekbones, and jaw. Those data can then be used to search for other images with matching values on other databases. "Tagging" images on social networks such as Facebook is controversial and has inspired significant protests from privacy advocates. In late 2012, Facebook promised to forego its facial-tagging program in response to protests from regulators and advocates, but the practice continues.

The privacy implications of being able to associate Ayan's face to her name are huge. Aside from the uses that may be made by law enforcement, these technologies have also been described as a "stalker's dream." Yes, Ayan's face, and your face, are personal information. And yes, we should have rights over how that information is captured and shared.

and academic issue. Huge economic interests are at stake. As Internet use has increased and other digital communication technologies have proliferated, the accessibility of information has grown exponentially, fuelling individual empowerment and democratic participation. At the same time, the Internet makes it much easier for organizations to capture, process, and disseminate information about individuals, often by hidden means. A wide variety of entities can now observe online behaviour by monitoring the network, by tapping into the vast quantity of data collected about individual

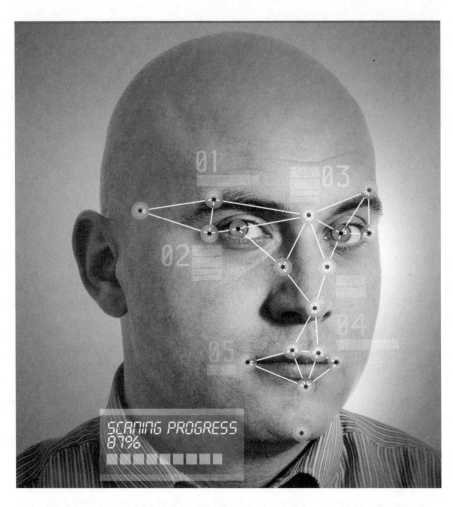

**Facial scanning: making your facial image accessible—but to whom?** (Source: © iStockphoto.com/ rappensuncle)

Internet usage, or by installing spyware directly on individual computers. Third-party advertisers do not need to know your real life "identity" so long as you can be identified by a technically specified address and thus targeted with personalized ads.

Processing personally related information online is therefore fundamental to the business models through which "Big Data" companies actually make money. Advertising is the lifeblood of the Internet economy. To the extent that companies can discover more detailed and extensive information about personal preferences and behaviours, they will make more money. To some extent, privacy laws constrain that ability. Rules about notification, informed consent, access, correction of personal data, and so on are not just an important limit on the ability of an organization to monitor consumers; they also have profound economic consequences. So, too, does the definition of personal information and the argument over what is, and is not, personal information. If information is "personal," organizations are constrained, but if it is not, they are unregulated.

## User-Generated Content

Another source of confusion around traditional understandings of personal information relates to social networking. Traditionally, we conceived privacy concerns as stemming from personal information about individuals being collected and processed by organizations. Big organizations primarily control personal data, which they analyze using the latest technologies in order to make decisions about individuals in their capacities as consumers, clients, students, employees, and so on.

In the world of social networking, however, the individual generates most of those data. User-generated content (UGC), also known as consumer-generated media (CGM), refers to any material created and uploaded to the Internet by users themselves, whether that is a comment left about a book on Amazon.com, or a video uploaded to YouTube, or a profile on Facebook. UGC has been around in one form or another since the earliest days of the Internet. But in the past few years, thanks to the growing availability of high-speed access and search technology, it has become one of the fastest-growing forms of content and has revolutionized how users interact with each other and how advertisers reach those individuals.

If we produce user-generated content, does that personal information belong to us or to the companies whose platforms host it? Do these organizations have a responsibility to apply all the privacy principles to the data we provide? Our regulators tend to say yes, insisting that social-networking services are data controllers, whatever the source of the personal data processed.[6]

Companies tend to see things differently, which is apparent from the definitions of "personal information" contained in their official privacy policies, as documented by a recent study of the most popular twenty-four social-networking sites used in Canada.[7] Predictably, conceptions of which characteristics accurately define personally identifiable information vary across these sites. Here are some examples:

- *Google* (for Blogger and Google+): Information that the user provides to Google which personally identifies that person, such as your name, email address, or billing information, or other data that can be reasonably linked to such information by Google.
- *Facebook*: Name, profile pictures and cover photos, network, gender, username, and user ID. Facebook may collect IP address, GPS location, Internet service provider, location, type of browser, or the pages you visit.
- *Flickr*: Name, gender, birthdate, postal code, and email address. Flickr collects information about users' transactions with Yahoo and with their business partners, including information about users' use of financial products and services that they offer.
- *Instagram*: The amount and type of information that Instagram gathers depends on the nature of the interaction.
- *Plenty of Fish* (a Canadian dating site): Contact information, personal preferences (e.g., language preferences), marketing information (e.g., photographs), other information provided in your personal profile (e.g., interests, marital status, height, weight, occupation).
- *Zynga*: Name, profile picture or its URL, user ID number, your friends' user ID numbers and other public data, login email, physical location and that of access devices, gender, birthday.

These definitions have implications for privacy. For instance, Nexopia, advertised on its site as "Canada's largest social networking site for youth," advises users that "to help members find and communicate with each other, you may submit and post additional profile data, including but not limited to the following: weight, height, sexuality (i.e., sexual orientation), dating and living situation, and information regarding your interests."[8] To be sure, this information is not mandatory for using Nexopia, yet all information provided in one's profile is not identified as "collected personal information" and may thus be shared accordingly.

Ping, Apple's social networking site (SNS) for music, ostensibly provides a category of protected personally identifiable information to its users but limits this category to contact and payment information. The category does not include information gathered about a user's family and friends: when a Ping user shares his or her favourite music with others, "Apple may collect the information you provide about those people such as name, mailing address, email address, and phone number."[9] Put simply, Apple collects the personally identifiable information of third parties, and, because Apple's privacy policy does not apply to these third parties, Apple does not consider this information to be personally identifiable.

And then there is the question of metadata—the data about the data, typically including identifiers such as users' IP addresses, their operating systems, and any information gained from cookies: information that can subsequently be used not only to identify individuals and their personal browsing habits but also to track their physical location. Of the twenty-four SNSS surveyed in this research, not one identified any element of metadata as personally identifiable information, nor did any of them give users any expectation of privacy regarding their metadata. Unsurprisingly, the motivation for this treatment of metadata is overwhelmingly couched in the language of the SNS's efforts to improve the user experience. IP addresses or cookie information are necessary, it is reasoned, to combine services, to prevent problems, to keep products safe, and, generally, to tailor one's use for a more "personalized" approach. The broader privacy implications are rarely addressed.

Many social networks (indeed, many websites) also permit access through pseudonyms that conceal a user's identity but allow them to be recognized on a return visit. These are sometimes referred to as unique "handles" and are designed to be deliberately opaque—but clearly linkable to a particular individual. People rely on this form of identification in multiple scenarios and contexts on the Internet because pseudonyms often encourage more candour and openness. However, people also tend to choose the same pseudonyms for different sites, making it easy for them to be re-identified.

Since online companies make money with these data, should we not have some rights over their use? But how, then, would one exercise those rights if a condition of using a service is to authenticate one's identity? There is circularity here: one has to reveal one's real identity to exercise rights over personal data that were originally shrouded.

### So What Does the Law in Canada Say About Personally Identifiable Information?

Over the past thirty years, the federal and provincial governments across Canada have gradually passed privacy legislation. Initially, most of these laws regulated the public sector; only later were they extended to private corporations. With few exceptions, most organizations in Canada, both public and private, are expected to follow a set of common information privacy principles. Not surprisingly, however, legal definitions of what constitutes personal information are not uniform.

Most laws tend to use the word "identifiable information." Thus, the federal law governing the private sector (PIPEDA) states, "Personal information means information about an identifiable individual."[10] This is very flexible, but it can also be quite circular.

Other laws define specific types of personal data exactly and include long lists of categories of data to which the legislation applies. Here, for instance, is the list in the Freedom of Information and Protection of Privacy Act in Ontario:

(a)  information relating to the race, national or ethnic origin, colour, religion, age, sex, sexual orientation or marital or family status of the individual;

(b)  information relating to the education or the medical, psychiatric, psychological, criminal or employment history of the individual or information relating to financial transactions in which the individual has been involved;

(c)  any identifying number, symbol or other particular assigned to the individual;

(d)  the address, telephone number, fingerprints or blood type of the individual;

(e)  the personal opinions or views of the individual except where they relate to another individual;

(f)  correspondence sent to an institution by the individual that is implicitly or explicitly of a private or confidential nature, and replies to that correspondence that would reveal the contents of the original correspondence;

(g)  the views or opinions of another individual about the individual; and

(h)   the individual's name where it appears with other personal information relating to the individual or where the disclosure of the name would reveal other personal information about the individual.[11]

Other Canadian laws include subtly different categories of sensitive and nonsensitive forms of information. But such lists can never be exhaustive, and the definition of what is, and is not, sensitive is invariably subjective and inherently related to the context. For instance, having our names and addresses in the phonebook might be in our interests, but that same information on a blacklist, a no-fly list, or a file of bad credit risks would be incredibly sensitive. In other words, the same information in different contexts and used for different purposes can affect the risk to privacy dramatically.

Many other laws, like the privacy law in Ontario, specify that the information has to be "recorded." But what does that mean? Can one have rights over one's personal data even if they are not recorded? The law covering the private sector in Québec is a bit different: personal information is "any information which relates to a natural person and allows that person to be identified."[12]

Other laws include lists of information to which the legislation does *not* apply: basic business contact information, for example, or, more controversially, "work product" information produced by individuals in the course of their employment, business, or profession. Controversially, this exemption has been extended to include medical prescriptions written by Canadian doctors. The work-product exemption also tends to exclude the data submitted about a business on consumer reporting websites like www.travelocity.com or www.yelp.com. It would be totally unreasonable to ask a business to consent before a consumer posted a critical review of his experience at a hotel or restaurant. But then what about evaluations of teachers or professors on www.ratemyprofessor.ca? Is this the personal information of the professor or of the student, or both?

The Canadian privacy commissioner often struggles with whether personal information, as defined in the federal laws governing the public and private sectors (PIPEDA and the Privacy Act, respectively), is being processed, and thus whether its legal provisions apply. In many cases, the question of whether privacy is at risk often rests on tricky questions of probability. Our commissioners and courts struggle with an evolving legal framework, which always seems to be one or two steps behind the technology.

## Conclusion

The contentious and confusing definition of personal information exposes a basic problem with trying to use privacy laws to address the entire range of social problems captured by the word *surveillance*: *surveillance can occur even when personal information is not collected.* The examples above demonstrate that the information available about us online cannot be split into two neat categories, some of it personal and some of it nonpersonal. Rather, the risks to privacy tend to depend on what organizations assume about us when they collect information about us and on how likely it is that they will be able to use our information to identify us individually. Analysis of the risks may just as likely be based on subjective judgments about organizational motivations. And just because an organization can identify an individual does not mean that it will do so.

This trend also confronts us with a larger question about how to understand this looming social problem in political terms. Privacy analysis and privacy law tend to begin and end with the existence of personally identified or identifiable information. If no claim can be made about the actual or potential linkage between a surveillance practice and a specific individual, then the privacy regime cannot help.

One major contribution of surveillance scholarship is the insistence that power relations are present between the watcher and watched even when personal information is *not* captured. Video surveillance cameras do not need to be working or monitored to change behaviour: the prospect or potential for surveillance is often enough. Individuals might not be monitored at any one time, but they would be well advised to behave as if they were. Similar dilemmas plague the capture of information by ubiquitous computing devices, remote sensors, drones, or radio frequency identification (RIFD) tags, which allow data to be transferred wirelessly using electromagnetic fields and are used by many industries to track the physical location of products. And on the Internet, your browsing behaviour might not be monitored, but many of us now know enough about the potential for surveillance to be careful and to take protective steps, or perhaps not to browse on certain topics.

Surveillance technologies structure power relations and imbalances between individuals and between individuals and organizations, whether personal data are captured or not. If no personal data are collected, it is difficult to contend that a "privacy problem" per se exists. Yet power is and can be exercised without any personally related data being captured, anonymized or otherwise. The growing ambiguity and complexity of these questions brings into focus the range of surveillance problems that lie outside the very broad realm of personal privacy protection.[13]

## Notes

1 Office of the Privacy Commissioner of Canada, *What an IP Address Can Reveal About You: A Report Prepared by the Technology Analysis Branch of the Office of the Privacy Commissioner of Canada,* May 2013, http://www.priv.gc.ca/information/research-recherche/2013/ip_201305_e.asp.

2 Office of the Privacy Commissioner of Canada, "Legal Information Related to PIPEDA," last modified 2 October 2013, http://www.priv.gc.ca/leg_c/interpretations_02_e.asp.

3 Alma Whitten, "Are IP Addresses Personal?" Google Public Policy Blog, 22 February 2008, http://googlepublicpolicy.blogspot.com/2008/02/are-ip-addresses-personal.html.

4 Paul Ohm, "Broken Promises of Privacy: Responding to the Surprising Failures of Anonymization," *UCLA Law Review* 57 (2010): 1701–77.

5 Khaled El Emam, David Buckeridge, Robyn Tamblyn, Angelica Neisa, Elizabeth Jonker, and Aman Verma, "The Re-identification Risk of Canadians from Longitudinal Demographics," *BMC Medical Infomatics and Decision Making* 11, no. 46 (2011), http://www.biomedcentral.com/1472-6947/11/46.

6 See, for instance, EU Article 29 Data Protection Working Party, *Opinion 5/2009 on Online Social Networking,* adopted 12 June 2009, http://ec.europa.eu/justice/policies/privacy/docs/wpdocs/2009/wp163_en.pdf.

7 Colin J. Bennett, Adam Molnar, Christopher Parsons, Brittany Shamess, and Michael Smith, *An Analysis of SNS Policies,* unpublished report funded through the Office of the Privacy Commissioner of Canada's Contributions Program, 2012.

8 See Nexopia Privacy Policy, last updated 31 May 2013, www.nexopia.com/privacy, as well as http://www.nexopia.com/mag/about-us.

9 See Apple Privacy Policy, last updated 1 August 2013, www.apple.com/privacy/.

10 Canada, Personal Information Protection and Electronic Documents Act (PIPEDA), 2000, s. 2(1).

11 Canada, Freedom of Information and Protection of Privacy Act, R.S.O. 1990, c. F.31, s. 2 (1).

12 Province of Québec, An Act Respecting the Protection of Personal Information in the Private Sector, c. P-39.1, s. 2, http://www2.publicationsduquebec.gouv.qc.ca/dynamicSearch/telecharge.php?type=2&file=/P_39_1/P39_1_A.html.

13 See Colin J. Bennett, "In Defense of Privacy: The Concept and the Regime," *Surveillance and Society* 8, no. 4 (2011): 485–96.

# Expanding Mobile and Location-Based Surveillance

## From Who You Are to Where You Are

Until about five years ago, a favourite claim of Internet pundits was that new information and communication technologies (ICTs) would make geography irrelevant. They envisioned a world where new technology would allow us to easily communicate with people anywhere in the world, get the information and media we desire from anywhere, and work equally well in the office, at home, or in a café in Antigua. And while many of those things have come to pass, the surveillance capabilities embedded in the technologies that make such developments possible give new significance to geography—precisely because now we can be almost anywhere and still be contacted. This greater ability to track and locate individuals represents another key surveillance trend in Canada and elsewhere.

Consider how our telephone use has changed over time. Not long ago, few of us would have begun a phone conversation with the question, "Where are you?" Phone numbers designated places, equivalent to street addresses. Today, with the omnipresence of cellphones, our caller could be almost anywhere on the planet. At the same time, the technology itself has a built-in need for (approximate) location data since calls must be routed to wherever the receiving phone happens to be.

In addition, our ability to pinpoint the location of a phone has improved. Early cellphone networks could locate a cellphone to within one hundred metres. Once the global positioning system (GPS) became publicly available in 2000,* civilian users were given fine-grained positional data. Today, phones are capable of identifying their location within a range of two metres.[1] The number of devices using GPS data exploded as the unit cost of GPS processing chips became so low that they could be added to any device without significantly altering its manufacturing cost. Most new chips are compatible with other satellite navigation systems, including the Russian GLONASS system, the Chinese Compass, and the forthcoming EU/ESA Galileo. This multiplication of systems and the greater market for competing global navigation satellite system infrastructures is likely to produce faster, cheaper, and more precise localization data.**

As devices that can read GPS data have become cheaper, the previous divide between well-to-do cellphone owners and poor landline users no longer applies. Even the most basic "free" phone has a built-in ability to track our geographic location. In fact, as mobile devices become more powerful, many low-income consumers are abandoning personal computers altogether.[2]

This ability to locate cellphones is being replicated for other everyday objects through the use of RFID chips, which make these objects uniquely identifiable, as well as through the latest Internet Protocol systems, which make it theoretically possible to assign an IP address to nearly every object in the world. Sensors that can read RFID tags and share information about their location over the network will be embedded in our homes and offices, in public buildings, and in locations along the street, thereby enabling the movements of these objects (including human beings) to be mapped in real time. This is the much-hyped future "Internet of things," where the physical world and informational flows will become layers in our daily existence. In that future, simply walking down the street will generate flows of information about minute details of our everyday interactions with our environment.

Developments such as these will multiply in the next few years because they ostensibly benefit both those who do the tracking and those who are tracked. They also represent a particularly significant and rapidly developing

* It is no longer correct to refer to such a system as a GPS, since that is the name of a specific US military system, which is only one among many. It is a global navigation satellite system, or a GNSS. In this study, however, we continue to use "GPS" because of its familiarity.

** A number of commentators have raised questions about the impact of this data on vulnerable populations, such as women seeking to escape from abusive relationships.

form of surveillance. In what follows, we explore a few important facets of the potential for mass geographic tracking of objects and people. We are concerned here with everyday, large-scale tracking and will not discuss police, intelligence, and other forms of tracking used in law enforcement.

## Continuous Versus Sporadic and Trace Geolocation

Almost any form of data gathering can reveal aspects of your location. Your credit, debit, and loyalty cards all situate you at specific places and times. If you use a card five times a day, someone could learn a good deal about your movements that day. After a few months of accumulated data, a precise picture of the spatial distribution of your main habits would be apparent.[3] Access control cards or biometrics also pinpoint a person's location, allowing his or her activities to be tracked and mapped. These processes are referred to as "geolocalization." And while such activities are possible, we should be careful not to equate what is possible with what is really happening. Many of these complex analytical operations are probably not being undertaken and may not yet be doable at a reasonable cost.

Location-based surveillance, however, is different from such efforts to develop a locational profile by piggybacking on other, previously existing systems. Location-based surveillance provides spatial data immediately, without the need for data-mining analysis. Whatever its ultimate goal, a location technology always produces location data.

### Continuous Geolocation

In order to receive calls, a portable phone must continuously inform its carrier's system about where it is. Most phones do this by sending a roaming signal to nearby antennas. All carriers collect and keep these data for billing and other purposes. For example, they can be used to identify usage trends in order to plan for future infrastructure needs. Other potential uses are more nebulous. A recent mini-scandal involving Apple's iPhones showed that Apple "location services," which are part of the phone's operating system, kept a full year's worth of geolocation data in the device's memory (although the information was not sent to Apple's servers).

Many consumer products now aim to produce continuous, instantly available tracking. Parents, for example, may use RFID bracelets to ensure

## The iPhone Panic of 2011

In the spring of 2011, two Apple aficionados noticed that a curious file was being synced between their iPhones and their computers. Further investigation revealed it to be a log of every phone tower and Wi-Fi hot spot they had been near in the last twelve months. The friends then designed an application that helped to demonstrate how the tracing data recorded their phone's movements, and the Internet exploded with the rumour that Apple was tracking iPhone users. In fact, it turned out that Apple was not collecting the data. The location information is simply left as an unencrypted file in the phone and on the individual users' computers and is updated each time the phone is synced. These data are used to feed location-based applications such as FourSquare and, of course, iAds.

Apple does not need to know where its hardware customers are, but it needs its phones to deliver geographically targeted information to their users, ostensibly to provide them with a better experience, but also to maximize revenue by sending ads for businesses that are close to the phone. Apple is not unique. Google Now, the digital assistant that is part of Android 4.1, "Jelly Bean," also monitors the user's location and spontaneously offers information related to the immediate surroundings when in "passive mode."

Google Now can also deduce facts or meanings about locations. For instance, it automatically identifies your home and place of work according to the data it collects on your habitual movements. Linked to geolocation applications (such as the previous Google Latitude), this system allows users to control and fine-tune how this information is shared with "friends" or with anyone who wants to know their location.

Google Glass, the Internet giant's next project, promises to superimpose selected data directly over the wearer's field of vision (often referred to as "augmented reality") using special

---

that children do not leave the grounds of a city park. A distrustful spouse can surreptitiously install a GPS device on a partner's car for the purpose of spying on his or her movements. Some of these devices simply sample and record a person's location, but others can be queried remotely at any time for instant, real-time checks. Car-rental, car-sharing, and taxi companies have begun using these for fleet control and, if applicable, for ensuring that their cars remain within a permitted range. Commercial transportation companies have been using these devices for a while, as have police forces

**The iPhone—a tracking device?** (Source: Wikimedia Commons and map from iPhone Tracker application)

glasses. These glasses will need to carefully select "relevant" information to avoid information overload and the need to constantly fiddle with the device. This means more profiling and targeting of users. Each query, whether generated by the user or the device, will be geocoded and linked to the individual user's account for an unknown length of time.

and ambulance services. In all cases, fleet management is the primary goal, but, of course, the whereabouts of employees and clients are simultaneously recorded.

Truly continuous geolocation is seldom an efficient use of limited communication and computer resources. Much the same outcome can be secured through discontinuous geolocation—the practice of intermittently collecting data from a device. This involves recording significant or useful data, even though it does not produce a full record of a person's movements.

Because humans are creatures of habit, accumulating these discontinuous data over short periods of time—say, a few months—makes it possible to predict fairly accurately where someone will be at any time.

### *Sporadic and Discontinuous Geolocation*

A GPS device continuously records its location while it is being used, as is the case, for instance, with automotive and marine GPS navigation devices. This localization is *internal* in the sense that a pure GPS device computes its own location and does not respond to, check in with, or inform any outside system about its location. There is no third-party user. Only its owner can see the data and watch his or her own position.

**TransLink trolley bus, Vancouver** (Source: © Wikimedia Commons/Bobanny, http://commons.wikimedia.org/wiki/File:Vancouver_trolley2101_050720.jpg)

GPS-based localization surveillance is, for the most part, sporadic and/or discontinuous. Sporadic localization occurs when GPS data are recorded on the device for later use. In that case, a third party could retrace the movements of the device's owner within a certain timeframe (as determined by the device's capabilities). One example is the typical GPS-based handheld locator for hikers, which keeps a predetermined number of positions in its memory.

Discontinuous surveillance can occur when a device intermittently and automatically checks in and gives its position; most modern portable phones work this way. A roaming cellphone locates itself roughly in cells but can also triangulate its position with signals from multiple antennas or through its GPS unit if more precise positioning is required. From the surveillance agent's point of view, such discontinuous surveillance has the disadvantage of producing sizable amounts of "junk" data: useless information about routine, unchanging, uninteresting, or repeated geographic positions. Portable phone users may also simply turn off all geolocation services other than the necessary roaming information, something often done in order to preserve battery life. In fact, many phones do this automatically when the battery level is low. Consequently, GPS-based surveillance via portable devices is highly unreliable.

There are numerous other examples of discontinuous geolocation and new technologies that sample our geolocation. For instance, some public transit cards or toll highway cards record your point of entry and point of exit in order to compute your fare or toll.

Finally, location data may exist simply as traces left on entirely unrelated activities. Twitter, for example, has been geotagging tweets since 2009. This means that every time someone tweets, Twitter records information about the location of the device used to create the tweet. Tweets can be searched and sorted based on this location information. Applications such as Twoogle Geo Search can use these data to map recent tweets around a specified location anywhere on the globe.[4] Users can then be "followed" and their uploaded media consulted. Applications automating this process might draw quick profiles of people at certain locations or search for locations where people with specific profiles have gathered.

Ordinary photos taken with a phone or a GPS-enabled camera can also contain location data. These cameras record their location—and the location of any person within the picture—at the time of the shot. If one combines this with, for instance, Facebook's new facial-recognition capabilities, it is possible not only to be "tagged" in pictures but to have the picture reveal where you were at certain times.

Perhaps more than any other form of location data, the value of trace location depends on individual users' relationships with their technologies. For those who take one picture a year with their phones or tweet once a week, the traces are so far apart that they reveal very little. But some Twitter users update their accounts several dozen times per day, and some food enthusiasts systematically take pictures of their meals (and tweet them!). Anyone who follows these tweets for a short while can predict the tweeter's position at any time of the day.

## Geography and Identity

Geolocalization, in its purest form, produces a set of coordinates. This geo-spatial data can be immediately helpful in watching or finding people. For instance, the Toddler Tag lets you know where your kids are within 150 feet; the Victoria Tracking Service does the same thing around the globe.[5] The Freedom GPS Locator Watch is designed to track family members who have Alzheimer's disease.[6] Hikers lost in the mountains may use GPS beacons to be rescued. In all of these cases, this information is only about physical loca-tion. Physical places, however, have their own meanings.

We can break down the secondary analysis of location data into three categories. The first is "georelational" and has to do with the ability to place others on the same map as you. It is now obvious that applications such as Facebook are extensions of conventional social networks created by people who share the same spaces, belong to the same groups, or work in the same locations. This is why notifying friends of one's location makes sense. If your network is spread over the globe, the likelihood that a member might be close to another would be extremely low. So allowing others to see our posi-tion is a way to anchor our networks, at least in part, in physical space—and to actually meet one another. Of course, third parties can then find out who you happen to be with and at what time. This is the basis for such infamous mobile applications as Girls Around Me—which loads Facebook profiles of nearby women (or men) who have recently "checked in" with Foursquare, a location-based mobile service—and for the less controversial Banjo, which uses much more powerful capabilities to query nearly all social networking sites to see who might be nearby. Note also that georelational data can be interpreted temporally: being with one's coworker at 3:00 p.m. is not the same as being with him or her at 3:00 a.m. These data can also be highly gendered. The James Bond–style silhouettes of girls dancing used in Girls Around Me, for example, led to a spirited debate about how technology depicts women as either victims or objects.[7]

A second way to categorize positional data is "geosocial." This involves mapping personal position onto socially significant sites. Being at home, for instance, is not the same as being at work, and the red light district is not the same as the entertainment district. The geosocial is also temporal, since different times of day mean different things in the same geographic spot: being home during the day has a different meaning than being home in the evening.

**Applications like Glympse provide continuous localization data**
(Source: Google Play)

Finally, positional data are also "geoinformational" or "geocomputational." In the near future of the Internet, we can expect that data will probably be generated by networks and subnetworks comprising humans and machines. This kind of ubiquitous computing would mean that machines no longer simply carry and store contents but also understand, manipulate, and create it. In short, machines will probably become part of the network instead of being mere communication tools.

In a universe of ubiquitous computing, the role of humans in the network will be transformed in unpredictable ways. The physical and informational layers of users' experience will overlap and merge as the gap we currently identify between the real and the virtual breaks down. Geolocation of all objects will become an integral part of our lives. Most of the technologies needed to bring about these developments already exist.

## Geography in Practice

What is particularly interesting about the surveillance of mobility is how those data are used. The immediate use of portable phone continuous localization data is to route calls to subscribers. The use of location data for non-routing purposes, however, can result in forms of intervention that can affect both subscribers and nonsubscribers. Often, this intervention will involve classifying and sorting people into groups so that they can be treated differently. For instance, consumers can be assigned high or low value according to the locations they frequent. People who tend to be found in more affluent areas may be given preferential access to valued items, services, premises, sample merchandise, and the like. The police are starting to recognize the value of data mining the online information that is freely available to them. As this practice continues, we can anticipate that specific, preprogrammed position sequences and movements will be interpreted as suspicious, triggering a police response.

In order to better understand the practical applications of geolocation, it is useful to split them into two interrelated categories. The first involves internal uses of geolocation, where users initiate the localization process as a service in and of itself. By contrast, external geolocation occurs when a non-user—usually a service provider—collects location data for its own purposes from users engaged in other activities. Often, this involves individuals who agree to be watched in exchange for goods and services.

### Internal Geolocation

The consumer initiates internal geolocation. For instance, applications such as Foursquare give users the option to "check in" and tell their friends where they are. Google+ and Facebook have equivalent location services for members who want to share their location with selected (groups of) people. In these cases, location data are not merely an exchange currency offered in order to obtain another service; they are the end in itself.

Of course, the ability to broadcast one's location on the Internet is anything but new; even the earliest website could be updated with location status by its webmaster. Early blogs often reported where the blogger had been at what time. What is new in so-called geosocial networking is that the location of the user is taken as an integral part of the experience of communicating with others. Such location information is assumed to be trustworthy because it is automated instead of being reported by the user. Users of mobile devices can still choose when to reveal their location, but it is harder to lie about where you are.

### External Geolocation

Geolocation is external when the consumer is not the immediate beneficiary. The main purpose of most of the technologies and strategies listed above is to market goods, services, and information to users. In fact, in almost every case, the popular applications that locate users are free in the sense that the main price paid is usually a greater exposure to advertisements. However, the line between advertisement and content has become so faint that, from the point of view of the user, it can be imperceptible. Of course, the classic banner ad appearing on top of the content, now omnipresent on YouTube, for instance, is easy to notice because many find it so downright annoying. But a new series of "hybrids" are erasing any remaining distinction between content and advertising. Apple's iAds, among others, are designed to be "played" and shared with others like any other content. Facebook "likes" are both an expression of users' interests and advertisement. Typical media files such as songs and movies are almost always linked to marketing goals through embedded advertising, product placement, or "special offer" bundles.

External forms of geolocation are used in this context. The increasingly targeted nature of marketing has evolved to include location, for two reasons. The first has to do with the fact that much commerce is still done in person. Consequently, the proximity to physical points of sale is still taken as an important opportunity by advertisers and vendors. Interactive ads are more useful if they target not only users' interests but also their current position in the city. McDonald's Canada offers an Android and iPhone application whose sole function is to use GPS or network location services to find its restaurants. It has been installed thousands of times per month since it

**McDonald's Canada Android application** (Source: Google Play)

was first launched. The application also accesses the phone's unique serial number and the user's phone number to upload and download (unspecified) information to and from McDonald's Canada servers. In other words, users offer their position, as well as other data, so that McDonald's can tell them if they are close to one of its restaurants.

We can therefore predict that mass geolocation will happen not *in spite of* consumer protest but rather *because* consumers demand it. The ability to trade location information for goods and services is already seen as giving new value to an otherwise apparently useless category of personal information.[8] Therefore, unless consumers question whether it is against laws, ethics, good sense, or collective interest, it will probably recede from public debate. Consumers readily exchange "units" of personal information to obtain goods, services, and information. We are trained to look for offers, deals, and coupons, and, in order to ensure value, we seek the opinions of other consumers who were there and saw for themselves. We also need to instantly find shared cars, city bikes, or buses nearby to reduce the environmental impact of mass transit. Many of us subscribe to Onstar vehicle navigation services because we like the safety of being watched over while driving. Apparently, some of us also want to know the ratio of males to females in a bar before entering.[9] This is why, according to Programmable Web, location APIs (application programming interfaces) and mashups (applications that use and combine other services into new products) related to location are multiplying rapidly—although, of course, at this point, the same is true of all mobile applications.[10]

The second factor fuelling the development of location awareness is the eagerness of industries to learn more about consumers in order to market and deliver products and services. Here, it is not the physical proximity of consumers to enterprises that is important but the meaning of their geographically distributed habits. For instance, Amazon might like to know where you are so that it can offer to sell you a book about that place.

The same kinds of information can be used to help manage and maintain physical infrastructure, like roads and highways. This kind of surveillance is already used on the Greater Toronto Area toll highway 407 (ETR407) and on the new Port Mann Bridge connecting Coquitlam to Surrey, for instance, where information from entry and exit points is collected to bill customers. The system could eventually manage congestion with flexible toll rates, a feature commonly used elsewhere. ETR407 uses special transponders—which emit a unique signal, allowing them to communicate with other signalling devices—installed on windshields, as well as licence plate registration and automated recognition. This latter system, usually referred to as automated licence plate recognition (ALPR) or automated number plate recognition (ANPR, mostly in the UK), is growing faster than most other systems today. ALPR is used by automated traffic control cameras, cameras mounted on police cruisers, automated car park operators, and many others. ALPR is also installed for environmental policies designed to limit the number of cars in downtown areas and for security initiatives. To date, most ALPR systems require dedicated video cameras. However, new software can analyze large quantities of data and look for licence plates in prerecorded video or banks of static images.

When geolocation traces are available or can be extracted from other systems such as municipal traffic cameras equipped with face, clothing, or object recognition and/or ALPR software, or from personalized public transportation cards, we can expect to see a tsunami of location devices and applications. Unidentified citizens could be recognized and automatically followed. Extremely personalized interventions will emerge, whether for purposes of social control, marketing, safety, entertainment, or user-pay schemes—and, of course, for stalking, satisfying curiosity, or engaging in blackmail.

**Conclusion**

While all of the above developments are available and many are in use today, the current popularity of location-based applications can be overstated.[11] Location-based service penetration is still extremely low—well below 10 percent in the United States, for example.[12] Yet many of these technologies have only been in development for a short period, and expansion seems highly likely.

Another example might provide some perspective. Although driving and road safety are important social concerns, the public still resists many new road safety technologies, such as speed cameras. Event data recorders (EDRs or "black boxes") are installed on some automobiles to record information about crashes or accidents. Notwithstanding their technical abilities, the use of EDRs remains rare and is entangled in debates about privacy. The US National Highway Traffic Safety Administration (NHTSA), for instance, has been "reviewing" EDR standards since 2005. Even though grand schemes for intelligent transport systems—in which cars communicate with one another and with central traffic control systems—are in the works, it is hard to imagine that they could be implemented in the short or medium term.[13] Beyond their technological limitations, the fear pertaining to such technologies relates to the net cost to citizens in terms of the considerable prospect of state control of personal behaviour.

One final note. In the technologies described above, people are almost never tracked: it's the devices that are tracked, whether phones, cars, RFID tags, or transponders. That the identified owners are carrying these devices is always a leap of faith. This faith must be strong if tracking is rare or intermittent, since the likelihood of error is high. Moreover, people will inevitably try to fool or outwit such systems when it is to their benefit to do so. For instance, even the extremely limited implementation of speed cameras in the province of Québec (fifteen sites) has led some people to use false plate numbers.

There are two possible responses to these sources of uncertainty. The first is to increase tracking to the threshold where enough data are collected to establish identifiable, unique individual patterns. This does not require complete, uninterrupted tracking. Patterns developed using much less data offer near certainty that the same person is carrying the device. However, that person might not be the official, registered, or contracting owner of the device.

The second response is to replace device-unique IDs with user biometrics in order to link geolocation data directly to individuals rather than to their devices. It is already common for portable computers to offer fingerprint locking in order to protect their owners' sensitive data. Microsoft's Windows operating system has had a weak version of fingerprint locking for years. Manufacturers are also starting to include fingerprint recognition in smartphones and tablets. Some smartphones already have facial-recognition locks, but it is widely known that a photograph can fool this technology. The next generation of touchscreen biometrics will read fingerprints continuously as the user manipulates the phone or tablet, rather than only at the initial unlocking stage. In that case, any change of user will be recorded. If we push this biometrics and geolocation trend just a bit further into the future, we can imagine that new technologies, be they Google Glass or others, will recognize not only their users via iris recognition but also all faces around them, whether or not those being recognized are aware of this—and, obviously, whether or not they agree to it.

## Notes

1 Anna Klimaszewski-Patterson, "Smartphones in the Field: Preliminary Study Comparing GPS Capabilities Between a Smartphone and Dedicated GPS Device," *Papers of the Applied Geography Conferences* 33 (2010): 270–79, http://www.academia.edu/353833/Geographic_Fieldwork_Preliminary_study_comparing_GPS_capabilities_between_smartphones_and_dedicated_GPS.

2 Online Publishers Association, *A Portrait of Today's Tablet User Wave II*, June 2012, http://www.atelier.net/sites/default/files/etude/utilisateurs_americains_de_tablettes.pdf.

3   Daniel Ashbrook and Thad Starner, "Using GPS to Learn Significant Locations and Predict Movement Across Multiple Users," *Personal Ubiquitous Computing* 7 (2003): 275–86.

4   See Twoogle Geo Search, http://twoogle.co.uk/.

5   See http://www.brickhousesecurity.com/product/toddler+tag+child+locator.do for an example of the Toddler Tag Child Locator, and, for a description of the Victoria tracking system, see Tracking System Direct, GPS Tracking Children, 2009, http://www.tracking-system.com/for-consumers/gps-tracking-children.html.

6   See Freedom GPS Locator Watch at Bluewater Security Professionals, LLC, http://www.bluewatersecurityprofessionals.com/elderlytracking.htm.

7   See Kashmir Hill, "The Reaction to 'Girls Around Me' Was Far More Disturbing Than the 'Creepy' App Itself," *Forbes*, 2 April 2012, http://www.forbes.com/sites/kashmirhill/2012/04/02/the-reaction-to-girls-around-me-was-far-more-disturbing-than-the-creepy-app-itself/.

8   Stéphane Leman-Langlois, "Privacy as Currency: Behaviour Control in the Industrial Cyberspace," in *Technocrime: Technology, Crime and Social Control,* ed. Stéphane Leman-Langlois (Cullompton, UK: Willan Publishing, 2008), 112–38.

9   See scenetap.com: "SceneTap lets you check out the scene in real-time."

10  Janice Y. Tsai, Patrick Gage Kelley, Lorrie Faith Cranor, and Norman Sadeh, "Location-Sharing Technologies: Privacy Risks and Controls," *I/S: A Journal of Law and Policy for the Information Society* 6, no. 2 (2010): 119–52.

11  See Mohamed Kahlain, "Location Based Segmentation in Canada," *Mediative Blog: The Digital Results People*, 19 January 2012, http://blog.mediative.com/en/2012/01/19/location-based-marketing-segmention-canada/.

12  See Kathryn Zickuhr and Aaron Smith, "4% of Online Americans Use Location-Based Services," *Pew Internet,* 4 November 2010, http://www.pewinternet.org/Reports/2010/Location-based-services.aspx.

13  For more on intelligent transport systems, see Ching-Hung Yeh, Yueh-Min Huang, Tzone-I Wang, and Hsiao-Hwa Chen, "DESCV-A Secure Wireless Communication Scheme for Vehicle ad hoc Networking," *Mobile Networking Applications* 14 (2009): 611–24.

# Globalizing Surveillance
## From the Domestic to the Worldwide

The term *global surveillance* evokes international espionage and the spreading tentacles of clandestine intelligence agencies—the stuff of spy thrillers and, more soberly, organizations such as the US National Security Agency (NSA). Such global monitoring exists, of course, but much more mundanely, global surveillance may now also refer to international standards for airport security or simply to tagged consumer goods with standardized codes. Your razor blades or your blouse may contain an RFID tag conforming to a universal electronic product code and associated with global data synchronization. These grand technical terms matter little, but what they point to is a world in which data connections allow the blades or the blouse to be traced back to their producers or forward to the person currently using them.

Processes that used to be separated by national borders are increasingly connected beyond those borders. The globalization of surveillance, then, refers to how information once held in national silos is now more typically digital and thus flows more easily across borders. One may use a credit card, for example, to make purchases in another country, and personal details accompany such transactions. We have also become more aware of these connections, these data flows. We expect similar security regimes in airports everywhere, and we are aware that our passports are machine-readable around the world. Those scanners recognize our identification details even though the country we are in may be geographically and culturally remote from our own.

## Data Beyond Borders

Even Canada's privacy commissioner has experienced problems with her own personal data being made available internationally. A few years ago, *Maclean's* magazine purchased Jennifer Stoddart's private phone logs from an American data broker, no questions asked. To her consternation, detailed lists of calls made from her Montréal home, her Eastern Townships chalet, and her government-issued BlackBerry were plopped on her desk. Calls had been made to a relative in Frelighsburgh, Québec, and to the home of one of her communications advisors, among many others, and the dates and times were all correct.

Data brokers come in various shapes and sizes: some are behemoth global corporations such as Acxiom (discussed in Trend 1) or Experian, and some, such as InfoCanada, are much smaller. They deal in personal information, gleaned from consumer sources, that they buy and sell mainly for marketing purposes (but government departments, police, and intelligence agencies also use their services on occasion). Different legal regimes—say, between the United States

---

Surveillance in Canada is deeply affected by broad global trends. American politics and policies are one obvious source of influence, but the global surveillance connections extend much more broadly. These global influences may involve subtle efforts to shape policy directions, the sharing of expertise, or compliance with international standards and regulations. For example, in 2007, Canada signed a "partnership" agreement with Israel to cooperate on public safety.[1] Given that Public Safety Canada works cooperatively with the Canada Border Services Agency (CBSA), the Royal Canadian Mounted Police (RCMP), the Canadian Security Intelligence Service (CSIS), and Correctional Services of Canada (CSC), surveillance practices have to be central to this international arrangement. Israeli security uses ethnic-profiling practices—so does this mean that Canada will also extend such discriminatory techniques to its border?[2] Whatever the specifics, to appreciate both the contemporary and future dynamics of surveillance in Canada, one must think about Canada in the context of globalization.

Surveillance has been greatly affected by globalization. People are as likely to be observed by video surveillance cameras whether they are in Toronto, Johannesburg, or Tokyo. National identity card systems can be found in the Netherlands, India, and Brazil. But it is not simply that similar technologies are used or that the same technology companies operate

and Canada—make for complex jurisdictional issues as personal data travel between the different countries and beyond.

After years of kid-glove treatment of data-brokering corporations in Canada, in 2013, a House of Commons committee urged the federal privacy commissioner to prepare guidelines for how data brokers and social media collect and use personal data.[2] Companies like Facebook or Twitter originate outside of Canada, as do many data-brokering companies who nevertheless handle Canadian data. The hope is that at least Canadian personal data could be better protected. However, several vocal members of Parliament argued that the committee recommendations do not go nearly far enough.

1. Jonathon Gatehouse, "You Are Exposed," *Maclean's*, 21 November 2005, http://www.macleans.ca/canada/national/article.jsp?content=20051121_115779_115779.
2. *Privacy and Social Media in the Age of Big Data: Report of the Standing Committee on Access to Information, Privacy and Ethics* (Ottawa: Parliament of Canada, April 2013), http://www.parl.gc.ca/HousePublications/Publication.aspx?DocId=6094136&Language=E&Mode=1&Parl=41&Ses=1.

in different countries: surveillance processes and procedures are becoming more alike. No matter which country you travel to, at the national border, you are likely to be asked similar questions and subjected to similar kinds of observations. Frequently, international processes—the use of automated teller machines (ATMs), for example—connect to networks that share information globally.

The globalization of surveillance is not a finished process; it is ongoing. This does not mean that the same surveillance practices occur everywhere, even though many may be widespread. Although surveillance cameras are used in different cities around the globe, for instance, they are not necessarily conducting the same form of surveillance. Systems can differ in terms of both the groups of people being watched and the underlying reasons for their monitoring. Indeed, such systems may not involve a human watcher at all: video camera footage is now often simply recorded without observation and is increasingly monitored by automated software systems.

Despite the frequent similarities in surveillance around the world, the networks that connect surveillance systems are not necessarily global; they may involve local networks created for local purposes. In London, England, the city with the highest density of video surveillance cameras in the world, two cameras located very close to one another may be part of entirely different

## RFID Tags May Allow Global Tracking

RFID tags are now embedded in Canadian and other passports, enabling personal data to flow more freely across borders. But globe-trotting travellers will probably become more aware of RFID for other reasons in the near future. RFID is also used in many consumer products, such as clothing, with the consequence that we may unwittingly wear items that can be scanned for data. Hotels use RFID to keep track of their towels and bathrobes, for instance, and many ski resort operators use RFID tags rather than paper passes for skiers to access the lifts and, sometimes, the après ski bar. Some car rental agencies require customers to use RFID tags rather than car keys, and you may well be purchasing items with a contact-free credit card that also depends on RFID.

RFID tags are tiny and unobtrusive, but they promise great gains to the organizations and businesses that use them in terms of the fine-grained detail they provide. Indeed, one risk is that stakeholder voices may easily drown out those of concerned citizens and agencies. RFID tags are a rapidly growing source of Big Data—massive, complex data-sets requiring relatively new modes of management and analysis—increasingly sought by governments and corporations for many worthy, and less worthy, purposes.[1]

Although those who worry that RFID and Big Data will create an integrated global surveillance system may exaggerate the privacy risks they represent, the Canadian Office of Consumer Affairs includes this appropriate caution on its website: RFID technology "will enable increasing, systematic and covert localization of individuals on a much wider scale. This substantially impacts people's traditional reasonable expectations of privacy in movement: they may have been visible at a certain time at a certain place, but much less traceable for a longer period of time. The overall result is that more of our lives, in more places, are exposed."[2]

Transparent lives, indeed—not just in Canada, but globally.

---

systems operated by different local authorities or police forces. If you tried to connect them, you would discover that they are incompatible. Some are still analogue, recording to VHS tape; some are digital and cable-connected; some transmit information wirelessly. Likewise, some are watched by dedicated operators in control rooms connected to the police, while others are sporadically monitored; some merely record, and some are "dummy" systems that merely resemble surveillance cameras. There is no seamless transfer of video surveillance images around London, let alone around the world, despite the ambition of security professionals to move in that direction.

**RFID tags, which come in many shapes and sizes** (Source: © iStockphoto.com/albln)

1. See, for example, Armand Mattelart, *The Globalization of Surveillance* (Cambridge, UK: Polity Press, 2010), 190–93.
2. Industry Canada, Office of Consumer Affairs (OCA), "RFID Technologies and Consumers in the Retail Marketplace," last modified 5 December 2012, http://www.ic.gc.ca/eic/site/oca-bc.nsf/eng/ca02287.html.

These differences are compatible with globalization because global-ization does not mean homogeneity. Thinking about the globalization of surveillance involves recognizing both similarities and differences in sur-veillance around the world. National borders and national cultures still matter. Canada is just one kind of national surveillance society. China, for instance, practices a form of totalitarian surveillance that is still functionally compatible with capitalist economic development. Intensive surveillance of political and cultural views and opinions in China can result in signifi-cant impacts on individual dignity, life chances, and freedom. There are also significant differences among Western states. Some European states, such as Germany, have constitutional rights that make it more difficult to adopt technology-dominated surveillance. Sweden, in contrast, treats much of the personal information gathered by the state, such as the data in an individual tax return, as public property and makes it publicly accessible. In the rapidly developing economies of Brazil and Mexico, it is normal for wealthier citizens to eschew the limited protections offered by the state and opt for private security and surveillance providers, and for the poor to be left unwatched and undefended unless they turn to one of the many gangs that are the source of the more privileged citizens' fears.

## Globalization Processes

There are many processes of globalization, or, to be more precise, different processes, practices, policies, and technologies are being globalized in different ways and at different speeds. Forms of globalization that are related to surveillance are discussed here under four interconnected themes: globalizing regional interests, globalizing governance, globalizing standards, and globalizing technologies.

### Globalizing Regional Interests

Artificial satellites orbiting the earth constitute one of the most global of surveillance systems in terms of their coverage. Most of these satellites are controlled by military organizations—in particular, the US military. Near the end of the Cold War, the United States achieved control of orbital space, which allowed it to seize the "high ground." The US government has since claimed the power to deny other countries access to orbital space if it considers that use a threat to American interests. So while satellite surveillance appears to be global, it would better be described as serving regional interests: "globalization" here means the globalization of US military power.

Similarly, the United States dominates global communications. The Internet—a US military Cold War innovation that was originally intended as a form of self-repairing communication in the event that total war destroyed conventional forms of communication (the Internet reroutes around damage)—remains largely under US-based administration. A key example is ICANN (the Internet Corporation for Assigned Names and Numbers), the organization that decides how Internet domain names and addresses are assigned to countries and other bodies. The Internet, like other communication systems, has produced new freedoms and ways of sharing and organizing between people. Its protocols, however, depend upon automatically sorting and categorizing vast amounts of data. Although one might think that it would be impossible to manage all of these data, the problem of volume is proving to be a technical one. US intelligence—in particular, the National Security Agency (NSA), through its ECHELON and PRISM systems—can use back doors in communications hardware and software to tap into, siphon, and sift much global communications traffic, including the Internet, email, telephone, fax, and telex.*

Although other nation-states monitor and control the Internet and, like China or Iran, may do so with greater effect within their national borders, those countries do not have the global reach of the United States. This is, in part, because the United States has enlisted allies into its surveillance practices. In the case of ECHELON, the Canadian Communications Security Establishment (CSEC) is a "first party" to the agreement that underpins this global system of communications interception and analysis under the secretive 1948 CANUSA treaty.[3]

## Globalizing Governance

Many forms of surveillance operate at global levels as part of global institutions—like the World Health Organization, the World Bank, and the International Monetary Fund (IMF)—that exist largely to monitor global information flows in a variety of domains, from the economic to the environmental. Some of these surveillance systems, particularly those concerned with environmental change or the monitoring of human or agricultural diseases, provide desirable public benefits. In other areas, this is more debatable. A large proportion of contemporary surveillance at the global level exists to protect commercial interests, or to advance the globalization of capitalism itself.

Agencies that operate at a global level, such as the IMF, have a clear surveillance function, and their activities alter the destiny of millions, as, for

* "ECHELON" was a code name for one part of a complex system used by the NSA during the 1980s to tap into and analyze communications data. Now that the system has become public knowledge, the term has been adopted as a journalistic shorthand for the system as a whole.

## NSA Tracks Well Beyond US Borders

Revelations about secretive US surveillance programs began to be leaked in June 2013, to the consternation of American authorities, who promptly hounded the whistleblower, Edward Snowden, charging him with theft, communication of defence information, and espionage. The National Security Authority (NSA) was shown to be collecting telephone data on millions of US citizens, supplied by telecom companies such as Verizon. Also disclosed was the existence of a system called PRISM, which gives the NSA and FBI access to data held by companies including Google, Yahoo, Apple, Microsoft, and Facebook. PRISM tracks non-Americans outside the United States, and this is where the globalizing dimension becomes very clear—and, as it transpired, very irritating to many countries.

Many have suspected for a long time that such programs exist, but the direct evidence that Snowden gave to *The Guardian* newspaper in the United Kingdom created a major controversy. US authorities tried to play down the significance of the "telephone metadata"—which do not include the actual content of the communication—being tracked. Their aim is to analyze numerical patterns to map terrorist networks, they insisted, not to engage in mass surveillance. But metadata reveals who has spoken with whom, where the interlocutors were, and many other details from which political and personal preferences and priorities may be gleaned. Capturing these data may appear minor and trivial, but, as Daniel Solove suggests, it's like a Seurat painting—cluster all those bits of metadata together and we have something that is closer to "information" than mere "data."[1]

Both metadata and full message content are clearly captured by PRISM, for instance, as emails or chat messages are handled by US companies whether or not they leave Canada. So Canadians, alongside other non-Americans outside the United States, are obviously vulnerable to having their own personal data tracked by the United States. But does this mean that our own

example, when a national economy requires "structural adjustment" to meet IMF criteria for economic stability. Until recently, this was a process associated largely with the imposition of an Anglo-American economic model on emerging colonial countries (although even the United Kingdom experienced structural adjustment in the global economic downturn of the 1970s). The most recent example, however, is the imposition of harsh conditions on Greece and Italy in return for financial bailouts, as well as the removal of democratically elected governments and their replacement by IMF-approved technocrats to manage the hoped-for economic recovery. In the global

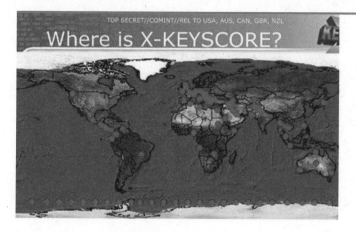

Worldwide surveillance data caches used by the NSA to store data captured by PRISM and possibly other interception programs (Source: Glenn Greenwald, "XKeyscore: NSA Tool Collects 'Nearly Everything a User Does on the Internet,'" *The Guardian* (UK), 31 July 2013, http://www.theguardian.com/world/2013/jul/31/nsa-top-secret-program-online-data.)

agencies, such as CSEC, the Communications Security Establishment Canada, cooperate with the PRISM program (and others like it)? This is highly likely, argues law and technology columnist Michael Geist, although given the veil of secrecy draped over CSEC, it is hard to say.[2] Such globalization of highly revealing personal data requires far stronger oversight, says Jennifer Stoddart, the outgoing privacy commissioner of Canada—in this country, as well as in the United States.[3] Many concerned citizens around the world agree.

1. "Surveillance: A Threat to Democracy," editorial, *New York Times,* 11 June 2013, http://www.nytimes.com/2013/06/12/opinion/surveillance-a-threat-to-democracy.html?_r=1&.
2. See Michael Geist's blog, "Why Canadians Should Be Demanding Answers About Secret Surveillance Programs," 8 June 2013, www.michaelgeist.ca/content/view/6869/125/.
3. Jennifer Stoddart, "Moving Towards a Global Regulation of Privacy: Proposals and Strategies," address to the 31st International Conference of Data Protection and Privacy Commissioners, Madrid, Spain, 6 November 2009, http://www.priv.gc.ca/media/sp-d/2009/sp-d_20091106_e.asp.

economy, control is often exercised at national levels through providing credit and subsequently monitoring almost all aspects of a state's economy, not only in order to facilitate repayment but also to ensure the state's compliance with the norms of international economic competition more broadly.

This is similar to how banks and other financial institutions use information that they acquire through surveillance (including clients' personal and financial data from both the bank itself and external credit-rating agencies, as well as "softer" information acquired via interviews and meetings) to make decisions about the services that they offer individuals. The combination of data from different sources results in profiles that determine the suitability of applicants for loans and other services. Nation-states are subjected to comparable kinds of dataveillance and profiling: public and private information companies collect and collate data and perform both human and, more commonly, algorithmic judgments on data relating to nation-states and then profile these countries to assess their credit-worthiness and relative place in global markets. As with the consumer-banking and credit-rating systems, much of this global economic surveillance infrastructure is corporate and not run by nation-states or democratic international organizations: the credit-ratings agencies that define the credit-worthiness of nations—including Standard & Poor's, Moody's, and Fitch Ratings—are private companies accountable to no one but their shareholders.

### Globalizing Standards

The third form of globalization that is important to surveillance is standardization. Increasingly, global expert and technical forums—such as the Frame Relay Forum, which determines the physical characteristics of telephone and other communication hardware connections, or intergovernmental gatherings such as the G20 summits or OECD meetings—set global standards relating to security and surveillance. In the past, such standards might have related solely to technologies. These standards are significant in their own right since they influence the ease or difficulty with which states can monitor communications systems. However, with the creation of the International Organization for Standardization's (ISO's) Societal Security standard, which includes technical standards for everything from emergency evacuation procedures to video cameras for security purposes, standards now relate increasingly to practices, including security and surveillance practices.[4]

Much of this standardization combines state and corporate interests. Most technologically advanced states have (or have proposed) laws that require Internet service providers (ISPs) to hand over personal traffic and/or content data to the police, and to block those who contravene copyright and licensing regulations from accessing the Internet. An example is ETSI, the European Telecommunications Standards Institute, whose global reach means that standards for the lawful interception of communications are applied worldwide. Here, the globalization of intellectual property rights meets the globalization of communications and computing, and the response of states has been to favour the smooth flow of commercial content. In other words, state surveillance supports state security and competition between corporations and does not necessarily take into account the interests of individuals or groups.

### *Globalizing Technologies*

Finally, many aspects of the globalization of surveillance occur through more elusive and opaque processes. For example, video surveillance has spread globally largely through policy transfer between nation-states and, more importantly, through the exchange of "lessons learned" among members of the private sector (including technology companies and private security agencies), police forces, and local governments, as well as those dubbed by some as "travelling technocrats."[5] In turn, policy transfer relies on fact finding, conferences, courses, and the sharing of best practices in professional publications. Many of the visible material forms of surveillance that one sees more and more often, especially within the globally connected "World Cities"—including Toronto, Montréal, Calgary, and Vancouver—are the result of such semi-formal processes of global knowledge-sharing, marketing, and policy learning.

The spread of surveillance thus occurs almost independently of academic or third-party assessments of its effectiveness. For example, academic studies in the United Kingdom clearly show that surveillance cameras fail to meet their crime-fighting objectives.[6] Yet, despite this evidence of their ineffectiveness, the use of such cameras has mounted, as other countries follow the UK's example. Surveillance cameras are now so established as a trusted item in the professional toolbox of urban management and policing that their failure is often viewed only as a problem of implementation or of insufficient technology, never as a problem potentially inherent in the technology itself.[7] Within the closed and self-reinforcing world of militaries, police, and security technology companies, all too often profit and influence follow from promoting surveillance technologies, regardless of what academics and advocates may conclude about their effectiveness or social costs.

### The Globalization of Surveillance in Practice

The following section outlines four key globalized phenomena that have affected, and will continue to affect, Canadians in the twenty-first century: border control; the related issue of migration and undocumented people;

the global movement of mega-events, such as the Olympic Games; and the increased use of unmanned aerial vehicles, or drones.

### The Transformation of Canadian Borders

Many of the developments outlined above are motivated by concerns about the increased mobility of people, goods, and information. Globalization has meant that raw materials and products travel further and faster than previously, and so, too, do people, from elite global business travellers and officials, to tourists, to the masses of migrants seeking a better life or escape from war, disaster, and poverty. Along with the movement of people and goods come security threats and the risk of disease, as well as economic, cultural, and political challenges. Moreover, information circulates even further and faster than either material goods or people, and this includes information about those goods and people. Although information is constantly being sorted, there are still particular points where global circulations of bodies, goods, and information all intersect—and borders are one such place.

The Canadian border, like all borders, is being transformed. There are simultaneous local and global pressures to "open up" (on economic grounds, to facilitate flows of people and goods) and to "close down" (on security grounds, to regulate people and cargo perceived to be a risk). Two main Canadian bodies deal with borders. The Canada Border Services Agency (CBSA) is the primary body responsible for border security. Established in 2003, the CBSA now manages 119 land-border crossings and thirteen international airports. The second major border agency is the Canadian Air Transport Security Authority (CATSA). Founded in 2002, CATSA is responsible for preboarding screening (passengers and their belongings), baggage screening, nonpassenger screening, and the implementation of restricted area identity cards at eighty-nine airports, both international and domestic.

Other state bodies, like Citizenship and Immigration Canada, the RCMP, and the CSIS, cooperate with CBSA and CATSA on border security. In the far North, the Canadian military operates remote patrols. The North is likely to become a more significant site for border surveillance as climate change reduces the covering ice, opening potential sea routes and mineral exploration and leading to territorial claims from multiple states. However, monitoring the North is proving to be expensive and complicated. In 2008, the Canadian government proposed a drone-based Joint Uninhabited Surveillance and Target Acquisition System (JUSTAS) to monitor the far

North, but that initiative continues to increase in cost, especially as it is pushed further into the future. In late 2012, the project was estimated to cost $1 billion and to be delivered in 2017.[8]

The Canadian border is essentially a triage point in a complex set of global flows of people, information, and things. But much of the work in establishing who and what can and cannot enter is not done at the border itself: it occurs elsewhere and prior to arrival. New global standards are being developed to track and verify goods and people. Shipping containers are frequently tagged with radio frequency identification (RFID) chips that closely monitor their movements. Some specific cargo, including most live animals (and most animal carcasses), must also be chipped. Although people are not tagged, a machine-readable passport containing an RFID chip is becoming a global standard, as are basic biometric identifiers, such as fingerprints and facial photographs. In addition, data from passenger name records (PNRs) or advance passenger information (API) are widely shared across borders.[9]

Such cross-border sharing can cause problems because other countries may not have the same provisions as Canada has to protect privacy, data, or even due process. In recent years, Canada has put in place several agreements and border-security programs and has increased data exchange with the United States and the European Union (EU). The EU's main privacy framework, known as the General Directive, is highly compatible with Canada's privacy legislation. The General Directive, originally passed in 1981 and revised in 1995, has become a global standard, since it was the first legislative framework created for protecting personal data.[10] In contrast, the United States has no comparably comprehensive personal information protection; rather, it has particular acts for certain sectors, such as banking and health, and more generalized statements in its privacy acts. Nor is there a federal legislative framework in the United States for protecting personal data collected at borders. To further compound matters, in 2007, the American government exempted its passenger-monitoring program, Secure Flight—otherwise known as the no-fly list—from its already limited US Privacy Act.

The influence of the United States on Canada can already be seen in data-sharing schemes and in special agreements between the two countries that enable US border guards and police to operate on Canadian territory (at international airports, where one now enters US territory within Canadian airports when going through US customs). However, in some cases, Canada has had a more ambivalent attitude to the border surveillance introduced by the United States. For example, Canadian border agencies have only partially followed the US example in adopting full-body scanners. Increasingly, evidence suggests that the body-scanning technology most commonly used in US airports—backscatter X-ray, which produces pictures that are difficult to blur (blurring is necessary to ensure privacy)—may pose a health hazard. Consequently, in 2013, the US Transportation Security Administration started to remove backscatter X-ray machines from its airports.[11] In contrast, airports in Canada employ millimetre wave scanners, which do not raise the same health concerns, and Transport Canada has attempted to follow strict privacy guidelines in their use.[12] Canada has also kept the scanning process voluntary. Moreover, whereas scanners have become routine in the US, with the option of a physical search available to passengers who object to scanning, in Canada it is the other way around: passengers who would prefer not to be physically searched can instead choose the scanner.

Issues about the Canadian border typically include the United States, and not simply because we share the world's longest land border. The strategic reach of the United States and its claims over airspace and defence have intensified since 9/11. During this period, the security agenda has joined with ongoing international economic liberalization. The latter has progressed since the inception of the North American Free Trade Agreement (NAFTA) in 1994, to the point where, in the opinion of some, the logical progression in border control is a "North American security perimeter."[13] This would essentially mean that Canada would adopt US rules for Canadian border interactions in return for easing the restrictions that make it increasingly difficult for people and goods to cross into the United States.

In early 2011, Prime Minister Stephen Harper and President Barack Obama signed a formal declaration entitled "Beyond the Border: A Shared Vision for Perimeter Security and Economic Competitiveness." The two countries promised to "work together to establish and verify the identities of travellers and conduct screening at the earliest possible opportunity" and to "work toward common technical standards for the collection, transmission, and matching of biometrics that enable the sharing of information on travellers in real time." This implies that intimate personal data will now be transmitted between the two countries instantaneously. In addition, the two countries "expect to work towards an integrated Canada-United States entry-exit system, including working towards the exchange of relevant entry information in the land environment so that documented entry into one country serves to verify exit from the other country."[14]

## Undocumented Migrants

Increased migration is one of the most significant facets of an interconnected world. The United Nations Population Division estimates that almost 214 million people migrated from one country to another in 2010.[15] Canada is a country built on immigration. With the exception of First Nations peoples, everyone in Canada either descends from immigrants or is an immigrant himself or herself. Furthermore, many immigrants—including important figures in Canadian history—arrived without documentation or with dubious legal backgrounds.

For migrants, the logic of border control and surveillance now starts long before they reach the physical border, with attempts to acquire legitimate papers and identification for entry into desirable countries like Canada. Identification has become another major global business and often forms the infrastructure for surveillance—whether at borders or within nations. However, despite Canada's economic need for more migrants, many people are unable to acquire the necessary documentation. Canada's immigration regime has been tightening, which has created more onerous and time-consuming processes and has excluded certain categories of people—particularly, the "unskilled" and less educated.

The result has been a rise in the number of migrants who do not have the documentation or permissions that Canada now requires for entry. Estimates of undocumented migrants to Canada are unreliable, ranging between thirty-five thousand and five hundred thousand. Because they lack the forms of identification, visas, and other documents that would allow them to negotiate the increasingly complex web of administrative surveillance, undocumented migrants face three types of inequality: unequal rights, unequal risk, and unequal speed.[16] Undocumented migrants are denied medical care, social security, and the basic protections that Canadians take for granted. People are singled out for questioning, search, and exclusion from entry, often because of prejudice, misidentification, or unwarranted assumptions.[17] Canada is not alone in this: in the EU, migrants face increased criminalization, restrictive migration laws, and a growing climate of fear. There is particular concern over the treatment of the children of undocumented migrants, which includes their frequent imprisonment in some countries.[18] The police, particularly the RCMP and the CBSA, target undocumented migrants for further intensive surveillance in the name of tackling "people trafficking." However, many undocumented migrants are unwitting subjects of such surveillance simply because they have overstayed their visas

**A Canadian passport: the end result of a complex surveillance process** (Source: © iStockphoto.com/AndrewWilliam)

or arrived in Canada on closed, single-employer work permits only to find their employers abusive or unwilling to deliver the (minimal) wages and conditions promised. As such individuals attempt to live a life under the radar of state surveillance, they constitute a cheap, vulnerable, and marginalized workforce employed by Canadian companies to do menial jobs.

The migrant situation reflects the fact that while identification and passport standards have become increasingly standardized, there is no formal international regime to govern the border-crossing mobility of people.[19] Existing provisions tend to be limited to conventions regarding skilled workers. Even in situations where a global governance framework does exist, as with refugees whose right of asylum is guaranteed by the United Nations, the situation is not much better.[20] The United Nations Population Division estimates that there were almost 16.5 million refugees globally in 2010, most of whom were merely temporary refugees from neighbouring states.[21] This is a surveillance issue because official decisions made about whether someone may cross a border depend upon personal information contained in documents or in related databases. How such information is gathered and interpreted has direct consequences for those waiting to hear the response to their request to be allowed entry.

Canadians are proud of their reputation for offering refuge to those escaping persecution, whether slaves fleeing the United States, Sikhs from the Punjab, or "boat people" from Vietnam. However, recent Canadian legal reforms have moved in the opposite, less welcoming direction. The latest changes redesignate some of those claiming asylum as "irregular arrivals" and also establish a list of "safe countries" (twenty-seven in 2013) from which claims for asylum will generally not be considered.[22] These "safe countries" include Hungary, which means that Roma people from Hungary cannot seek asylum in Canada despite the fact that they face a level of persecution that makes it difficult for them to remain in that country. Many such nomadic peoples that previously sought refuge in Canada may even be denounced as "bogus" and "criminal."[23]

### Canadian Cities and Mega-events

Major Canadian cities compete globally for resources and prestige.[24] A major marker of global status is the ability to attract mega-events, including gigantic sporting competitions, such as the Olympic Games and the FIFA World Cup; international political conferences, such as the G20, G8, and United Nations summits; and major cultural and commercial festivals and exhibitions, such as World Expos. When incidents like the bombing of the Boston Marathon route (April 2013) occur and street camera footage is used forensically to confirm the culprits' identities, it is not surprising that expanded surveillance is seen as a means of bolstering security.

Of course, not all mega-events are the same. But while events where a (paying) public is invited, such as the Olympics, and those that are closed to nonparticipants, such as the G20, have quite different dynamics, among the features they share is the use of exceptional forms of security and surveillance that may temporarily supplement, replace, or conflict with national and local laws.[25] An example is the infamous "FIFA World Cup Courts" in South Africa in 2010, in which the soccer authorities virtually took over a function of the justice system. They prosecuted fans and others for entirely new crimes against the FIFA World Cup competition, largely those connected with breaching the exclusive marketing rights of sponsors—for example, by wearing clothes with the brands of rival companies.[26] These exceptional measures are often demanded as a condition for hosting such events and are increasingly standardized across cities, regardless of national or local practices and customs. For example, the International Olympic Committee (IOC) now makes security a key part of the official evaluation process, and, in a good example of the processes of global "lesson-learning" mentioned above, the IOC facilitates the sharing of best security practices between former and future host cities.[27]

Thus, the surveillance measures deployed in cities hosting mega-events increasingly come to resemble each other. Vancouver during the 2010 Winter Olympics and Toronto during the subsequent G20 meeting both featured intensive police surveillance of political activists, surveillance that many found intimidating and that was designed to pre-empt both crime and legitimate protest.[28] Police also deployed open street video surveillance systems together with pictures taken with handheld photographic and video cameras, which they then uploaded to social media in order to identify activists at these events.[29]

Such events are frequently test beds for new surveillance technologies, and the technologies used often persist beyond their deployment at the event. In the case of Vancouver, the Winter Olympics were clearly used to justify installing video surveillance that might not have been politically acceptable in normal circumstances. After the G20 summit in Toronto, however, only a few surveillance cameras were left in the downtown area, but the police stored the remaining cameras for potential future use.[30] Mega-events outside Canada have introduced other experiments. Chemical-sniffing robots were used at the FIFA World Cup in Germany in 2006, and the 2007 Pan-American Games in Rio de Janeiro featured high-flying surveillance airships.[31] Smaller unmanned aerial vehicles (UAVs, about which more below) kept an eye on the UEFA European Championship in Switzerland and Austria in 2008, and for the Olympic Games in London in 2012, biometric entry systems were installed.[32] Increasingly, these technologies are redeployed at subsequent events as standard practice.

Many of the cities hosting these events have temporarily redesigned their streets to increase security and surveillance. The strategy of "island security," for example, involves isolating the site of the event within the city and is based on the "Ring of Steel" tactics used by the British authorities to deal with terrorism in Belfast and London.[33] This is now standard practice for G20-type meetings and sports mega-events. Such events now also increasingly involve changes to urban roads and paths, as well as the use of controlled "fan zones" that isolate spectators in fenced-off video-viewing areas that allow for surveillance and control of a potentially unruly public. These areas are frequently designed to subject fans to a combination of saturated marketing and surveillance for commercial purposes.[34]

### Mobile Surveillance and Drones

Another form of increasing global surveillance features remotely operated aircraft. Popularly known as "drones," these pilotless devices were originally called remotely piloted vehicles (RPVs), or unmanned aerial (or air) vehicles (UAVs). According to a recent US Government Accountability Office (GAO) report, more than fifty countries are now developing nine hundred UAV systems, and seventy-six countries currently operate UAVs.[35] Of the latter, only three—the United States, the United Kingdom, and Israel—operate armed UAVs; most are purely surveillance devices. The global market for UAVs has been called "the most dynamic growth sector of the world aerospace industry"; it is currently worth around US$6.6 billion per annum and is expected to almost double to US$11.4 billion over the next decade.[36]

Government secutiry operations account for a great deal of this growth. US Customs and Border Protection now patrols the US-Canada border with the same Predator drones that it uses in Pakistan. As noted above, the Canadian government has been less successful in its attempts to procure UAVs for border patrol in the far North. UAVs are also increasingly applied in civilian markets. New and powerful industry associations advocate for national domestic and private commercial use of UAVs. Internationally, the Association for Unmanned Vehicle Systems International (AUVSI) lobbies on behalf of drone manufacturers, and in Canada, an affiliated group, Unmanned Systems Canada (unmannedsystems.ca), was created in 2010 from the merger of two smaller groups. These industry bodies lobby to limit regulation to what they believe is strictly necessary.

UAVs are used by certain Canadian military and police units, such as the RCMP in British Columbia and Saskatchewan, and the Ontario Provincial Police.[37] They are used for coastal surveillance, as well as for obtaining images of highway accidents and for other types of law enforcement checking and monitoring tasks.[38] Drones are also used for a number of public activities outside of policing: from the real-estate sector, for dramatic but inexpensive aerial marketing videos of large properties (where their use has increased substantially), to NGOs, for monitoring corporate environmental abuses.[39]

**Drones, now increasingly used in civilian contexts** (Source: © iStockphoto.com/alexsalcedo)

Drones are also used by forestry trusts, environmental researchers, and private corporations to survey and assess otherwise inaccessible areas.[40]

Most military UAVs, which tend to be similar in size to conventional piloted aircraft and can operate for long distances and time periods, are significantly different from the drones used in domestic contexts. The latter—often referred to as micro- or mini-UAVs, or MAVs—tend to be small, lightweight (some are compact enough to fit in a backpack), and easily operated, and in many cases, they resemble hobbyist remote-control kit aircraft. The personal and institutional use of UAVs is therefore apt to increase.[41] Industry reports suggest that the growth of civil markets for UAVs is held back only by national aviation regulations.[42] Yet citizens, civil rights groups, and privacy regulators all have good reason to be concerned with the growth of domestic human-related UAV surveillance. In the United States, a Congressional Research Service report recently highlighted such concerns, and the Electronic Privacy Information Center (EPIC) has testified before Congress that UAV use by police should have "a warrant requirement . . . as well as data use limitations, and transparency obligations for drone opera-tors."[43] Canadians also need clarification about the corporate, personal, and police use of these devices. Thankfully, the popular media in North America is starting to raise such questions: a recent article in *The Atlantic* asked, "If I fly my UAV over my neighbor's house, is it trespassing?"[44]

The decreasing size of drones has certainly made surveillance more portable and covert. However, a major area of research and development expansion in mobile surveillance devices is in biomimetic technologies. Biomimetics are machines that imitate naturally occurring animals or plants. The most common biomimetic devices tend to mimic birds, snakes, and insects. AeroVironment, a leading manufacturer of UAVs in the United States and the supplier of the most popular police helicopter drones, recently dem-onstrated a functional partially radio-controlled and partially autonomous robotic "Nano Hummingbird."[45] These developments show that visual surveil-lance is likely to become even more hidden, while losing none of its power.


## Conclusion

Surveillance trends in Canada must be understood not merely in a national but in a global context of laws, standards, practices, technologies, and organi-zations. Globalization helps to accelerate the development of surveillance in all areas, particularly over the new global economy. Such surveillance touches ordinary consumers and travellers in their everyday transactions as well as in security-related fields. New global, international, or bilateral agreements fre-quently spell a formal commitment to new surveillance measures; examples of such agreements include no-fly lists, application programming interface (API) data, and border agreements with the United States. Globalization also results in an increasingly competitive and innovative marketplace for all surveillance technologies, from the most expensive military platforms to the cheapest private devices, including, for example, drones. Many of these technologies are also increasingly hybrid and are marketed with only minor variations for military and civilian uses. The spread of global norms, whether in the form of the ISO's Societal Security standard or through more informal understandings of best practices that do not distinguish between different contexts and histories, can allow special security interests to appear neutral and can help to foreclose debate in the name of applying what is already apparently globally acceptable.

# Notes

1   Rebecca Anna Stoil, "Israel, Canada Sign Security Accord," *Jerusalem Post,* 29 November 2007, http://www.jpost.com/Israel/Israel-Canada-sign-security-accord.

2   See Andrew Stevens, "Surveillance Policies, Practices and Technologies in Israel and the Occupied Palestinian Territories: Assessing the Security State," The New Transparency: Surveillance and Social Sorting, Working Paper 4, November 2011, http://www.sscqueens.org/sites/default/files/2011-11-Stevens-WPIV_0.pdf.

3   Philip Rosen, *The Communications Security Establishment: Canada's Most Secret Intelligence Agency* (Ottawa: Parliamentary Library and Research Service, Parliament of Canada, BP343-E, September 1993), http://www.parl.gc.ca/Content/LOP/researchpublications/bp343-e.htm, 3.

4   International Organization for Standardization, *Societal Security: Guideline for Incident Preparedness and Operational Continuity Management*, ISO/PAS 22399:2007, http://www.iso.org/iso/home/store/catalogue_tc/catalogue_detail.htm?csnumber=50295.

5   Wendy Larner and Nina Laurie, "Travelling Technocrats, Embodied Knowledges: Globalising Privatisation in Telecoms and Water," *Geoforum* 41, no. 2 (2010): 218–26.

6   See, for example, Martin Gill and Angela Spriggs, *Assessing the Impact of CCTV* Home Office Research Study 292 (London: Home Office Research, Development and Statistics Directorate, 2005), https://www.cctvusergroup.com/downloads/file/Martin%20gill.pdf.

7   For a discussion of Canadian policy practices and rationales, see Sean P. Hier, *Panoptic Dreams: Streetscape Video Surveillance in Canada* (Vancouver: University of British Columbia Press, 2010).

8   David Pugliese, "Canada's Drone Squadron Still Stalled, with Neither Planes nor Troops," *Ottawa Citizen*, 27 December 2012.

9   Again, RFID-tagged passports and biometric identifiers were driven by the United States, originally through the G8 meeting in Sea Island, Georgia, on 10 June 2004. See Statewatch, "G8 Meeting at Sea Island in Georgia, USA, Sets New Security Objectives for Travel," 2004, http://www.statewatch.org/news/2004/jun/09g8-bio-docs.htm.

10  "Directive 95/46/EC of the European Parliament and of the Council of 24 October 1995 on the Protection of Individuals with Regard to the Processing of Personal Data and on the Free Movement of Such Data," *Official Journal* L 281, P. 0031–0050, 11 November 1995, http://eur-lex.europa.eu/LexUriServ/LexUriServ.do?uri=CELEX:31995L0046:en:HTML.

11  Mike M. Ahlers, "TSA Removing 'Virtual Strip Search' Body Scanners," *CNN*, 18 January 2013, http://www.cnn.com/2013/01/18/travel/tsa-body-scanners/index.html.

12  Transport Canada, "Full Body Scanners at Major Canadian Airports," 16 April 2013, http://www.tc.gc.ca/eng/mediaroom/backgrounders-full-body-scanners-7131.html.

13  For a critical assessment, see Dana Gabriel, "The Integration of Canada into a U.S. Dominated North American Security Perimeter," *Global Research,* 18 June 2013, http://www.globalresearch.ca/the-integration-of-canada-into-a-u-s-dominated-north-american-security-perimeter/5339525.

14  Prime Minister of Canada Stephen Harper, "Beyond the Border: A Shared Vision for Perimeter Security and Economic Competitiveness. A Declaration by the Prime Minister of Canada and the President of the United States of America," 4 February 2011, Washington, DC, http://www.pm.gc.ca/eng/media.asp?id=3938.

15  United Nations Population Division, "International Migrant Stock: The 2008 Revision," United Nations, 2009, http://esa.un.org/migration/.

16  Robert Pallitro and Josiah Heyman, "Theorizing Cross-border Mobility: Surveillance, Security and Identity," *Surveillance and Society* 5, no. 3 (2008): 315–33.

17  For some examples and personal stories, see International Civil Liberties Monitoring Group, "Watch Lists and Border Controls," 2010, http://www.travelwatchlist.ca/.

18  Platform for International Cooperation on Undocumented Migrants, *PICUM's Main Concerns About the Fundamental Rights of Undocumented Migrants in Europe 2010*, October 2010, Brussels, http://picum.org/picum.org/uploads/publication/Annual%20Concerns%202010%20EN.pdf.

19  United Nations Development Program, *Overcoming Barriers: Human Mobility and Development,* Human Development Report 2009, http://hdr.undp.org/en/reports/global/hdr2009/, 39.

20  For more on guaranteed right of asylum, see the United Nations High Commissioner for Refugee's 1951 *Convention Relating to the Status of Refugees* and the 1967 *Protocol Relating to the Status of Refugees*, both available at http://www.unhcr.org/pages/49da0e466.html.

21  United Nations Population Division, "International Migrant Stock: The 2008 Revision."

22  Nicholas Keung, "Changes to Refugee System: Immigration Minister Jason Kenney Lays Out Criteria for 'Safe' Countries," *Toronto Star,* 30 November 2012, http://www.thestar.com/news/canada/article/1296161--changes-to-refugee-system-immigration-minister-jason-kenney-lays-out-criteria-for-safe-countries.

23  Cynthia Levine-Rasky, "Who Are You Calling Bogus?" *Canadian Dimension* 46, no. 5 (2012): 12–14.

24  See Peter J. Taylor, *World City Network: A Global Urban Analysis* (London and New York: Routledge, 2003).

25  See, for example, Alessandra Renzi and Greg Elmer, *Infrastructure Critical: Sacrifice at Toronto's G8/G20 Summit* (Winnipeg: Arbeiter Ring, 2012).

26  Marina Hyde, "World Cup 2010: Fans, Robbers and a Marketing Stunt Face Justice, Fifa Style," *The Guardian* (UK), 20 June 2010, http://www.guardian.co.uk/football/2010/jun/20/world-cup-2010-fans-marketing-justice-fifa.

27  Philip Boyle, "Knowledge Networks: Mega-events and Security Expertise," in *Security Games: Surveillance and Control at Mega-events,* ed. Colin J. Bennett and Kevin D. Haggerty (London and New York: Routledge, 2011), 184–99.

28  Jeffrey Monaghan, and Kevin Walby, "Making Up 'Terror Identities': Security Intelligence, Canada's Integrated Threat Assessment Centre and Social Movement Suppression," *Policing and Society* 22, no. 2 (2012): 133–51.

29  Daniel Trottier, "Policing Social Media," *Canadian Review of Sociology / Revue canadienne de sociologie* 49, no. 4 (2012): 411–25.

30  "Toronto Police Want to Keep Most G20 Security Cameras," *CTV News,* 15 November 2010, http://toronto.ctvnews.ca/toronto-police-want-to-keep-most-g20-security-cameras-1.575057.

31  See Francisco R. Klauser, "Spatial Articulations of Surveillance at the FIFA World Cup 2006TM in Germany," in *Technologies of (In)Security: The Surveillance of Everyday Life,* ed. Katja Franko Aas, Helene Oppen Gundhus, and Heidi Mork Lomell (London and New York: Routledge-Cavendish, 2009), 61–80; and David Murakami Wood, "Cameras in Context: A Comparison of the Place of Video Surveillance in Japan and Brazil," in *Eyes Everywhere: The Global Growth of Camera Surveillance,* ed. Aaron Doyle, Randy Lippert, and David Lyon (London and New York: Routledge, 2012), 83–99.

32  See Francisco R. Klauser, "Commonalities and Specificities in Mega-event Securitization: The Example of Euro 2008 in Austria and Switzerland," in Bennett and Haggerty, *Security Games,* 120–36; and Pete Fussey and Jon Coaffee, "Balancing Local and Global Security Leitmotifs: Counter-terrorism and the Spectacle of Sporting Mega-events," *International Review for the Sociology of Sport* 47, no. 3 (2012): 268–85.

33 Jon Coaffee, David Murakami Wood, and Peter Rogers, *The Everyday Resilience of the City* (Basingstoke, UK: Palgrave Macmillan, 2009), chap. 6.

34 David Murakami Wood and Kirstie Ball, "Brandscapes of Control? Surveillance, Marketing and the Co-construction of Subjectivity and Space in Neo-liberal Capitalism," *Marketing Theory* 13, no. 1 (2013): 47–67.

35 US Government Accountability Office (GAO), *Nonproliferation: Agencies Could Improve Information Sharing and End-Use Monitoring on Unmanned Aerial Vehicle Exports,* GAO-12-536, July 2012, http://www.gao.gov/assets/600/593131.pdf, 13, 9.

36 "Teal Group Predicts Worldwide UAV Market Will Total $89 Billion in Its 2012 UAV Market Profile and Forecast," Teal Group, 11 April 2012, http://tealgroup.co/index.php/about-teal-group-corporation/press-releases/66-teal-group-predicts-worldwide-uav-market-will-total-89-billion-in-its-2012-uav-market-profile-and-forecast.

37 See Alexandra Gibb, "Privacy Concerns Hover over RCMP Drones in British Columbia," *TheThunderBird.ca,* 29 March 2012, http://thethunderbird.ca/2012/03/29/privacy-concerns-hover-over-rcmp-drones-in-british-columbia/; and Sigrid Forberg, "Taking to the Skies: New Tool Facilitates Investigations," *RCMP Gazette* 74, no. 1 (2012), http://www.rcmp-grc.gc.ca/gazette/vol74n1/trends-dernierestendances-eng.htm.

38 On coast surveillance, for example, see Colin Kenny, "Why Canada Needs Drones," *National Post,* 28 February 2012, http://colinkenny.ca/en/p102659/.

39 On the former, see Neal Ungerleider, "Unmanned Drones Go from Afghanistan to Hollywood," *Fast Company*, 15 February 2012, http://www.fastcompany.com/1816578/unmanned-drones-go-afghanistan-hollywood; on the latter, see Alexandra Gibb, "A Drone Field Guide," Canadian International Council, *Opencanada.org*, 31 May 2012, http://www.opencanada.org/features/the-think-tank/a-drone-field-guide/.

40 Julia Horton, "Attack of the Drones to Fight Tree Rot in Scotland," *The Scotsman*, 28 October 2012, http://www.scotsman.com/news/environment/attack-of-the-drones-to-fight-tree-rot-in-scotland-1-2602637.

41 See "Drones Work the Skies for Police, Scientists, Media," *CBC News*, 22 March 2012, http://www.cbc.ca/news/technology/story/2012/03/22/technology-thecurrent-civilian-drones.html.

42 Steve Zaloga and David Rockwell, "UAV Market Set for 10 Years of Growth," *Earth Imaging Journal*, 2011, http://eijournal.com/uncategorized/uav-market-set-for-10-years.

43 "EPIC to Congress: Protect Privacy Against Drone Surveillance," 5 November 2012, http://epic.org/2012/11/epic-to-congress-protect-priva.html. See also Richard M. Thompson II, *Drones in Domestic Surveillance Operations: Fourth Amendment Implications and Legislative Responses*, Congressional Research Services, 3 April 2013, http://www.fas.org/sgp/crs/natsec/R42701.pdf; and Electronic Privacy Information Center (EPIC), "Testimony and Statement for the Record of Amie Stepanovich, Association Litigation Counsel, Electronic Privacy Information Center, Field Forum on the Impact of Domestic Use of Drone Technology on Privacy and Constitutional Rights of All Americans," 25 October 2012, Rice University, Houston, http://epic.org/privacy/drones/EPIC-Drones-Testimony-102512.pdf.

44 Alexis C. Madrigal, "If I Fly a UAV over My Neighbor's House, Is It Trespassing?" *The Atlantic*, 10 October 2012, http://www.theatlantic.com/technology/archive/2012/10/if-i-fly-a-uav-over-my-neighbors-house-is-it-trespassing/263431/.

45 AeroVironment, "Nano Hummingbird," 2013, http://www.avinc.com/nano. See also Kevin D. Haggerty and Daniel Trottier, "Surveillance and/of Nature: Monitoring Beyond the Human," *Society and Animals* (2013), doi: 10.1163/15685306-12341304.

# Embedding Surveillance in Everyday Environments

From the Surveillance of People
to the Surveillance of Things

In the "Day in the Life" story in Trend 1, relatively few of the many surveillance moments that Farah and her family encounter would be readily recognized as such without an understanding of how personal information is captured and processed behind the scenes. Much of everyday surveillance is embedded seamlessly, nearly unrecognizably, within the gadgets and settings to which we have become accustomed as essential to modern living.

The trend toward ubiquitous surveillance is enabled, in part, by placing sensors, identifiers, and cameras in everyday objects and the built environment. What once was done at specific locations or using specific devices has become a general feature of the vehicles, streets, homes, and workplaces with which we interact daily. We use cellphones to keep in touch with family and friends without thinking about the fact that we are letting the phone company know exactly where we are at all times. We browse through pictures of ourselves on Facebook without considering that Facebook is now the largest facial recognition software developer in the world; it can identify us in photos whether or not we are tagged. And digital cameras can embed both a time/date and GPS location stamp on every picture we take.

This embedding of surveillance capabilities into familiar devices and everyday environments is an ongoing trend, closely linked to both the general expansion of surveillance and the more recent expansion of mobile and location-based surveillance, two themes examined in earlier chapters. The

## Eyes on the Street: Citizens Surveilling Video Surveillance

Relatively little is known about the private sector's use of video surveillance in Canada. While surveillance cameras are largely deployed for commercial purposes, most research so far has focused on governmental use.[1] Even basic facts, such as the approximate number of privately operated cameras, have not been established. Little is currently known about private sector policies and practices around the handling of the personal video information captured by cameras.

One recent study, funded by the Office of the Privacy Commissioner of Canada, has attempted to fill in some of these gaps.[2] Researchers from the University of Toronto visited more than three hundred commercial establishments in the Greater Toronto Area and found surveillance cameras in nearly half of them. In particular, the four largest firms in each of the major retail sectors of banking, clothing, fast food, electronics and department stores, all operated video surveillance. The Sears department store in the Toronto Eaton Centre alone had ninety cameras. Roughly 60 percent of installations had no visible sign alerting people to the presence of cameras, and of these, none—not one!—met the minimum requirements specified by the guidelines developed jointly by the privacy commissioners of Canada, Alberta, and British Columbia.[3] These signage requirements are hardly onerous and, in public sector video surveillance operations, are frequently, although not universally, met: a visible, readable sign identifying the owner, the purposes for the data collection, and contact details for timely enquiry would suffice.

After documenting the presence of cameras and signage, the University of Toronto researchers asked the manager of a number of the establishments for information about the company's privacy practices and then handed over a personal information request form that requests a copy of the video record of the visit. The custodian of personal information is legally required to respond within thirty days and to provide individuals with access to their records. The results were dismal and revealing. Despite systematic and determined follow-up after the initial request, only three out of forty-five companies provided the requested video footage. In the other one hundred cases where there was no follow-up after the initial request, the results were even weaker.

Both the inadequate signage and the poor response to requests for personal information demonstrate widespread noncompliance with the Personal Information Protection and Electronic Documents Act (PIPEDA), the legislation that regulates privacy in the private sector. It does not bode well for Canadians that those operating the most iconic form of surveillance, video cameras,

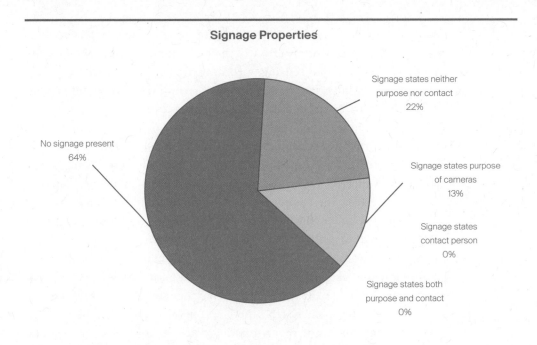

## Signage Properties

No signage present
64%

Signage states neither
purpose nor contact
22%

Signage states purpose
of cameras
13%

Signage states
contact person
0%

Signage states both
purpose and contact
0%

**Surveillance camera signage** (Source: Courtesy of Andrew Clement, University of Toronto)

are overwhelmingly violating the law with apparent impunity. As video surveillance continues to expand through ever cheaper digital storage, networked transmission, and automated image analysis and becomes further embedded within our shared physical environment as well as within cultural expectations, the risks will grow unless new and more effective forms of public oversight are implemented.

1. Aaron Doyle, Randy Lippert, and David Lyon, eds., "Introduction," in *Eyes Everywhere: The Global Growth of Camera Surveillance* (London and New York: Routledge, 2012), 17.
2. Andrew Clement, Joseph Ferenbok, Roxanna Dehghan, Laura Kaminker, Simeon Kanev, and Silvia Valdman, *"Smart" Private Eyes in Public Places? Video Surveillance Analytics, New Privacy Threats and Protective Alternatives,* Final Report, 23 July 2011, submitted to the Office of the Privacy Commissioner of Canada, http://surveillancerights.ca/downloads/Clement_Ferenbok etal - OPC - Private Eyes - Final Report with appendices.pdf.
3. Privacy Commissioner of Canada, Information and Privacy Commissioner of Alberta, Information and Privacy Commissioner for British Columbia, *Guidelines for Overt Video Surveillance in the Private Sector,* March 2008, http://www.priv.gc.ca/information/guide/2008/gl_vs_080306_e.asp.

rapid pace of technological change in digital networking and related tech-nologies is the most obvious driver of the embedding process. Not only are the capabilities of digital sensing, recording, transmission, and processing devices growing, but such devices are also becoming cheaper and smaller on a unit basis. In sharp contrast to the expansion of cars in the early part of the twentieth century, when vehicles, roadways, and other aspects of the sup-porting infrastructures became highly visible in everyday settings, the even more extensive and rapid expansion of digital networking is occurring largely out of view. Although we can see people using their smartphones, laptops, and related devices, the devices themselves are just the tip of an enormous iceberg, with the bulk of the hardware invisible behind walls or underground and with the buzzing activity extending nearly everywhere via radio waves.[1]

As we have embraced these technologies, we have also embedded sur-veillance into our taken-for-granted understandings of the worlds we inhabit. Surveillance is now spoken of as a normal part of parenting, work, and travel, and many of us routinely watch others and allow ourselves to be watched as we go about our day, without thinking twice about it. Such embedding makes it difficult for us to identify, understand, debate, and democratically regulate surveillance practices as they become woven into the fabric of con-temporary life.

To help us visualize and understand the surveillance around us, and to facilitate discussion, it is useful to distinguish between two distinct approaches to embedded surveillance. In the first, surveillance is the central purpose for developing new modes of capturing personal information. In the second, surveillance capabilities are introduced as an *add-on* to an existing activity: this approach relies on personal information that is collected as an inherent part of the initial activity or is easily generated as a by-product of it. Video surveillance cameras are an example of the former, more recognizable mode of surveillance, while incorporating keystroke monitoring in an office setting or intercepting traffic on the Internet backbone are examples of the latter. The "surveillance as add-on" approach is more widespread and more difficult to recognize. As the following discussion illustrates, in both cases, the embedded character of surveillance makes it hard to detect and thereby difficult to hold those responsible to account.

## Surveillance as Central: Special Purpose Surveillance

The most obvious example of the unobtrusive embedding of devices designed specifically for surveillance purposes into our daily environment is the extraordinary growth of various types of camera surveillance. Most of this growth takes the form of surveillance cameras deployed on city streets and in shopping centres for security purposes. Indeed, the surveillance camera is probably the most familiar symbol of surveillance.

Although the United Kingdom has long been the recognized leader in the adoption of surveillance cameras, Canada is similarly moving toward making this form of monitoring a ubiquitous feature of contemporary urban life.[2] Surveillance cameras are, for instance, becoming common along roadways, where they are used to spot drivers speeding or going through red lights. Taxicabs in major cities are fitted with cameras that record the face of every passenger. In these examples, stored images are normally examined only when there is evidence of an infraction or incident.

Even though such cameras are among the most visible indicators of explicit surveillance, people are largely unaware of their presence.[3] This is, in part, due to the fact that such cameras are relatively small and nondescript and are often tucked unobtrusively away in ceilings and high walls outside of our usual sightlines. Few video surveillance operators draw attention to their installations. Even though businesses are required by Canadian law to post signs notifying people of the presence of video surveillance, a 2011 study found that only one-third of sampled commercial installations had any form of signage and that when such signs were posted, they were often designed and positioned so as not to be noticed.[4] Furthermore, the wording of the signs consistently failed to meet even the minimum notification requirements specified by Canadian privacy law.

A more sophisticated and privacy-sensitive application of visual surveillance is the growing use of automated licence plate recognition (ALPR) systems on roadways and in parking lots. Such systems use optical character recognition (OCR) techniques to capture licence plate numbers; the plate numbers are then compared against lists containing the licence plate numbers of cars that police are looking for or are stored in databases for later use. ALPR devices are also mounted on structures above highways to collect tolls, flag suspects, or track the movements of "persons of interest." Police use ALPR-equipped cars to scan parking lots and highways in search of vehicles that match their watch lists. They may ticket or apprehend drivers on the spot.

## Surveillance as an Add-on: Transactional Surveillance

Although businesses and government agencies are rapidly embedding special purpose surveillance devices into our built environment, the surveillance capabilities that have been added into the familiar devices and transactions originally developed for other purposes are much less visible and far greater in scope, intensity, and consequence. The expanded use of computers for record keeping and transaction processing, which began in the 1960s, greatly increased the capacity for embedded surveillance across a wide range of settings. Such surveillance was initially implemented in the work environment in large offices characterized by routine work and subordinated employees. Management began to use computerized production data readily generated as a by-product of existing systems—including keystroke counts, response times, sales volumes, and throughput—to manage employee performance, a process referred to as "informating."[5] Often, this took the form of monitoring individual performance against pre-established targets and then rewarding or punishing employees accordingly. The more intensive forms of this surveillance were controversial, especially in unionized settings, and became the focus of a Canadian federal government enquiry in the early 1980s.[6]

Back-office automation paved the way for online customer transaction processing and customer surveillance. In the past decade, as such transactions have moved from corporate-owned, special-purpose, immobile devices—such as automated teller machines (ATMs) and point of sale (POS) terminals—to individually owned, multipurpose mobile devices—notably, smartphones—surveillance capabilities have been embedded in these as well. The *News of the World* phone-hacking scandal in the United Kingdom, in which reporters intercepted the voicemails of thousands of individuals, highlights the potential for conducting transaction surveillance via the telecommunications networks on which mobile devices rely.[7] Such surveillance techniques are further detailed in Trend 5.

## "Enhancing" ID for Surveillance

Another example of how surveillance has been unobtrusively embedded in familiar and uniquely personal items includes the recent digital "enhancement" of our identification documents. ID is central to contemporary life: we are increasingly required to present identification documents when we shop, enter buildings or other spaces, board transit vehicles, cross borders, and so on. The ID documents that we use are most often standardized plastic cards that slide smoothly into designated places in our wallets and purses. People are accustomed to presenting such cards or other ID documents for a quick visual inspection by an authorized employee before being allowed to proceed.

The embedding of surveillance capability in ID cards has developed in stages as digital technologies have become more sophisticated. First and most significant is the direct linking of ID documents with their associated databases. The computerized reading of data on the card—notably, the unique identifier—allows real-time checking against a database to determine whether the cardholder is authorized to proceed. This shifts the primary function of the ID card from its role of certifying that its holder has a particular status (e.g., authorized driver, club member, citizen) to that of primary nexus between the individual and his or her "data double"—which refers to the totality of that individual's personal digital information. Typically, such card scanning also produces a record that is added to the person's dossier. This linking of data collection, database storage, and automated authorization enables the fine-grained management of large populations—that is, the efficient and unobtrusive sorting of individuals into organizationally prescribed treatment categories.[8]

In the past decade, two further digital technologies—digital biometrics and radio frequency identification (RFID) chips—have been embedded in our familiar ID cards such as drivers' licences, health cards, and passports. These changes have had little effect on the form or superficial appearance of the cards, but they have ushered in significantly greater surveillance potential. Often introduced in concert with an ever growing number of back-end databases and relentless attempts to more thoroughly integrate the data capture of these systems behind the scenes, RFIDs and biometrics capture personal information with breathtaking ease. By unobtrusively reading card data in a more dispersed and varied range of transactional settings, these techniques promise convenience to cardholders but, at the same time, invisibly tie them ever more tightly to their corresponding data doubles.

The Ontario Smart Card Project (OSCP) was one of the first, and is still one of the most ambitious, attempts in Canada to "enhance" conventional ID cards by incorporating digital technologies. Proposed in the late 1990s by then-premier Mike Harris's Conservative government, the OSCP was intended to be a multipurpose card to access a wide range of government services. Users would

## Ubiquitous Embedded Surveillance: Infonaut's HospitalWatch*Live* System

Health surveillance is, arguably, a form of surveillance that many of us might support. Close tracking of infectious diseases is particularly important for diagnosing individual cases as well as for protecting the wider population from their devastating spread. Infonaut, a Canadian health technology company specializing in "evidence-based infection control," is a world leader in taking fine-grained health surveillance to a new level. Infonaut got its start after forty-one Torontonians died of SARS in early 2003.[1] One of the company's first products was Infection Watch Live, a map-based community surveillance and alert application for gastrointestinal and respiratory disease incidence built on real-time information feeds.

Infonaut is piloting its HospitalWatch*Live* system, which attempts to help control the spread of infection in hospital settings by tracking the real-time ongoing location and movement of patients, staff, and equipment. Ultrasound transponder tags, manufactured by Sonitor, are attached to patients, staff, beds, trolleys, soap and gel dispensers, commodes, and other hospital equipment found in areas close to sites of possible contamination and infection transfer. The precise location of these tags is read every two to thirty seconds by a network of ultrasound microphones installed on the walls and ceilings of hallways and in patient rooms and bathrooms. The resulting stream of data enables accurate tracking of people and objects, their relative proximities, and, by inference, the possible routes taken by pathogens. As the company materials note:

> The deployment of a Real Time Location System (RTLS) into clinical environments allows hospitals to track and store all movement, contact and interaction of patients, staff and assets. This provides instant, risk-rated contact tracing, with predictive analysis of patterns and disease reservoirs.[2]

In particular, Infonaut has designed this system to provide these benefits:

- *Hand Hygiene Compliance:* To promote adherence to hand-cleansing standards by clinicians and track related clinician-patient contact
- *Automated Contact Tracing:* To track infection risks through multiple degrees of separation
- *Occupational Safety:* To protect staff by providing immediate alerts about people with whom they have been in contact who have been exposed to an infectious disease
- *Infection Hotspot Detection:* To prevent ongoing transmission by identifying potential disease reservoirs

**Sonitor® P-Tag for patients and personnel** (Source: Sonitor technologies, http://www.sonitor.com/technology/tags/p-tag)

Infonaut recognizes that this form of fine-grained surveillance is potentially highly privacy invasive and that its effective operation depends on willing cooperation by all those involved. Consequently, it has been trying to build privacy into how the system operates. Infonaut has extensively briefed the frontline doctors, nurses, and cleaning staff involved in the pilot. Under Ontario's Personal Health Information Protection Act (PHIPA), the hospital is the official custodian of the information collected. The system-generated reports appear to be used exclusively for advancing the shared goal of infection control and not as a disciplinary measure. Patients are provided with basic information about the system and go through the same consent process as is involved in invasive procedures. Only approximately 10 percent of patients have declined to use the system.[3] This pilot program demonstrates the technical feasibility of close tracking of people in institutionalized settings. While it appears to employ an approach that respects privacy rights, it remains to be seen whether this same care with personal information will continue if and when HospitalWatch*Live* technologies move from experimental pilot to marketed product deployed under different conditions.

1. World Health Organization (WHO), "Summary Table of SARS Cases by Country, 1 November 2002–7 August 2003," http://www.who.int/entity/csr/sars/country/country2003_08_15.pdf.
2. Infonaut, "HospitalWatch*Live*," 2012, http://www.infonaut.ca/.
3. Dr. Colin Furness, Infonaut staff member, personal communication, 7 October 2012.

biometrically verify or "authenticate" that they owned the card by having a part of their body measured by a fingerprint, iris, or other scanner and then compared with previously recorded versions of these images. As with many other overly ambitious, controversial ID-scheme initiatives, the project was shrouded in a dysfunctional public obscurity and got bogged down in the complexities of integrating so many diverse services within a single unified operation. Although the provincial government quietly closed the floundering project in 2001, its central ambitions of population-wide registration, integrated databases, and biometric authentication live on and play an important role in subsequent Canadian ID initiatives. Most notable in this respect is the BC Services Card, which combines the provincial health card and driver's licence, backed by a common biometric facial database.

The response of the Bush administration to the terrorist attacks of 11 September 2001, although too late to help save the Ontario Smart Card Project, provided a spectacular and lucrative stimulus to the identity-management and security industries more widely. Canada felt the effects almost immediately. By the end of that year, the hastily drafted Canada-US Smart Border Declaration and Action Plan called for a common North American biometric identity card, even though neither the security value nor the technical effectiveness of such a measure could be demonstrated. At the same time, in a clear case of policy laundering, the US pushed the International Civil Aviation Organization (ICAO) to adopt a new "e-passport," which includes an embedded chip that can, on request, transmit a biometric-grade digital facial image of the passport holder.[9] This transmission does not require any contact, and the passport can be scanned without the passport holder's knowledge. Canada supported this change in standard, offering to have an e-passport ready by 2005. While the federal government has repeatedly postponed the public launch of the e-passport, it has, less visibly, been incorporating the essential biometric capabilities into newly issued conventional passports.[10] For example, Passport Canada introduced more rigorous standards for photos ("No smiling!") to facilitate automated face matching at the time of passport application and for later authentication.

The US federal Western Hemisphere Travel Initiative (WHTI), which came into effect 1 June 2009, also requires the use of biometrics. Because of concerns that the new security measures might slow down border crossing, the governments of several states and provinces along the Canada-US border promoted the enhanced driver's licence (EDL) as a border-crossing card that would be a faster, easier, and cheaper alternative to the passport.[11]

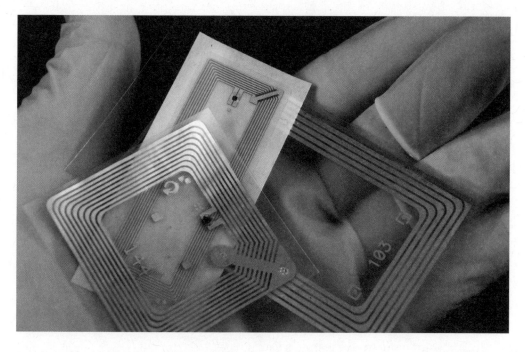

Some RFID chips can be read up to ten metres from an antenna and lack encryption—security or surveillance? (Source: © iStockphoto.com/albn)

Following specifications set by the Department of Homeland Security (DHS), an enhanced driver's licence includes an RFID chip. Border guards can access a digital image of the driver's face and other information contained in the driver's database record through scanning the card. One feature of the RFID standard adopted by the DHS is its relatively long read-range.[12] Developed originally for livestock and supply-chain management, it is designed to read objects up to ten metres from the antenna. Combined with the lack of encryption or other forms of privacy protection, the DHS could hardly have chosen a less secure and more surveillance-prone standard. Complaints by civil liberties advocates and ID industry officials alike regarding the potential for privacy invasion fell on deaf DHS ears. Perhaps the only bright spot is that few Canadians or Americans have opted to use EDLS—far below anticipated numbers—although it is unclear how long people will be given the opportunity to opt out.[13]

While the ambition to create a common North American biometric identity card has been scaled back because of opposition and implementation difficulties, many of its ingredients are systematically being assembled through other means. Under its REAL-ID initiative, and despite stiff resistance, the US government has attempted to turn state drivers' licences into a de facto national ID card.[14] In Canada, the federal and provincial governments have quietly worked together to develop a similar national identity-management scheme based on existing ID documents.[15]

Perhaps the greatest surveillance concern regarding these ID schemes in Canada is that the routine biometric enrolment of most of the adult population has been achieved without public debate and with scant indication of effective oversight. This has occurred largely through the capture of high-resolution facial images for drivers' licences, health cards, and passports, which have then been made available for automated facial matching. These capabilities came to public attention in the wake of the June 2011 Vancouver Stanley Cup riot, when the Insurance Corporation of BC (ICBC) offered the Vancouver Police Department the use of its facial-recognition software and its "fairly fool-proof database of images" to identify criminal suspects.[16] The police opted to develop its own database and did not seek the necessary court order to access ICBC's data.

### "Deep" Internet Surveillance

A third major issue concerning embedded surveillance that has emerged since 2000 is the interception and inspection of Internet traffic. Most public attention and controversy over Internet surveillance has focused on the surveillance at the "edges" of the Internet. On the user or client side of the Internet, the capture of data by surveillance software modules embedded within browsers (e.g., cookies and "web bugs") has been controversial since the 1990s, and more recently, such software embedded in personal mobile devices (e.g., location tracking on iPhones and Android smartphones) has raised similar concerns.[17] Similarly, on the server side, there are ongoing debates about the covert access to such communications as emails and social network posts that are held by Google, Facebook, Microsoft, and other major service providers.

With the extraordinary expansion of online services over the past decade, especially social networking applications, people around the globe have voluntarily, even enthusiastically, contributed enormous volumes of often highly personal information to corporate databases. Accessing this trove of fine-grained data—typically used for advertising or sold to third parties for commercial purposes—is a key feature of the business model of the corporations involved. This poses obvious privacy risks, but consumers, so far, have been willing to put up with this, whether because of a lack of knowledge or because they enjoy the convenience and immediate rewards of the services offered. These databases, and their promise of rich insights into the activities and attitudes of a significant portion of the population, have proved very attractive to state security and law enforcement agencies. In the case of the PRISM program, mentioned in Trend 6, the US National Security Agency (NSA) has embedded the means for automated access to the databases of nine major Internet service providers, thus bypassing the requirements of individual-specific court authorization that usually apply in the case of US persons. Despite their power and wealth, Internet companies have not been able to resist US government demands for bulk access to their data stores and have even invoked the same overly broad "third party" privacy exemption that the US government uses to justify the legality of its access.[18] In matters concerning Canadians, however (and likewise residents of other countries), the NSA's access to data is, in theory, unfettered by legal restraints. Similarly, under the terms of long-standing data-sharing agreements, Canadian government agencies should have access to data collected by the NSA.

Incorporating surveillance capabilities in both the client and server devices at the edges of the Internet is controversial, but it is deep within its "backbone" where the most alarming forms of Internet surveillance are being secretly embedded. Giant routers, housed in unobtrusive office towers in the cores of our major cities, switch billions of data packets every second between fibre-optic cables speeding our Internet traffic to its designated destinations. Over the past decade, governments and corporations have installed equipment that intercepts, analyzes, and selectively stores the traffic passing through these vital switches, or Internet exchange points (IXPS). Given the great and growing range of activity that is conducted via the Internet, the ability to surreptitiously monitor all the personal traffic of hundreds of millions of individuals is breathtaking in its potential ramifications.

It is a daunting technical challenge to analyze the enormous volumes of data coursing through the Internet rapidly enough for it to be useful to policing or management. Nevertheless, just as the speed and capacities of the routers have expanded, so too have the means of interception and the incentives for doing so. "Deep packet inspection" (DPI) refers to techniques that enable Internet carriers to read the content of the many messages and files they send along the net.[19] A data packet is a piece of formatted computer information carried along the Internet: it consists of a "header," containing addressing information, and a "payload," containing the message content. Such packets can be conceptualized as a kind of electronic postcard or letter. Privacy advocates prefer the letter analogy, recognizing that while the header needs to be readable by intermediaries, the contents should be treated as confidential. Service providers, however, prefer the postcard analogy, meaning that the contents are available to anyone. Encrypting the content can protect it from prying eyes, but the header—the destination address—must remain unencrypted for the routing to work. The header information, along with other communication metadata, such as the timing, location, and duration, has traditionally enjoyed lower privacy protection. However, now that such metadata, which can be highly revealing, can be routinely collected and analyzed on a mass basis, privacy advocates argue that it should enjoy protection similar to message content.

Deep packet inspection came to public light in Canada when privacy advocates suspected that major ISPs, such as Bell and Rogers, were slowing, or "throttling," the traffic of particular users or particular applications—notably, BitTorrent (www.bittorrent.com), a popular and free peer-to-peer Internet file-sharing service. In 2009, the same carriers told the CRTC (Canadian Radio-Television Telecommunications Commission) during hearings on Internet traffic management practices that they required DPI ability to prioritize certain traffic over others so that applications dependent on timely delivery (e.g., voice-over-IP, or VoIP) would suffer less delay than less time-sensitive applications (e.g., email and file transfers).[20] Subsequent research found that at least a dozen of Canada's largest carriers have installed DPI equipment.[21] Although Telus did briefly block access to a union-support website, based on header information, there has been no direct evidence thus far that Canadian carriers are using DPI capabilities to surveil users or thwart access to legitimate sites.[22] The same cannot be said of the equipment that Canadian manufacturers such as Netsweeper have sold to Middle Eastern authoritarian regimes, which use such devices for tracking opposition groups and censoring websites on political and religious grounds.[23]

The most extensive use of DPI techniques for population surveillance is the "warrantless wiretapping" of the US National Security Agency (NSA). Beginning around 2003, the NSA began installing surveillance equipment in the main Internet routing hubs of major US carriers, such as AT&T, Verizon, and others. This highly secretive activity came to light most dramatically when AT&T technician Mark Klein blew the whistle in 2006. Shortly after he retired from AT&T, Klein revealed that the NSA had arranged for AT&T to install fibre-optic "splitters" and related traffic-interception equipment in its main San Francisco Internet switching centre at 611 Folsom Street. With similar facilities at other Internet gateways around the country, the US government had evidently been spying on its entire population. As no warrants had been issued for these interceptions, more than forty court cases have been brought against both the carriers and the US government.[24] This litigation has been stalled by congressional passage of the FISA Amendments Act of 2008, which broadened the scope of legally acceptable surveillance and granted private sector carriers retroactive immunity from prosecution.[25] The American federal government has consistently blocked cases brought against it by claiming that plaintiffs lacked "standing" to bring charges, since they couldn't establish that they had been subject to the secret surveillance, and/or by invoking a "state secrets" exemption.[26]

Whatever legal protections may apply to US persons, none apply to those targeted by similar Internet interception operations by the United States outside the country. The NSA refers to such operations as "upstream" collection.[27] In addition to installing fibre-optic splitters within major Internet switches (infrastructure), in situations in which the switch operators are not sufficiently cooperative, the NSA has also adopted the technically more challenging route of tapping directly into the cables along the route between the switches. Since much of the international Internet traffic travels by submarine fibre-optic cable, this involves installing taps at landing stations or even in mid-ocean.[28]

In addition to what the NSA can access from its foreign Internet spying, Canadians are often subject to US domestic Internet interception, even when they and their communication targets are both in Canada. This is due to the fact that roughly one-third of Canadian traffic is routed through the United States, and almost always through one of the cities in which the NSA is strongly suspected of having surveillance operations (notably, New York, Chicago, and Seattle).[29] This "boomerang" routing can occur even between Canadian public institutions located within the same Canadian city. For example, data packets travelling from the University of Toronto to the Ontario Student Assistance Program, which is only a few blocks from campus, are routed via New York and Chicago—both probable sites of NSA splitter operations—before finally returning to Toronto. Because the information moves through the United States, such traffic is subject to provisions

**A Canadian boomerang Toronto-to-Toronto route** (Source: http://www.ixmaps.ca/index.php)

of the USA PATRIOT Act (2001), which allows American government agencies to peek into information passing through the United States even when the information itself is stored outside the United States.

Even Internet traffic carried by Canadian telecommunications service providers that remains entirely within Canadian borders is likely to be subject to similar forms of state-mandated network surveillance. This situation gained public prominence in 2012, when the Conservative government reintroduced "lawful access" legislation in Bill C-30—renamed at the last moment the Protecting Children from Internet Predators Act, even though the bill actually made no reference to child predators except in its title.[30] The key provisions of the legislation, which sought to expand the powers of law enforcement agencies, included access to "subscriber data" when such agencies ask service providers for it. Prior judicial authorization or reasonable grounds to suspect criminal behaviour would not be required, and providers would be compelled to hand over the data requested. The bill also included new powers for law enforcement to order service providers to store existing data on a client and to produce that data on request.[31]

In addition, Bill C-30 required that the systems of telecommunications service providers (TSPs) be designed so as to make it easy for police to intercept online traffic.[32] Given that complying with this provision would entail significant expense on the part of the carriers, for more than a year prior to presenting the bill, the government consulted extensively with Canada's largest telecommunications companies about who should pay and about the feasibility of monitoring user behaviour in an increasingly complex "cloud-computing" environment.[33] This relatively lengthy negotiation contrasted sharply with the complete lack of public consultation about lawful access during the same time period. Nevertheless, in response to a Conservative promise in the 2011 federal election to reintroduce this legislation if returned to government, civil liberties and Internet-rights advocacy organizations formed the Stop Online Spying coalition.[34] As noted in Trend 3, the coalition started a letter-writing campaign, created a variety of videos, and garnered more than 145,000 signatories on its online petition, which called for the government to stop spying on citizens online.[35] When the government finally introduced the bill on 14 February, it immediately ignited such public controversy that it was sent directly to committee for reworking and then was quietly and officially dropped a year later.[36] The Internet surveillance that it was intended to authorize is, nevertheless, probably being carried out, and within the scope of prevailing privacy legislation. This is because the privacy statute that applies to the private sector, the Personal Information Protection and Electronic Documents Act (PIPEDA), already allows TSPs to disclose to police investigators, in certain circumstances, personal information about clients without their knowledge or consent and without any need for a warrant.[37]

This situation illustrates several important points about the current state of Internet surveillance in Canada:

- The federal government and large private enterprises *will*, in secret and *without* public oversight, conduct surveillance and promote legislation that affects the fundamental relations between citizens and the state.
- Current privacy laws are too weak to serve as an effective bulwark against such challenges to taken-for-granted civil liberties.
- There is widespread public concern about surveillance across the political spectrum.
- Organized public opposition can play an important role in effectively resisting excessive Internet monitoring.

## Conclusion

Surveillance practices pose significant challenges to privacy and other civil liberties. The embedding trend heightens these concerns in particular ways—notably, by making surveillance less and less visible even as it grows more and more commonplace. Because these practices are rarely visible from the outside and are usually bundled up with the other more legitimate activities on which they depend, it is extremely difficult to ensure the openness and transparency necessary to making those who carry out surveillance democratically accountable. Although Canadian privacy laws require organizations conducting such surveillance to bear the primary responsibility for making their practices publicly accessible, how is anybody to know whether or not they are doing this? It usually takes a highly publicized breach and a subsequent in-depth investigation to bring surveillance abuses to light. And, by that time, such violations are often a widespread industry practice and hard to remedy after the fact.

## Notes

1   See Andrew Blum, *Tubes: Journey to the Center of the Internet* (New York: Harper Collins, 2012).

2   See Aaron Doyle, Randy Lippert, and David Lyon, eds., *Eyes Everywhere: The Global Growth of Camera Surveillance* (London and New York: Routledge, 2012), http://www.routledge.com/books/details/9780415696555/; Emily Jackson, "Hundreds of Unnamed Cameras Watching Vancouver," *TheThunderBird.ca,* 10 December 2009, http://thethunderbird.ca/2009/12/10/hundreds-of-unnamed-cameras-watching-vancouver/; Andrew Clement, Joseph Ferenbok, Roxanna Dehghan, Laura Kaminker, and Simeon Kanev, "Private Sector Video Surveillance in Toronto: Not Privacy Compliant!" *Proceedings of the 2012 iConference* (New York: ACM, 2012), 354–62; and Sean P. Hier, *Panoptic Dreams: Streetscape Video Surveillance in Canada* (Vancouver: University of British Columbia Press, 2010).

3   See Brenda McPhail, Joseph Ferenbok, Roxanna Dehghan, and Andrew Clement, "'I'll Be Watching You': What Do Canadians Know About Video Surveillance and Privacy?" *iConference 2013 Proceedings* (iSchools, 2013), 555–59, https://www.ideals.illinois.edu/bitstream/handle/2142/39966/276.pdf?sequence=5.

4   Andrew Clement, Joseph Ferenbok, Roxanna Dehghan, Laura Kaminker, Simeon Kanev, and Silvia Valdman, *"Smart" Private Eyes in Public Places? Video Surveillance Analytics, New Privacy Threats and Protective Alternatives,* Final Report, 23 July 2011, submitted to the Office of the Privacy Commissioner of Canada, http://surveillancerights.ca/downloads/Clement_Ferenbok etal - OPC - Private Eyes - Final Report with appendices.pdf, 5.

5   On the practice of "informating," see Shoshana Zuboff, *In the Age of the Smart Machine: The Future of Work and Power* (New York: Basic Books, 1988).

6   See Margaret E. Fulton, *In the Chips: Opportunities, People, Partnerships,* report of the Labour Canada Task Force on Micro-electronics and Employment (Ottawa: Labour Canada, 1982), 89. Workplace monitoring became a bargaining issue with mail sorters at Canada Post (Canadian Union of Postal Workers [CUPW]), airline reservation agents at Air Canada (Canadian Airline Employees Association [CALEA]), and telephone operators at Bell Canada (Communications Workers of Canada [CWC]).

7   For details of the scandal, see the articles at "British Phone Hacking Scandal (Leveson Report)," *New York Times*, http://topics.nytimes.com/top/reference/timestopics/organizations/n/news_of_the_world/index.html.

8   David Lyon, *Identifying Citizens: ID Cards as Surveillance* (Oxford: Polity Press, 2009).

9   "Policy laundering" refers to the practice of national governments pushing for rulings by international bodies, often without democratic oversight, to make policy changes that would probably not be achieved through domestic legislative processes. See Ian Hosein, "International Relations Theories and the Regulation of International Dataflows: Policy Laundering and Other International Policy Dynamics," paper presented at the annual meeting of the International Studies Association, Montréal, QC, 17 March 2004, http://citation.allacademic.com/meta/p_mla_apa_research_citation/0/7/3/8/8/pages73882/p73882-1.php; and Barry Steinhardt, "Problem of Policy Laundering," American Civil Liberties Union (ACLU), 13 August 2004, http://26konferencja.giodo.gov.pl/data/resources/SteinhardtB_paper.pdf.

10  Passport Canada finally announced that as of 1 July 2013, all new Canadian passports issued are electronic passports. See Passport Canada, "About ePassports," last modified 9 August 2013, http://www.ppt.gc.ca/eppt/about.aspx?lang=eng.

11  These jurisdictions include British Columbia, Manitoba, Ontario, Québec, Vermont, New York, Michigan, and Washington. See the map at http://www.getyouhome.gov/html/EDL_map.html. Several other provinces, including Saskatchewan and Nova Scotia, also considered EDLs but decided against them. Adoption has been much lower than projected and appears not have contributed to easing border congestion. See "Saskatchewan Halts New Enhanced Driver's Licence Program," news release, Government of Saskatchewan, 23 March 2009, http://www.gov.sk.ca/news?newsId=88eb5109-3361-4c9f-bafc-d4c226f5b897, and "Sask. Government Ditches 'Enhanced' Driver's Licence Plan," *CBC News,* 23 March 2009, http://www.cbc.ca/news/canada/saskatchewan/sask-government-ditches-enhanced-driver-s-licence-plan-1.808226. For Nova Scotia, see New Driver's Licence and Identification Cards, *Access Nova Scotia,* http://www.novascotia.ca/snsmr/access/drivers/new-licence.asp (last updated 25 November 2013).

12  The standard specified for the EDL RFID chip is the EPC Gen2, short for EPCglobal UHF Class 1 Generation 2. For a discussion of the privacy and security controversies surrounding this particular chip, see "EPC Gen2," *Wikipedia*, last modified 12 October 2013, http://en.wikipedia.org/wiki/Radio-frequency_identification#EPC_Gen2.

13  Brenda McPhail, Krista Boa, Joseph Ferenbok, Karen Louise Smith, and Andrew Clement, "Identity, Privacy and Security Challenges with Ontario's Enhanced Driver's Licence," in *2009 IEEE Toronto International Conference, Science and Technology for Humanity (TIC-STH)*, Toronto, ON, 26–27 September 2009 (IEEE Xplore Digital Library, 2009), 904–9, doi: 10.1109/TIC-STH2009.5444399.

14  See REAL ID Act of 2005, Pub. L. 109-13, http://www.gpo.gov/fdsys/pkg/PLAW-109publ13/html/PLAW-109publ13.htm.

15  Andrew Clement, Krista Boa, Simon Davies, and Gus Hosein, "Toward a National ID Card for Canada? External Drivers and Internal Complexities," in *Playing the Identity Card: Surveillance, Security and Identification in Global Perspective*, ed. Colin J. Bennett and David Lyon (London and New York: Routledge, 2008), 233–50.

16  "Insurance Corporation Offers to Help ID Rioters," *CBC News,* 18 June 2011, http://www.cbc.ca/news/canada/british-columbia/story/2011/06/18/bc-icbc-rioters-id.html.

17  A web bug, also known as a web beacon, a tracking bug, or a page tag, "is a graphics on a Web page or in an Email message that is designed to monitor who is reading the Web page or Email

message": Richard M. Smith, "The Web Bug FAQ," Electronic Frontier Foundation, 11 November 1999, http://w2.eff.org/Privacy/Marketing/web_bug.html.

18  In seeking to dismiss a consumer privacy complaint, Google has drawn on a finding in the *Smith v. Maryland* case to the effect that "a person has no legitimate expectation of privacy in information he voluntarily turns over to third parties" (*Smith v. Maryland*, 442 U.S. 735 [1979], 743–44). See "Defendant Google Inc.'s Motion to Dismiss Plaintiffs' Consolidated Individual and Class Action Complaint" (case 5:13-md-02430-LHK, document 44, filed 06/13/13, before the United States District Court, Northern District of California, San Jose Division), http://www.consumerwatchdog.org/resources/googlemotion061313.pdf, 19.

19  For more on deep packet inspection, see the DPI project website, http://www.deeppacketinspection.ca/.

20  See Telecom Regulatory Policy CRTC 2009-657, "Review of the Internet Traffic Management Practices of Internet Service Providers," Canadian Radio-Television and Telecommunications Commission, 21 October 2009, Ottawa, http://www.crtc.gc.ca/eng/archive/2009/2009-657.htm.

21  See Office of the Privacy Commissioner of Canada, "Deep Packet Inspection Essay Project," last modified 28 March 2013, http://dpi.priv.gc.ca.

22  "BCCLA Denounces Blocking of Website by Telus," BC Civil Liberties Association, 26 July 2005, http://web.archive.org/web/20060101100357/http://www.bccla.org/pressreleases/05telus.htm.

23  Helmi Noman and Jillian C. York, *West Censoring East: The Use of Western Technologies by Middle East Censors, 2010–2011*, OpenNet Initiative, March 2011, http://opennet.net/west-censoring-east-the-use-western-technologies-middle-east-censors-2010-2011.

24  See "NSA Spying on Americans," Electronic Frontier Foundation, n.d., https://www.eff.org/issues/nsa-spying.

25  The FISA Amendment Act is also referred to as the Foreign Intelligence Surveillance Act of 1978 Amendments Act of 2008: see www.intelligence.senate.gov/laws/pl110261.pdf.

26  One notable exception to this is *Al Haramain Islamic Foundation v. Obama,* which made it past the state secrets obstacle but in 2012 was denied on the technical legal basis known as "sovereign immunity." See "Al Haramain v. Obama," Electronic Frontier Foundation, n.d., https://www.eff.org/cases/al-haramain.

27  James Ball, "NSA's Prism Surveillance Program: How It Works and What It Can Do," *The Guardian* (UK), 8 June 2013, http://www.theguardian.com/world/2013/jun/08/nsa-prism-server-collection-facebook-google.

28  The nuclear submarine *Jimmy Carter* has been specially modified to conduct these underwater cable-tapping operations. See Associated Press, "New Nuclear Sub Is Said to Have Special Eavesdropping Ability," *New York Times*, 20 February 2005, http://www.nytimes.com/2005/02/20/politics/20submarine.html?_r=1&.

29  Ron Deibert, *Black Code: Inside the Battle for Cyberspace* (Toronto: McClelland and Stewart, 2013), 43. See also Andrew Clement, "IXmaps—Tracking Your Personal Data Through the NSA's Warrantless Wiretapping Sites," in *2013 IEEE International Symposium on Technology and Society (ISTAS),* Toronto, 27–29 June 2013 (IEEE Xplore Digital Library, 2013), 216–223, doi: 10.1109/ISTAS.2013.6613122.

30  See Meagan Fitzpatrick, "Online Surveillance Bill Could Change, Harper Signals," *CBC News*, 15 February 2012, http://www.cbc.ca/news/politics/online-surveillance-bill-could-change-harper-signals-1.1150295. The bill was originally called "An Act to enact the Investigating and Preventing Criminal Electronic Communications Act and to amend the Criminal Code and other Acts" (2012): for the full text, see http://s3.documentcloud.org/documents/292611/bill-c-30.pdf.

31  Phillipa Lawson, *Moving Toward a Surveillance Society: Proposals to Expand "Lawful Access" in Canada*, BC Civil Liberties Association (BCCLA), 2012, http://bccla.org/wp-content/uploads/2012/03/2012-BCCLA-REPORT-Moving-toward-a-surveillance-society1.pdf, 5.

32  Ibid.

33  Anna Mehler Paperny, "Telcos in Talks with Ottawa to Shape Internet 'Spy' Bill: Documents," *Globe and Mail*, 29 June 2012, http://m.theglobeandmail.com/technology/tech-news/telcos-in-talks-with-ottawa-to-shape-internet-spy-bill-documents/article4376958/?service=mobile.

34  The Stop Online Spying coalition had a broad membership from across Canada and was convened by OpenMedia.ca: see http://stopspying.ca.

35  See, for example, the video "(Un)Lawful Access: Canadian Experts on the State of Cyber-surveillance" (2011), at http://unlawfulaccess.net/.

36  John Ibbitson, "Harper Government Kills Controversial Internet Surveillance Bill," *Globe and Mail*, 11 February 2013, http://www.theglobeandmail.com/news/politics/harper-government-kills-controversial-internet-surveillance-bill/article8456096/.

37  Leo Singer, "Unwarranted Access?" *National: Legal Insights and Practice Trends,* Canadian Bar association, June 2012, http://www.nationalmagazine.ca/Articles/June-2012-Issue/Unwarranted-access.aspx.

# Going Biometric
## From Surveillance of the Body
## to Surveillance in the Body

The door of the seminar room at the University of Arizona slowly opens, and what looks like a futuristic casket is wheeled in, followed by an attentive team of accomplished scientists, administrators, and graduate students. The casket-like case is unlatched, and an apparatus resembling a bank machine is carefully lifted out. After some tinkering and tuning, the machine is "awake." Its screen displays a computer-generated human face complete with blinking, moving eyes that glance from side to side. AVATAR, the Automated Virtual Agent for Truth Assessments in Real-Time, is ready.

What follows is the typical examination expected by any traveller at the Canada-US border, including inquiries about whether you packed your own luggage, where you plan to stay, and the intended duration of your visit. What makes this examination different is that it is entirely conducted by AVATAR, a biometric, artificial intelligence kiosk charged with assessing whether or not travellers require secondary inspection—on the basis of AVATAR's presumed ability for "detecting deception," be it a false answer to a question, concealed contraband, or a range of other possibilities.

This demonstration of AVATAR, which took place in September 2010, was preceded with a lecture by Professor Nunamaker, head of the AVATAR project and professor of management-information systems at the University of Arizona. Nunamaker's presentation extolled the virtues of both AVATAR and SPECIES (Special Purpose Embodied Conversational Intelligence with

Environmental Sensors), the technological model that underpins AVATAR—itself an example of what is more broadly referred to as an "embodied conversational agent." Although AVATAR is an extreme (and American) example, it illustrates a series of trends and beliefs that Canadians should find particularly interesting, if not troubling. Among other things, it exemplifies the belief that technology is neutral, effective, and almost infallible, and can out-perform the people we previously relied upon to guard our borders and test our trustworthiness. However, like all technology, AVATAR is produced by humans and is a product of human assumptions about behaviour, race, gender, deception, and so on. Rather than being neutral, technologies such as AVATAR contain the assumptions and biases that their creators have embedded within them.[1]

One such assumption relates to gender. Most border-crossing protocols assume that an individual is either male or female; this simple assumption has put transgendered persons at risk because their self-presentation does not match the gender recorded in official databases. The data, and the technology that makes decisions about people based on those data, are not neutral. They embody discriminatory assumptions about human identity.

## What Are Biometric Technologies?

This belief in technological neutrality underpins the development of many biometric technologies and is now pervasive among government officials, policy makers, and law enforcement officers on both sides of the Canada-US border.

Biometric systems put physiological characteristics into a digital form. They range from simple, relatively reliable and inexpensive digital fingerprinting, to retinal and iris scanning, to more complex systems that measure body temperature, scent, or gait. The technology seems to be evolving toward artificial intelligence, prosthetics, and virtual bodies. The increased reliance on proliferating body surveillance appears to go hand in hand with the contemporary biopolitical preoccupation of governments and the private sector with assorted social interventions designed to alter statistical levels of birth, recidivism, death, incarceration, and so on.

Understanding these developments, however, can prove challenging for both analysts and engaged citizens seeking to learn about current and future surveillance technologies. To comprehend these technologies, we

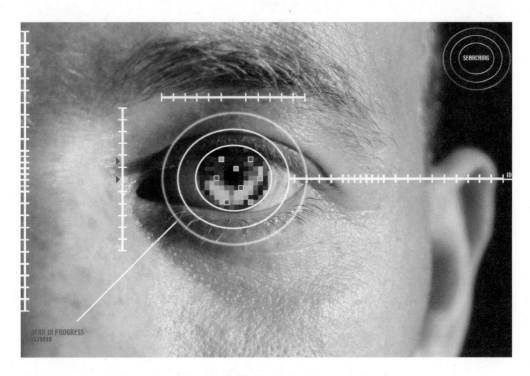

**Iris scanning: a popular biometric security measure** (Source: © iStockphoto.com/tlnors)

must understand the critical distinction between authentication and identification. Whereas identification is concerned with knowing who you are as a unique individual, an organization can *authenticate* an individual as, for example, a legitimate recipient of a service without actually knowing that person's identity. As noted in a research report on biometrics released by the US National Research Council:

> Authentication technologies are typically based on one of three things: something the individual knows, such as a password; something the individual has, such as a physical key or secure token; and something the individual is or does. Biometric technologies employ the last of these. Unlike password- or token-based systems, biometric systems can function without active input, user cooperation, or knowledge that the recognition is taking place.[2]

## Biometrics for Port Workers in Halifax

In 2007, it was announced that Unisys had been awarded a contract to develop and manage a biometric system to control access to the Port of Halifax for some four thousand workers. The plan was developed in compliance with Transport Canada's Marine Transportation Security Act. The system uses the hand vascular pattern recognition (HVPR) system developed by Identica. An infrared scan of the back of the cardholder's hand is embedded in a smart card, which also includes the holder's photograph.[1]

This vascular image, recognized by an infrared sensor, is used to identify cardholders when they present the card and place the back of their hand on the scanner. Verification is instantaneous and is achieved when the blood flow pattern of the holder's hand matches the pattern of the scan stored on the card. The biometric is stored only on the individual card, not in the database. The system manages access control to permit entry to various secure facilities only to those

---

In other words, biometric technologies are designed not to replace other authentication systems but to augment them within an increasingly "data rich" security environment. The passive capture of information through biometric systems raises special concerns about their potential (un)reliability and about our varying ability or inability to protect or control the capture, sharing, and transfer of this personal information.

Limited only by the human imagination, body surveillance is emerging in a range of areas. At Canadian schools, for instance, children's fingerprints are being used to facilitate cashless payment systems.[3] The Calypso Waterpark near Ottawa uses fingerprinting for entrance payments, and several Canadian firms have installed, or are planning to install, a system designed to track employee hours, overtime, and tardiness through fingerprinting.[4] At the Port of Halifax, the backs of port workers' hands are scanned to manage port access.[5] As with border-security strategies, these entail complex blends of private and public schemes. Together with alleged efficiency payoffs, the promise of enhanced security—often without much concrete evidence to support such claims—frequently seems reason enough for business owners, policy makers, and shareholders to embrace biometric surveillance.

individuals with proper clearances. Workers must also use the card and verify their identity when they leave an area. More than sixty such scanners have been installed in the port since 2008.

The HVPR system is touted as an example of a new generation of biometric authentication systems: an example of Privacy by Design, or PbD, it is more reliable and more secure than earlier biometric technologies, and it has built-in privacy-enhancing features. Since 9/11, ports have been identified as prime targets and worthy of state-of-the-art security. Is such a response a proportionate and justifiable response to a genuine security concern? Or is it over the top—expensive, intrusive, and ultimately ineffective?

1. See L. Samuel Pfeifle, "Unisys' Hand-Scan Plan," *Security Systems News,* 1 October 2007, 19–20; T. Peters, "Halifax to Use Biometrics to Identify Port Workers," *Canadian Sailings,* 3 September 2007, 15; and "Halifax Port Security to Scan Veins in Hands," CBC News, 7 September 2007, http://www.cbc.ca/news/canada/nova-scotia/halifax-port-security-to-scan-veins-in-hands-1.665612.

## Biometrics at the Border: An Example of Biometrics at Work

As various bilateral agreements and initiatives—particularly those established since 9/11—demonstrate, Canadian governments at all levels seem increasingly willing to embrace biometric and body surveillance technologies originating or already used in the United States and to accept initiatives to share vast amounts of personal data and information with the United States—often in the absence of public debate or media attention.

Most people have become more aware of so-called body surveillance since the attacks of 11 September 2001, but the use of biometrics goes far beyond antiterrorism efforts. Indeed, surveillance has long been linked with keeping populations not only secure but productive.[6] The dominance of government policies that focus on privatization, deregulation, and enhanced market powers has helped to promote both the free flow of capital and an intensive individualism. These combine to create the appropriate conditions for the rise of body surveillance.

Even a cursory examination of the politics of airport security uncovers a variety of public and private sector actors charged with often overlapping and muddled competencies. These actors include the RCMP and local police; commissionaires and private security guards; the contractors working for the

Canadian Air Transport Security Authority (CATSA), who help to prescreen passengers; and agents from the Canada Border Services Agency (CBSA), now authorized to carry firearms. Airline employees are also enmeshed in this web of security management by virtue of the fact that some security functions, such as enforcing no-fly lists, have been off-loaded onto airlines. Overlaid onto this complicated situation is the network of surveillance cameras (their maintenance and management), electronic passport readers, body scanners, and traveller kiosks, all representing their respective public and private developers.

These devices and practices are used in various models of security governance and are informed by different notions of risk, threat, and danger. They also involve different applications of body surveillance, all of which are interconnected in complex ways that make it challenging to critically engage with such developments. These difficulties are compounded by the fact that these systems operate in spaces—like the airport—where the discretionary power of the state is enhanced because of concerns about security.

The form of biometric technology that the average Canadian is probably most familiar with is the full-body scanner now used in the major Canadian airports. These scanners were installed after Umar Farouk Abdulmtallab, travelling on an Amsterdam-Detroit flight on Christmas Day 2009, attempted to blow up the plane by detonating an explosive concealed in his underpants. Abdulmtallab's attempt, which earned him the nickname the "underwear bomber," was thwarted—but by attentive passengers, not by security scans. Nonetheless, on 5 January 2010, Canadians were told that full-body scanners would be rolled out at major airports and that behavioural observation (described below) would be tested at Vancouver International Airport during the following year. Although the full-body scanners caught the imagination of many Canadians, especially passengers worried that security officers would see them naked, the prospect of behavioural observation was met with an almost audible silence.

Full-body scanners use millimetre wave technology, which projects radio frequency energy over the body; this energy, when reflected back, produces a 3D image. These scanners are intended to reveal objects such as weapons and explosives that travellers might be hiding under their clothing. The idea was to give passengers a "choice" between a physical search—a "pat down"—and the new scanners. They have become a familiar sight to air travellers, many of whom have now experienced them. Following public discussion of body-privacy concerns about what could be seen and who would view the images, and despite some lingering apprehensions, full-body scanners seem to have been domesticated as "normal." As well, the Office of the Privacy Commissioner was satisfied with the privacy impact assessment provided by the Canadian Air Transport Security Authority (CATSA).

Behavioural observation is a practice that has been used for a number of years at Ben Gurion Airport in Tel Aviv. While other forms of surveillance look for potentially dangerous *objects*, behavioural observation is supposed to be able to identify potentially dangerous *persons*. In Canada, from February to July 2010, special plain-clothes officers at Vancouver International Airport checked passengers at the gate for suspicious signs. Passengers who, for example, looked nervous or were sweating, tapping their feet, or wearing too much clothing for the warmth of the day were questioned by officers. Key concerns about this behavioural observation practice have to do with the training of officers, the (mis)identification of "suspicious" persons, and, perhaps most alarmingly, the chances that racial—or age or gender—profiling could be involved in determining who "looks suspicious."[7] The federal privacy commissioner has taken up these issues, which are still under discussion.[8]

## The Infatuation with Biometrics

Although many technologies entail body surveillance, biometric technologies are the clearest and most prevalent forms currently used. The relatively low cost of biometric systems contributes to their prevalence but is not the sole reason for it. Their proliferation is partly due to the fact that, since the 9/11 terrorist attacks, officials of all stripes have equated larger amounts of data with enhanced security. The attacks were themselves framed as a breakdown of a government's ability to assess, anticipate, and adequately respond to terrorism risks—a breakdown that was supposedly due, in large part, to insufficient data. In other words, there appears to be a sort of contemporary fetish for surveillance and data-collection systems, which are perceived to provide us with more security in and of themselves. This questionable assumption about the dangerous "lack" of data has become a convincing logic for increasing reliance on biometric systems and other forms of body surveillance. Moreover, decisions by governments to manage populations—even those made in the exceptional spaces of borders, where the discretionary power of the state is at its maximum—often then spill over into the private sector.

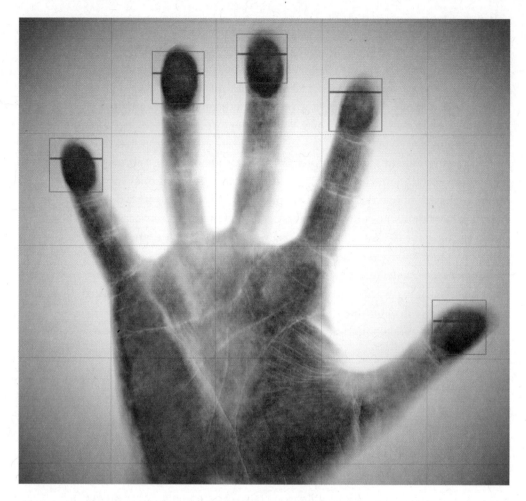

**Biometric scanning of fingerprints in a security system** (Source: © iStockphoto.com/malexeum)

The use of biometrics in passports to secure our borders from undesirable travellers, for example, cannot be easily separated from the Restricted Access Identity Card (RAIC), which uses biometrics to manage and secure the movement of CATSA employees in Canadian airports, or from the biometric systems used by the Halifax Port Authority to monitor port workers. Indeed, the management of populations, whether focused on people crossing national borders or arriving at work twenty minutes late, is an excellent example of the blurred division between the private and public (see Trend 3). In many instances, proponents of these systems, appealing to a presumed natural inclination toward greater "efficiency," tout them as enhancing our mobility but conveniently conceal how they actually decrease the mobility of some groups and allow draconian exercises of power at borders or in the workplace. They may even disenfranchise some persons—for instance, those who cannot qualify for particular programs because they do not have the required body part to be scanned, be it an iris, five fingers on a hand, or a readable fingerprint.

Technical changes in border security and in a wide range of contemporary security fields over the past decade have contributed to this increased reliance on biometric systems. In particular, the notion that visibility is increased by biometrically capturing some aspect of one's physical body—the notion that "the body is the password"—is directly connected to the trend toward forms of security that rely on ever more data. As more direct forms of human intelligence gathering, such as interactions with a border guard or customs agent, decline, "preassessment" of the profile of persons attempting to cross borders increases (as does that of purchasers, clients, consumers, etc.). Such preassessments may occur in the form of passenger prescreening systems used when booking an airline ticket or through traveller systems that rely on a specific profile captured in data, such as the NEXUS program (the program that allows fast-track travel between the US and Canada), to calculate who can and cannot be trusted to travel with a minimum of oversight.[9] Since the personal data about someone—known as the person's "data double"—are routinely distributed widely to various agencies that are seeking to confirm that individual's identity, it allegedly becomes even more necessary to convert that person's physiology into visible, machine-readable algorithms.[10] These measures have become synonymous with increased, intensified, and, allegedly, more effective and efficient security. They also exemplify Toby Miller's point that "the *quid pro quo* for the security afforded by governments has become that our lives [as well as our bodies] be knowable."[11]

The promise behind this knowability is better security. For example, officials strategically framed the events of 9/11 in Washington, DC, New York, and Pennsylvania as radical insecurity and unpredictability and as involving the catastrophic failure of existing security infrastructures. This insecurity was presented as if system-wide failure was not to blame, per se, but that the existing security and identity infrastructure was somehow "hoodwinked" or tricked. Responses therefore focused on the need to verify and authenticate identity—to ascertain that you are who you say you are; this quest is now

## Cashless Schools

Biometric techniques have moved quickly from airports, prisons, and military contexts to everyday civilian institutions, such as high schools, that may turn themselves into surveillance laboratories.[1] As part of a Cashless Schools initiative, for instance, Fredericton High School in New Brunswick now allows students to pay for lunch in the cafeteria simply by leaving a thumbprint. Such systems are being sold widely in Canada, to both universities and high schools. In the case of Fredericton High School, parents must register with Cashless Schools, a Canadian-based company that specializes in payment systems for schools, make a deposit in their account, and sign a consent form confirming that their child may use the biometric scanner.

The student has to enrol a fingerprint in the system in order to make the cashless transaction possible; enrolment in the database allows for verification at the site of the transaction—in this

synonymous with the introduction of body surveillance, since traditional forms of authentication, like passports and other identity certificates, have obviously failed. This rather odd but nonetheless straightforward question of whether you are who you say you are has led to a panoply of practices, techniques, and technologies to enhance both visibility and states' abilities to identify and manage risk.[12]

So we have seen increased spending allocated to ensuring that all those who cross state borders are "visible and knowable," and, whenever possible, new measures have focused on the preassessment of risk. Toward that end, an ever expanding number of government strategies and techniques have increased the amount of data collected through body surveillance. Again, surveillance attitudes and measures demonstrated at state borders have been mimicked and replicated in other sectors and include the use of biometrics in simplified payment schemes, employee tracking, and managed access to public and private facilities. An underlying belief that such schemes provide increased efficiency and enhanced security is apparent in both private and public sectors; biometric systems are accordingly used in Canada to pay for a child's school lunch, gain access to a local fitness facility, or track employees in a law firm.[13]

case, the cafeteria. While Cashless Schools reassures its clients that the company goes "above and beyond" industry standards for privacy and security, it has to be said that the opportunities for using school biometric systems might extend into many other areas.

In other contexts, parents or school health officials can check meals bought through a finger scan. Indeed, pizza or burgers could be made unavailable to certain students: "Purchase denied!" In some schools where biometric systems have been installed, future plans include scans for school bus entry, library use, and parking. Surveillance creep appears to make economic and technical sense—if the system has that capacity, why not use it? Whether it is necessary, effective, or proportionate to the activity or whether a less invasive alternative might be available seems to go unconsidered.

1. See John Gilliom and Torin Monahan, *Supervision: An Introduction to the Surveillance Society* (Chicago: University of Chicago Press, 2013), 73.

## What's Wrong with Biometrics?

State policy makers and law enforcement agencies have generally supported these technologies of authentication, regardless of the relative dearth of sound qualitative and quantitative data that convincingly demonstrate their efficacy. In fact, reports have raised serious issues about the reliability and the high false-positive rates of biometrics: such false positives include situations where an individual has been incorrectly deemed risky or mistakenly placed on a watch list or no-fly list.[14] These obviously disconcerting situations do not even address the broader socio-cultural and politico-economic implications of relying on these technologies, which often require more data-reliant systems of capture and preassessment.[15] They also reflect an undue dependence on technical solutions in the absence of convincing research into the efficacy and broader impacts of their use.[16]

In her insightful analysis of biometrics, Shoshana Magnet concisely asserts, "Human bodies are not biometrifiable."[17] She goes on to discuss how, despite the enormous financial investment in biometric technologies, the human body is simply not static enough to make this form of identification reliable. This critique, heard within the humanities and social sciences for the past decade, is beginning to be echoed within the natural sciences. Both the 2012 National Research Council report *Biometric Recognition* and extensive research at the University of Notre Dame highlight problems posed by the dynamic quality of the physical characteristics that biometrics purport to identify, such as changes to the iris as people age.[18] Questions have also been raised about the underlying science that converts physiology into algorithms. Put succinctly by the authors of the National Research Council report:

> Users and developers of biometric systems should recognize and take into account the limitations and constraints of biometric systems—especially the probabilistic nature of the underlying science, the current limits of knowledge regarding human individual distinctiveness, and the numerous sources of uncertainty in biometric systems.[19]

This certainly does not reflect the tenor of statements from security professionals, policy makers, and border-security managers, who persistently extol the virtues of the biometrics that appear in such things as passports, body scanners, and trusted-traveller cards.

The emergence of scientific queries about biometrics might provide a window of opportunity for a more critical conversation about these technological systems, and their respective developers and proponents, in much the same way that scientists have raised critical socio-political and ethical concerns about other technologies, as exemplified most famously in J. Robert Oppenheimer's criticism of the Manhattan Project. A theoretical physicist known as the father of the atomic bomb, Oppenheimer was one of the key figures in the development of nuclear weapons for the United States toward the end of World War II. However, immediately after the war, as chief advisor to the American Atomic Energy Commission, Oppenheimer became an outspoken critic of nuclear weapons, advocating nonproliferation and the avoidance of an arms race with the USSR. In a similar manner, scientists involved in developing biometrics are increasingly criticizing the efficacy and reliability of these systems.[20]

## Conclusion

So where do we go from here? How do we, as citizens who have often been rendered more vulnerable by the intensified power of the state and private sector, critically engage with technologies and systems that rely on body surveillance? Unfortunately, there is no "how to" guide in this matter. A range of possibilities exists, however, for an engaged citizenry to raise important questions and to become attuned to the often dubious assumptions, commitments, and truth claims that are part of the increasing prevalence of these technologies. Although the turn to body surveillance, notably biometric systems, is part of a widespread technology fetish, there are also deeper systemic factors that make the introduction of these systems appear logical. One such factor is the general embrace of the practice of governing through risk, explained in more detail in Trend 2.[21] This entails strategies developed to deal with incalculable risks, or to govern what is ungovernable.

The fact that many risks cannot be calculated and are therefore both unknown and unknowable has become equated, in the minds of security planners and an increasingly anxious public, with an intolerable level of insecurity and danger. One way to make people feel safer is to collect the personal data of members of a wide set of groups, captured through assorted systems. Those enrolled in these systems—be they frequent flyer schemes, trusted-traveller programs, passport enrolment, or credit-rating operations—are thought to be more knowable, and this knowability has come to be equated with a form of security in the eyes of both the state and the business world. The logic of risk management therefore motivates states and private actors to increase their knowledge of populations in order to enhance security, and the use of biometrics creates the illusion that members of those populations are guaranteed to be who they claim to be.

Risk management also appeals to government officials since it presents one possible way of dealing with financial pressures at a time when austerity and restraint collide with the alleged need for greater spending in the fields of security and surveillance. Particularly since 9/11, risk-management calculus—based on calculating or predicting the frequency of risks and their potential impact—has been used to support the case for increased public expenditure and has led to dramatic increases in security spending. In Canada, just shy of $100 billion *more* was spent on national security in the decade following 9/11 than would have been spent had budgets remained in line with pre-9/11 budgets; the corresponding figure in the United States was close to $1 trillion.[22] Bureaucrats and their political masters have successfully framed the potential frequency and possible impact of risks such as terrorism as necessitating a growing share of government funding over the range of other services and budget lines that vie for limited funds.

The need to critically engage with body surveillance is not an indictment of the technologies themselves. Simplistic normative judgments serve no purpose here. Some biometric systems are minimally intrusive, have robust privacy protections, and effectively serve the interests of security and efficiency. There are appropriate and inappropriate uses of such devices. For example, the RAIC used by CATSA, mentioned earlier, simply allows nonpublic spaces in airports to be secured through random checks of the individuals accessing those halls and spaces. The RAIC holds the employee's biometric information on the card itself. During a random check, the digital fingerprint encrypted on the card (RAIC), which is swiped on a reader, is linked with the actual fingerprint placed on the reader. The information is not transferred to or stored on databases. This minimizes the privacy-invasive nature of the identity check and protects the individual's biometric identifiers from identity thieves.

So we need not toss the baby out with the bathwater. But unfortunately, the bathwater is incredibly murky. The primary challenge for citizens in engaging with body surveillance devices is to appreciate the logics that underwrite them. This can include the assumption that, by its very nature, body surveillance is more reliable and thus provides greater security than alternate systems; or the claim that introducing technologies allows us to escape the more complicated politics of racial profiling; or the assumption that undergirds technologies such as AVATAR—that body surveillance is a more reliable way to detect the types of deception that are to be expected in border spaces. Consequently, we might want to refuse the body scanner at the airport in favour of the physical check by an agent, or to choose not to enrol in trusted-traveller schemes that rely on biometric systems, or to challenge an employer's decision to track employees with biometric systems, or to stand in a longer line at the local fitness facility in order to avoid the biometric payment scheme. Unfortunately, the immediate consequence of such refusals often appears to amount to little more than reducing our own mobility. So how do we engage more effectively with body surveillance issues?

The public may find it hard to participate in debates about these devices given that such discussions are dominated by assorted experts and consultants, many of whom have financial ties to the industry they represent. Advocates of biometrics and body scanners frequently try to dismiss those who criticize such technology with the accusation that such critics threaten the state's security interests. Moreover, public debate may not exist at all when governments use quiet strategies to bypass public discussion of potentially controversial issues, as was the case when the Canadian government signed the *Beyond the Border* agreement (2011) that stipulates that Canada share biometric data with the United States.[23]

The often impenetrable specialist and technocratic discourse that surrounds such devices, together with the alleged "security imperatives" associated with their use, gives the impression that decisions surrounding surveillance of almost any form have been whisked from the democratic process. This should not be the case. Conventional politics are as relevant here as in any other area. Decisions about many forms of monitoring remain in the hands of politicians, subject to parliamentary committees, media scrutiny, and public pressure. Although influential underlying assumptions shape the application of these technologies, we can challenge public figures and funding agencies about these logics. Informed awareness of these devices, as well as the judgments that undergird them, provides ample space to question their rapid embrace. As critical voices within the scientific community emerge, the need to take advantage of this moment cannot be overemphasized. It is as citizens that we can speak for vulnerable groups, such as the refugees and asylum seekers who face the most developed and nefarious technological systems of body surveillance, both in Canada and abroad. A critical eye should scrutinize all forms of body surveillance before that eye is forced to provide a retinal scan.

## Notes

1  See Simon A. Cole, *Suspect Identities: A History of Fingerprinting and Criminal Identification* (Cambridge, MA: Harvard University Press, 2002); Joseph Pugliese, *Biometrics: Bodies, Technologies, Politics* (New York and London: Routledge, 2010); and Shoshana Amielle Magnet, *When Biometrics Fail: Gender, Race and the Technology of Identity* (Durham, NC: Duke University Press, 2011).

2  National Research Council, *Biometric Recognition: Challenges and Opportunities* (Washington, DC: National Academies Press, 2012), 5.

3  See "Canadian Schools Benefiting from Biometric Payment System," *ID News Canada*, 30 June 2010, http://www.idsuperstore.ca/idnews/education-id-news/canadian-schools-benefiting-from-biometric-payment-system-19865906/.

4  On the waterpark payment system, see Calypso's "Money at My Fingertip" page, http://www.calypsopark.com/parc-aquatique/en/services/money-at-my-fingertip/; and "Largest Themed Waterpark in Canada to Open on June 7," *ID News Canada*, 4 June 2010, http://www.idsuperstore.ca/idnews/sports-and-recreation-id-news/largest-themed-waterpark-in-canada-to-open-on-june-7-19820328/. On the tracking of employees, see S. Dobson, "Accuracy Vital to Overtime Tracking," *Canadian HR Reporter*, 10 September 2007, 26, 30; D. Harder, "Fingerprint Technology, Pinpoint Accuracy," *Canadian HR Reporter*, 8 September 2008, 23, 34; and "Biometrics Security to Track Working Hours," *The Current, with Anna Maria Tremonti*, CBC Radio 1, 8 November 2012, http://www.cbc.ca/thecurrent/episode/2012/11/08/biometrics-security-to-track-working-hours/.

5   See "Halifax Port Security to Scan Veins in Hands," *CBC News,* 7 September 2007, http://www.cbc.ca/news/canada/nova-scotia/halifax-port-security-to-scan-veins-in-hands-1.665612.

6   See Toby Miller, "Surveillance: The 'Digital Trail of Breadcrumbs,'" *Culture Unbound* 10, no. 2 (2010): 9–14.

7   See Reg Whitaker, "Behavioural Profiling in Israel Aviation Security as a Tool for Social Control," in *Surveillance and Control in Israel/Palestine: Population, Territory and Power*, ed. Elia Zureik, David Lyon, and Yasmeen Abu-Laban (London and New York: Routledge, 2011), 371–85.

8   See Jim Bronskill, "Privacy Czar Fears Airport Security Plan Could Involve Racial Profiling," *Globe and Mail*, 9 March 2012, http://www.theglobeandmail.com/news/politics/privacy-czar-fears-airport-security-plan-could-involve-racial-profiling/article552340/.

9   On prescreening systems, see Colin J. Bennett, "What Happens When You Book an Airline Ticket? The Collection and Processing of Passenger Data Post-9/11," in *Global Surveillance and Policing: Borders, Security, Identity,* ed. Elia Zureik and Mark B. Salter (Cullompton, UK: Willan Publishing, 2005), 113–38.

10  On the concept of "data double," see Kevin D. Haggerty and Richard V. Ericson, "The Surveillant Assemblage," *British Journal of Sociology* 51, no. 4 (2000): 605–22.

11  Miller, "Surveillance: The 'Digital Trail of Breadcrumbs,'" 9.

12  See Claudia Aradau and Rens van Munster, "Governing Terrorism Through Risk: Taking Precautions, (un)Knowing the Future," *European Journal of International Relations* 13, no. 1 (2007): 89–115.

13  "Biometrics Security to Track Working Hours."

14  See National Research Council, *Biometric Recognition,* 4–5; and Samuel P. Fenker and Kevin W. Bowyer, "Analysis of Template Aging in Iris Biometrics," paper presented at the IEEE Computer Society Biometrics Workshop, 17 June 2012, http://www3.nd.edu/~kwb/FenkerBowyerCVPRW_2012.pdf.

15  See National Research Council, *Biometric Recognition,* esp. chap. 4.

16  See Benjamin J. Muller, "(Dis)Qualified Bodies: Securitization, Citizenship and Identity Management," in *Securitizations of Citizenship*, ed. Peter Nyers (London and New York: Routledge, 2009), 77–93; and Benjamin J. Muller, "Testifying While Critical: Notes on Being an Effective Gadfly," in *Research Methods in Critical Security Studies: An Introduction,* ed. Mark B. Salter and Can E. Mutlu (London and New York: Routledge, 2012), 109–12.

17  Magnet, *When Biometrics Fail*, 2.

18  See Fenker and Bowyer, "Analysis of Template Aging in Iris Biometrics."

19  National Research Council, *Biometric Recognition,* 5.

20  Fenker and Bowyer, "Analysis of Template Aging in Iris Biometrics."

21  See Aradau and van Munster, "Governing Terrorism Through Risk."

22  On Canada, see Meagan Fitzpatrick, "Security Spending After 9/11 Tops $92B," *CBC News*, 7 September 2011, http://www.cbc.ca/news/canada/story/2011/09/07/pol-911-security-spending.html; on the United States, see John Mueller and Mark G. Stewart, "Terror, Security, and Money: Balancing the Risks, Benefits and Costs of Homeland Security," paper presented at the annual convention of the Midwest Political Science Association, Chicago, IL, 1 April 2011.

23  Government of Canada, *Beyond the Border: A Shared Vision for Perimeter Security and Economic Competitiveness*, February 2011, http://actionplan.gc.ca/grfx/psec-scep/pdfs/bap_report-paf_rapport-eng-dec2011.pdf.

# Watching by the People

## From Them to Us

When we think of surveillance, what typically comes to mind are the activities of organizations such as corporations or the police. These are enormously important players in the operation of surveillance, but there is an entire realm of watching conducted by individuals that is not coordinated by organizations. This watching undertaken by everyday citizens has expanded in recent years, often with the aid of new information technologies, and it represents yet another broad trend in the contemporary dynamics of surveillance in Canada.

People watch one another, and they have always done so. We watch because it gives us strategic power over others, because people are inherently interesting, and because, as can be seen in the broad sweep of human history, watching others provides an evolutionary advantage.[1] We come to know the world around us and our place in it by interacting with other people. Watching and being watched are also fundamental parts of how we define who we are. We act out roles—child, sibling, parent, employee, friend, spouse, lover—and adopt characteristics depending on how our performances are received by others. We shape our identities based on how other people see us and react to our behaviour.[2]

So people have always conducted routine forms of day-to-day surveillance of other people. In recent years, however, such scrutiny appears to have expanded. We now watch in ways that only a short time ago would have been impossible or taboo. This change can be explained, in part, by the emergence of new technologies that make it easier for individual citizens to become watchers. It is also a sign of a growing surveillance culture, where watching has become a routine and unremarkable part of social life.

The surveillance conducted by organizations often (but not only) involves the more powerful watching the less powerful. So, for example, the police watch criminals, social workers scrutinize people on social assistance, and employers monitor workers. What makes the surveillance conducted by everyday citizens particularly interesting is that it can involve people from the less powerful echelons of society monitoring people from more powerful levels. So, for example, individuals now use camera-equipped smartphones to record police behaviour.[3] Global media also shine an often intense light on the foibles and indiscretions of celebrities and political figures.

This type of surveillance can involve some of the most intimate realms of our lives. Parents, for example, use new commercially available smart-phone monitoring applications and even home drug tests to expand upon their traditional responsibility to watch their children. They also set up "nanny cams" in household objects such as smoke detectors or teddy bears to secretly monitor spouses, children, and caregivers. Canadians involved in the substantial world of online dating have been encouraged to run formal background checks on potential romantic partners. Should the romance go sour, they might hire private detectives who specialize in exposing unfaith-ful spouses.

Perhaps the most interesting and fluid area of citizen-initiated monitor-ing can be found in the realm of online social media. Given the ever increasing significance of such media, we focus on them here as an extended example of how citizens are increasingly caught up in the dynamics of surveillance, not just as the targets of observation but also as watchers themselves.

## Individual Surveillance for Connection and Convenience

Given that surveillance can have a negative impact on our political, social, and economic relationships, it may seem strange to suggest that surveillance can also be fun. But there is an unmistakable playfulness in watching and being watched by others, as has become particularly apparent on social net-working sites. We post photos and comments on Facebook and Twitter and look at what friends, family members, and neighbours have posted about

A multitude of social media options, all enthusiastically embraced by Canadians (Source: © iStockphoto.com/franckreporter)

themselves because it gives us a window into the lives of others. By making supportive, funny, or crude comments or by tagging photos and "liking" products and videos, we also shape how others see us. While these services can be abused—for example, in cases of stalking and harassment—they also help us to strengthen our sense of connectedness to the people in our community.

Canadians have embraced social networking, and many of us use social media platforms as a matter of course. For example, as of 2011, some 15.4 million Canadians were on Facebook, and Canada had more users per capita than any other country in the world.[4] In a recent survey, 79 percent of Canadian adults reported that they had used Facebook in the past month. Although adults under thirty-five were more likely to have logged on (88 percent), a significant majority of those aged thirty-five to fifty-four (78 percent) and those over fifty-five (66 percent) were also active users. Close to half of them (48 percent) spent five hours or more on social media per week.[5] Canadian schools have been online since 1999, and, from the time that Canadian young people first had access to social media, they have consistently reported using them to try on different identities, deepen their friendships, play, learn about the world, and express themselves.[6] For many of us, social networking has become an integral part of our daily lives.

We also participate in social media—watching and being watched—to help others. When Hélène Campbell, a twenty-year-old Ottawa woman, needed a double-lung transplant, she posted a video on the Web and tweeted pop star Justin Bieber to ask for his help in promoting the importance of organ donation. Both the video and the tweets spread rapidly among members of the online community, who responded in droves. Campbell documented her illness, transplant, and recovery on Facebook; her site has been viewed over six hundred thousand times by people in 159 countries, and record numbers of new organ donors have registered in response to Campbell's campaign.[7] On sites such as Patients Like Me (http://www.patientslikeme.com/), people can post the details of their medical condition so that this information can be pooled with data from others and used for health research.

Sharing information in these contexts can be both caring and productive. In the online world, we all watch each other and know that, in turn, others are watching us. Watching and being watched is the point of social networking: the greater sense of connectedness that many of us now feel to the world around us is arguably a result in part of the ease with which we can share our lives and interests with others. Keeping in touch with friends and family, following our favourite shows and celebrities, enjoying our interests, and shopping are all more convenient precisely because we share so much about our private lives with people online. However, when someone *else*—an employer, a police officer, a fraudster, a stalker, a marketer, or even a nosy neighbour—oversteps the boundaries and submits us to too much scrutiny, we are left feeling both invaded and vulnerable.

In the online environment, there is no simple way to distinguish institutional surveillance from individual surveillance. On the one hand, the consequences can be similar: both the police and an abusive spouse can monitor an individual's social networking profile for the purposes of control. The individual will experience this monitoring as a form of surveillance in spite of the fact that one watcher is an institution and the other is an individual. On the other hand, we may be willing to accept surveillance from institutions who seek to care for us—public health organizations monitoring social networks to identify outbreaks of contagious diseases come to mind—and yet be uncomfortable with the caring gaze of a neighbour.

At the same time, the distinctions between institutional and individual monitoring can matter. There is a qualitative difference between checking out someone's social media profile out of simple curiosity and the kinds of monitoring that governments and businesses conduct using large databases and sophisticated mining, profiling, and analytical techniques. Moreover, individual monitoring may amplify institutional monitoring. Every time we post personal information online, we inadvertently participate in our own surveillance because the information is easily captured by a variety of actors—from marketers, to the state, to identity thieves—who use it for their own purposes.[8]

Laws designed to protect us from unwanted monitoring focus on whether we consent to the collection, use, and disclosure of the information we generate when we use networked communication tools. On social media sites, the fine print suggests that we trade our personal information for free access to the site. However, just because people use social media does not mean that they are willing to give up their privacy. The "privacy paradox"—the fact that people who report a high level of concern about their own privacy continue to disclose personal information in order to gain a benefit of some kind—continues to confound policy makers, who tend to equate privacy with secrecy. But our privacy expectations on social media are far more complicated. Consider some recent statistics. Seventy-two percent of Canadians agreed with the statement "When someone posts something on social media, it is fair game for anyone to search it out and view it." But almost the same percentage of people (75 percent) reported that they are concerned about other people invading their privacy by viewing their information on social media. Two-thirds (67 percent) agreed that if people were aware of what they were finding out about them through social media, they would be embarrassed or unhappy about it.[9]

## Youth and Social Media

Young Canadians are perhaps the most sensitive to the problems of online surveillance. In a recent qualitative study conducted for MediaSmarts, Canadian teens lamented the high degree of monitoring to which they are subjected by their parents and teachers.[10] Many of them have incorporated social media into their everyday communications with friends, but parents often fear online interactions and, accordingly, fall back on surveillance to keep their children safe. Most of the teens—and parents—who participated in the study equated this kind of parental surveillance with spying,

## Child's Play

From the early days of the Web, marketers and organizations have competed for the attention of the youngest Web users—children. Webkinz, owned and operated by the Canadian toy company Gantz, encourages children to come back to its site often by making their virtual pet sick if they stay away too long. Upon returning to the site, the child is met by a downcast-looking pet with a hot water bottle on its head. Children are told that their pet missed them when they were away but that they can make their pet happy again by coming every day and hitting the "I love Webkinz" button on the site.

Sites such as Webkinz typically encourage children to embed the brand into their real-world activities as well. Children are asked to send in artwork and original stories and to hold parties in the real world that involve incorporating some element found on the branded site. An earlier version of online Barbie would even call the child on the telephone to read a bedtime story at night.

Surveillance on children's play sites is presented as a way to protect children from online predators. Parents are told that the sites watch the children to make sure they are safe and

and it made the children feel both untrusted and untrusting. As one teen in Toronto said, "My mom trusts me enough to, like, actually bring a guy-friend home . . . but she doesn't trust me enough to, like, have him up on Facebook, which kind of makes me depressed."[11]

Surveillance by parents makes it more difficult for teens to use social media to meet their developmental needs to separate from the family, grow up, and take on adult responsibilities. To do that, they need both privacy and trust. Consider the words of another Toronto teen: "There should be a point where parents will just like, leave you alone and not have to know every single thing about you."[12]

Perhaps most importantly, the teens who were not routinely monitored by their parents were the ones who were the most comfortable going to their parents when they had problems with online harassment and offensive online content. Ironically, children's participation in social media has made many parents fearful that unseen watchers will prey upon their children. To protect them from these unknown others, parents place their children under individual surveillance, but that action may very well erode the trust that is at the heart of the parent-child relationship. The playfulness of online visibility is, accordingly, closely tied to worry and harmful renditions of caring.

that the streams of information they collect from the children are used to improve their online experiences.[1]

Club Penguin, another site originally created by Canadians and since purchased by Disney, encourages its users to sign up to spy on other children. As members of the Penguin Secret Agency (P.S.A.), they receive a special spy phone, the F.I.S.H. (Factual Informative Spy Handbook), and the ability to enter Headquarters. There, they learn that their "duty" is to report any penguin that is mean or rude, uses bad words, asks for or reveals personal information to other children, or breaks any of the other site rules. Children who keep their spy identity hidden and do a good job of spying receive virtual rewards. In this way, children learn that surveillance is fun and useful, and they become socialized into a culture of monitoring. The legal fine print on the site explains that the information that children release while they are on the site—including any artwork, stories, or other original material that they post there—becomes the property of the corporation.

1. Based on a study conducted in 2009. See Gary T. Marx and Valerie Steeves, "From the Beginning: Children as Subjects and Agents of Surveillance," *Surveillance and Society* 7, no. 3 (2010): 6-45.

The young Canadians in the MediaSmarts study said that they were also aware that their friends and peers were monitoring them, and they relied on a set of social rules to help them navigate their online exposure. For example, there are strong taboos, especially for girls, against posting embarrassing pictures of friends, and when someone is mean to a friend online, others try to post positive things about their friend to help them repair their reputation. They also use a number of privacy-protective strategies, such as posting only song lyrics and quotations that "insiders" will understand or creating more than one Facebook account so they can limit what their family members see. It appears, then, that a series of social rules is emerging among these groups that helps to control visibility and regulate who is watching whom.

But these young Canadians were also aware that information posted online is leaky and that, whatever they do, others may see it even when high privacy settings have been used. Information posted for one audience— friends or family—is sometimes viewed by other audiences, with unintended consequences. In addition to malevolent individuals, like identity thieves and burglars, who troll social media for personal information that can be used to commit fraud or identify houses of homeowners who are on vacation, a growing legion of organizations collect our data for their own purposes.

## Institutional Surveillance via Social Media

Sometimes the process is transparent. The visibility that comes with online participation makes it easier for information to cross lines: photos, videos, and text posted in one context can be used in another to hold people to account publicly for how they behave in their private lives. For example, on rare and controversial occasions, an employer looking to hire new staff has asked for a potential employee's Facebook password so that the employer can see everything that has been posted on the site before making a hiring decision. And a number of professionals, including teachers, have been disciplined or fired for their postings on social media. These cases remind us that the boundary is very porous between playful publicity and more conventional, top-down forms of surveillance.

More typically, however, the information flow is hidden, and we are unaware of how our information is used by others to shape our experiences and limit our opportunities. Again, the statistics are revealing. Eighty percent of Canadians surveyed believe that they have a say in what happens to their personal information, and the vast majority are opposed to corporations being able to scan email messages for information about people's interests (96 percent), to track the content of their Internet searches (88 percent), to share information about the websites they visit (90 percent), or to share the information they post on their social media sites (90 percent).[13] Yet all of these practices are common, driven by a business model that profits from the information we reveal as we go about our online lives.[14] The specifics are hidden in terms of use agreements and privacy policies that are continuously criticized for being difficult to understand and are fuelled by data-mining technologies that seek to divide people into categories so they can be offered services and targeted with advertisements.

The multidirectional visibility associated with social media is the direct effect of the operation of algorithms that are designed to categorize people in accordance with the logic of the marketplace. Through Facebook, Instagram, Pinterest, and other social media, we contribute to the classifications made by other agencies that use our data. When we post our preferences, habits, musical and food tastes, political viewpoints, or religious commitments, this places us in categories. Using privacy settings does not stop others from assessing and judging us; corporations can tell a great deal about us just by looking at the "friends" with whom we are linked online.

Most people assume that this kind of information is only used to determine which ads we are "served" when we are online. The fact that advertising is now embedded into our social world is interesting in many ways. Although most people (mistakenly) assume that they are immune to the influence of ads, advertising has a significant impact on our relationships, our view of the good life, and the kind of people we want to be. But advertising is just the tip of the iceberg. Corporations use the information they gather about us to reconstruct the social environment itself in order to promote certain kinds of identities and relationships that advance corporate interests. Online playgrounds collect children's personal information and use it to embed the brand into their sense of who they are. Sites using social media to sell tampons offer "advice" to teenaged girls and encourage them to talk to the corporation when they cannot talk to their mothers as they did when they were children. Facebook suggests to users that they add certain products to their "likes" to help them express their individuality. All of this shapes and constrains the kinds of people we are, often without our knowing it.

In addition, social media do not always make us visible in the ways we prefer to be visible: that is, the categories into which we are placed do not necessarily fit with how we see ourselves. This is particularly problematic for people who are marginalized in some way. For example, profiling is used to determine which group of people is likely to spend the most on certain goods. Stores seeking to sell furniture, electronics, and household goods have moved out of poorer areas in Ottawa because the people who live there do not fall into the demographic category that the store is seeking to attract. Because of this, those left behind may now have to take public transit to a store farther away just to buy food. The freebies offered to individuals who are profiled as desirable consumers are based on a system in which others who are more vulnerable get less.

The same is true for those of us who come to the attention of the authorities. Social media make it much easier for governments to identify and monitor people who are collecting employment insurance or social welfare benefits or are participating in political dissent. The traditional standard for state surveillance—reasonable and probable grounds to suspect that a crime has occurred—is side-stepped when policing agencies can simply go online and watch citizens. Ironically, privacy laws have made this easier by permitting organizations like Facebook or Google to disclose personal information to police and intelligence agencies upon request, and without a warrant,

## Social Media and the 2011 Vancouver Riots

People turn to social media to stay connected, but social media may also be used for a populist kind of criminal justice. Sites like Facebook allow new kinds of surveillance in which visibility becomes a form of punishment through public naming and shaming.

On 15 June 2011, the Vancouver Canucks lost the Stanley Cup Final to the Boston Bruins. Following this upset, roughly one hundred thousand people began to riot in Vancouver. Participants set cars on fire, looted storefronts, and assaulted bystanders. Although hockey riots have occurred in the past, public opinion of them has always been low. But, until recently, rioters have been shielded from public scrutiny. Like many aspects of social life, the ubiquity of mobile devices and social media platforms has changed visibility of rioters.

Almost immediately after the Vancouver riot began, people turned to Facebook to express their outrage. Riot-themed groups emerged, and one entitled "Vancouver Riot Pics: Post Your Photos" garnered more than one hundred thousand users, over five million views, and countless photographs in less than five days. Content came from multiple sources, including users' own cameras, television stills, and police footage, but images were also taken from suspected rioters' own profiles. While the legal admissibility of this "evidence" was questionable, this type of group marks a shift toward greater policing of social life through social media and mobile technology. Users directly contributed photographs, names, and descriptions of incidents. They

in the course of an investigation relating to the enforcement of any law of Canada, of a province, or of a foreign jurisdiction. This is a low legal threshold for an extensive surveillance capability.

These kinds of practices raise significant concerns about the democratic relationship between the citizen and the state. Access-to-information and privacy laws were passed in the 1970s to ensure that the state would be transparent to the citizen so that the citizen could hold the state to account for its actions. The citizen, however, was entitled to privacy from the state because privacy is what enables citizens to enjoy autonomy. Today, it is increasingly easy for the state to access information about the private lives of citizens. For example, one Alberta man was convicted of an assault after he posted "I superman punched a guy" on his Facebook status; when he testified in court that he did not hit the victim, the judge did not believe him because of his online comment (*R. v. Tscherkassow*, 2010 ABPC 324). In another case, three

also directed anger toward visible targets. Suspected rioters were embroiled in a virtual witch hunt, and many people were stigmatized as a result. Camille Cacnio, a local university student, was caught on video looting a clothing store. She was publicly identified, which, in addition to prompting the normal legal responses, offered her up to a city looking for a scapegoat. Cacnio became the target of hateful speech, much of it racist and sexist. This hate campaign spread elsewhere on the Internet and had an immediate impact on her quality of life. She was fired from her job and is now permanently visible on the Internet for what will probably be the most shameful incident in her life.

While rioters should be held accountable for their actions, the way they were pursued and vilified on social media marks the rise of a troubling kind of online vigilantism. The mob mentality that fuelled the riot was matched by an online mob mentality. All of the harm associated with surveillance—including profiling, prejudice, and the curbing of life chances—was effectively surrendered to the crowd. This online crowd was not held accountable to any professional standards. Although users might have believed that they were helping the police, such crowds can actually be a burden to police because their responses can lead to further social harm (suspected rioters receiving threats, families having to move out of town, etc.). Police are experimenting with techniques and technologies to monitor social media content, including open source intelligence, lawful interception, and social engineering. One has to wonder what kinds of surveillance will occur the next time hockey fans take to the streets.

teens in British Columbia were suspended from school after participating in a fight that was videotaped and posted on YouTube, even though the fight was consensual and no criminal charges could be laid. The teen who posted the video was also threatened with suspension.[15] In both cases, incidents unlikely to have attracted official sanction were brought to the attention of authorities because of social media.

At the same time, the processes through which the government collects information about citizens often take place behind closed doors, without any judicial oversight, as data are mined, matched, and run through algorithms to determine risk. This switch—from state transparency and citizen privacy toward citizen transparency and state privacy—threatens to upset the democratic balance.

But visibility is a two-edged sword. Social media have also played a role in calling the state to account for abuses of power. The video of Stacy Bonds's

## Officer Bubbles

*If the bubble touches me, you're going to be arrested for assault.*
—"Officer Bubbles" of the Toronto Police Service

This is hardly the kind of statement you would expect from a constable in the Toronto Police Service. Yet a quick YouTube search for "Officer Bubbles" will direct you to a video depicting an officer assertively declaring exactly that—just before arresting a woman for blowing bubbles at him. According to Officer Bubbles, whose real name is Constable Adam Josephs, blowing bubbles is equivalent to assault since bubble "detergent" can do harm if it enters someone's eyes.

Officer Bubbles became an Internet celebrity when a video of his arrest of Courtney Winkels, the bubble blower, was released online. The original video received more than nine hundred thousand views and became a topic of conversation on a number of national and international news outlets. The video also inspired creative responses from Internet users, including a cartoon series in which an animated Constable Josephs arrests Santa Claus and Barack Obama.

The Officer Bubbles incident is just one example of a number of bizarre policing incidents brought to the public eye by a citizen's camera. The incident suggests that while police officers

---

strip search by members of the Ottawa police and another of a police officer pushing a disabled woman to the ground in Vancouver's Downtown Eastside spread rapidly on YouTube, mobilizing citizen concerns and demands for accountability.[16] And cellphone footage of police actions posted during the G20 protest in Toronto helped to bring questions about abuse of power to the forefront of the debate over globalization.[17]

Our complicated relationship with surveillance makes it both easier and harder to hold powerful institutions to account. Certainly, we can expect more struggles in the future over who will control the products of all of this monitoring. Some American jurisdictions have already made it illegal for citizens to take videos of police, and Apple has recently patented a device that would let the police disable the recording function on wireless devices within a defined area. But backing away from social media may no longer be an option. Not only does refusing to disclose information about ourselves make it more difficult to find out about upcoming events or to participate in public

have always been highly visible as uniformed representatives of the justice system, the afford-ability and availability of cameras over the past decade has allowed citizens and activists to significantly enhance their visibility. Portable cameras have given citizens the opportunity to docu-ment interactions with officers like Constable Josephs and to expose their questionable behaviour via social media websites.

Furthermore, cameras and social media have given the public opportunities to review and cri-tique the behaviour of officers while voicing their concerns with policing institutions. It follows that police officers are susceptible to novel surveillance regimes that encourage public discussions about police incidents and to a new form of performance review. The political implications of these surveillance regimes are ambiguous and complex, encouraging questions like, Will this surveil-lance hinder police officers' ability to serve the public? And will the public's ability to monitor police officers deter deviant policing practices? There are no simple answers since the implications of this new visibility in policing are often ambiguous and require in-depth research. That said, one reality of policing's new visibility is that information about police is more available than ever before, creating new challenges for police organizations and their ability to manage their public image.[1]

1. See Andrew John Goldsmith, "Policing's New Visibility," *British Journal of Criminology* 50, no. 5 (2010): 9

discussions about the issues of the day; it also makes it harder to buy prod-ucts, qualify for a bank loan, and get a job.

## Conclusion

Social media, then, have at least two faces as far as surveillance is concerned. We use networked technologies to watch—and be watched by—our friends, neighbours, and family. But because of that, it becomes harder to separate the social flow of information within the community from the instrumental use of that information by governments, employers, and businesses. Even though very few of us amass huge databases on others, we all contribute to those data-bases by posting the details of our private lives, and the lives of others, online.

It is likely that social media will continue to be a means of connecting, sharing, and keeping in touch. They will also help us to "watch out for"—care for—others in an increasingly fragmented and anonymous world. Many stories—like that of Ottawa's Hélène Campbell—circulate about how people struck by accident or illness have been helped by distant others, connected through social media. But new issues related to watching and the implications of social media surveillance must be addressed.

The challenge here goes beyond the fact that you never know who might be watching, or why, or with what consequences. If surveillance is practiced in a context considered "fun," it not only renders "harmless" what might actually be the opposite for some, but it also helps to domesticate surveillance, to make it more natural and taken for granted.[18] It might embarrass or hurt others if they knew we were monitoring them, but we still do it. What government departments or corporations do, always with the potential for harm, we now feed into without blinking. In a profound sense, the call to be our brother's and sister's keeper has to be rethought for a digital age. In a world where we routinely monitor others and know that they are monitoring us, we must ask whether our surveillance is *of* others or *for the benefit of* others.

## Notes

1   John L. Locke, *Eavesdropping: An Intimate History* (Oxford: Oxford University Press, 2010).

2   See Julie E. Cohen, *Configuring the Networked Self: Law, Code, and the Play of Everyday Practice* (New Haven: Yale University Press, 2012); Daniel J. Solove, *Understanding Privacy* (Cambridge, MA: Harvard University Press, 2008); and Valerie Steeves, "Reclaiming the Social Value of Privacy," in *Privacy, Identity and Anonymity in a Networked World: Lessons from the Identity Trail*, ed. Ian Kerr, Valerie Steeves, and Carole Lucock (New York: Oxford University Press, 2009), 191–208.

3   Andrew John Goldsmith, "Policing's New Visibility," *British Journal of Criminology* 50, no. 5 (2010): 914–34.

4   Michael Oliveira, "Canada 'Most Socially Networked' Title Slipping Away," *Globe and Mail,* 29 February 2012, http://www.theglobeandmail.com/technology/digital-culture/social-web/canadas-most-socially-networked-title-slipping-away/article550205/.

5   Angus Reid Global, "Privacy and Surveillance: June 2012 Globalization of Personal Data Follow-Up" (Vancouver: Angus Reid Global, 2012),

6   Valerie Steeves, *Young Canadians in a Wired World, Phase II: Trends and Recommendations* (Ottawa: MediaSmarts, 2004), and *Young Canadians in a Wired World, Phase III: Talking to Youth and Parents About Life Online* (Ottawa: MediaSmarts, 2012), http://mediasmarts.ca/research-policy.

7   Barbara Turnbull, "Ottawa's Hélène Campbell Dreaming of Future, and More Transplant Donors," *Toronto Star,* 3 June 2012, http://www.thestar.com/life/2012/06/03/ottawas_hlne_campbell_dreaming_of_future_and_more_transplant_donors.html.

8   See Daniel Trottier, *Social Media as Surveillance: Rethinking Visibility in a Networked World* (London: Ashgate, 2012); and John Cheney-Lippold, "A New Algorithmic Identity: Soft Biopolitics and the Modulation of Control," *Theory, Culture and Society* 28, no. 6 (2011): 164–81.

9   Lyon and Smith, "Surveillance, Social Media and Participation."

10  Steeves, *Young Canadians in a Wired World, Phase III: Talking to Youth and Parents About Life Online,* 16–24.

11  Ibid., 19.

12  Ibid., 18.

13  Lyon and Smith, "Surveillance, Social Media and Participation."

14  See Mark Andrejevic, "The Kinder, Gentler Gaze of Big Brother: Reality TV in the Era of Digital Capitalism, *New Media and Society* 4, no. 2 (2002): 251–70; Mark Andrejevic, *iSpy: Surveillance and Power in the Interactive Era* (Lawrence: University Press of Kansas, 2007); Mark Andrejevic, "Exploitation in the Data Mine," in *Internet and Surveillance: The Challenges of Web 2.0 and Social Media,* ed. Christian Fuchs, Kees Boersma, Anders Albrechtslund, and Marisol Sandoval (London and New York: Routledge, 2012), 71–88; and Nicole S. Cohen, "The Valorization of Surveillance: Towards a Political Economy of Facebook," *Democratic Communiqué* 22, no. 1 (2008): 5–22.

15  Jason Hewlett, "School District Investigates YouTube Fight Video," *Daily News* (Kamloops), 9 June 2011, http://www.kamloopsnews.ca/article/20110609/KAMLOOPS0101/306099985/-1/kamloops/.

16  "Stacy Bonds Police Video," https://www.youtube.com/watch?v=P71BvVCbFXk; "CCTV: Vancouver Police Shoving Down 90 Pound Woman with Multiple Sclerosis in Downtown Eastside," https://www.youtube.com/watch?v=n8K7j5olaeg.

17  "Adam Nobody Gets Beat Up by Police," https://www.youtube.com/watch?v=NI2b8igEYc8.

18  See Ariane Ellerbrok, "Playful Biometrics: Controversial Technologies Through the Lens of Play," *Sociological Quarterly* 52, no. 4 (2011): 528–47.

# Conclusion
## What Can Be Done?

It is tempting to conclude that the various trends identified in this report are simply unstoppable. Some people believe that. Sometimes that message comes across loud and clear from individuals and organizations that have vested interests in using the latest technologies to process more and more personal data for profit. The words of Scott McNealy of Sun Microsystems, spoken some ten years ago, continue to echo: "You have zero privacy anyway. Get over it."[1]

As the nine trends discussed here show, this advice is simplistic and slanted. Personal data are used by all kinds of organizations, with varying results, for better or for worse. But, generally speaking, organizational power over individuals is bolstered by most kinds of surveillance. Following the thrust of this book, we must label as "surveillance" many more practices than just wiretapping or the trailing of suspects by police. McNealy's dismissal of privacy is simplistic because it fails to note the wide range of surveillance practices, and it is slanted because it deflects attention from the real power of those practices in people's everyday lives.

So we disagree with McNealy. For all the pressures in favour of surveillance expansion, there exist significant pro-privacy forces that operate in the other direction. Thankfully, we in Canada already have some tools in place to resist the negative impact of these trends and to assert and reassert the simple principle that personal data are not a free resource that public and private organizations can exploit at will. Our lives have become more transparent as a result of increased surveillance. We thus need initiatives focused on ordinary people in everyday life that aim to bring greater transparency to surveillance practices, especially those embedded within familiar transactions, devices, and environments.

Such initiatives require informed action on several fronts. Surveillance can only be stemmed if a number of approaches are used: law, self-regulation, activism, education, and technological protections as well as old-fashioned political pressure. There is enough evidence to conclude that sometimes, in some contexts, organizations can be forced to halt, and occasionally reverse, the patterns of information accumulation and mishandling documented in this volume.

An obvious place to start is the law.

Privacy does have some constitutional protection. Section 8 of the Canadian Charter of Rights and Freedoms states: "Everyone has the right to be secure against unreasonable search or seizure." The courts have interpreted section 8 to mean that the police generally need to get a warrant before they can put a citizen under surveillance. Indeed, any time the police conduct a search without a warrant, it is up to the state to prove that the search did not violate the individual's reasonable expectation of privacy. If the police cannot do that, the courts will generally throw out any evidence obtained through the search.

However, when it comes to applying section 8, the devil is in the details. The Supreme Court tends to divide privacy into discrete but related categories of bodily privacy, territorial privacy, and information privacy. The strongest protections have been given to bodily privacy because it "protects bodily integrity, and in particular the right not to have our bodies touched or explored to disclose objects or matters we wish to conceal."[2] Less protection is given to territorial privacy, depending on your location. The courts are especially concerned about protecting privacy inside the home. Once you leave your home, however, that protection weakens.

Informational privacy tends to be at the bottom of the hierarchy and attracts the weakest protections. Nonetheless, the Supreme Court has recognized that citizens have a privacy interest in information that "tends to reveal intimate details of the lifestyle and personal choices of the individual."[3] Privacy protection in this situation is based on "the claim of individuals, groups, or institutions to determine for themselves when, how, and to what extent information about them is communicated to others."[4]

One problem is that new technologies have blurred the lines between bodily, territorial, and informational privacy. When bodies and territories can be turned into information, the level of privacy protection too often drops to the lowest common denominator. For example, although the police cannot conduct invasive physical tests without a warrant, they can analyze the DNA in a used Kleenex discarded by a suspect after an interrogation. Similarly, although the police cannot enter a house and conduct a search for drugs without a warrant, they can check the electricity records for a house and see if the occupants are using enough power to run a grow-op.

Now that information about us leaks from our bodies, our territories, and the electronic devices we carry, it is much harder for courts to discern what constitutes a reasonable expectation of privacy. For instance, in *Tessling v. R.* (2004), the RCMP used forward-looking infrared (FLIR) cameras to take a "picture" of heat leaking out from a house that turned out to contain a marijuana grow-op; the Supreme Court said that this was constitutionally permissible under section 8 of the Charter because informational privacy attracts a lower level of protection than territorial privacy. In contrast, the Supreme Court ruled, in *R. v. A.M.,* that individuals do have a reasonable expectation of privacy with respect to odours that emanate from their clothes or belongings and are detected by a drug-sniffing dog.[5] (Of course, legal actions are not the only way to challenge violations of privacy. For instance, opponents of Smart Metering, which allows for two-way communication between a home electric meter and the utility company, have formed citizens' coalitions that have been quite vocal in Canada.[6] Other such responses are examined below.)

Challenging surveillance on the basis of section 8 of the Charter can thus produce ambiguous results. It can also be time consuming and expensive. Statutory privacy protections therefore tend to be more relevant for the average citizen. Over the past two decades, an increasingly complex patchwork of statutory laws has arisen to regulate surveillance practices and protect privacy interests. In Canada, unlike other countries, the privacy legal regime is generally divided between laws that regulate government surveillance and those that regulate private sector surveillance. Things are even more complicated by the fact that three levels of government—federal, provincial, and territorial—can pass laws to govern public and private sector privacy in their own jurisdictions.

Federal government information-collection practices are governed by the 1982 Privacy Act, which sets out the rules concerning how government agencies can collect, use, and disclose personal information. The privacy commissioner of Canada, an independent officer of Parliament, oversees the act and has the capacity to sue, intervene in lawsuits, launch complaints, and conduct investigations. However, because information practices have changed a great deal since 1982, most commentators agree that this legislation is out of date and requires significant reform to confront the kinds of challenges to privacy interests that have been documented in this volume.

All provinces have passed laws governing the treatment of personal information by provincial public bodies. In most provinces, information and privacy commissioners, who are also responsible for the oversight of freedom-of-information laws in their respective provinces, administer these laws.

Private sector information-collection practices are governed at the federal level by the Personal Information Protection and Electronic Documents Act (PIPEDA), which came into full effect in 2004. This act covers all organizations, including foreign companies, that collect, use, or disclose "personal information" in the course of "commercial activity." PIPEDA was modelled on the Canadian Standards Association (CSA) Model Code for the Protection of Personal Information, which contains ten "fair information principles" that mirror those in other national and international privacy laws and guidelines.[7]

Under PIPEDA, an organization that wants to collect, use, or disclose personal information about someone must first obtain that person's consent. When the personal information is particularly sensitive—medical or financial records, for example—the organization must explicitly ask for consent. In many situations, however, consent can be assumed to be implied. The test is whether, under similar circumstances, a "reasonable person" would expect to be asked whether he or she consents to the release of the information.

Because the "reasonable person" consent provisions within PIPEDA depend on the context, the courts have to decide whether consent is or is not implied on a case-by-case basis. For instance, in *Englander v. Telus Communications Inc.,* an individual brought a complaint under PIPEDA against a national telephone company because the company did not disclose that it was selling customer information in electronic form to third-party marketing companies.[8] In balancing the customer's right to privacy against industry needs, the court held that first-time customers must be told before their information becomes publicly available and that they can choose not to be publicly listed and thereby prevent this information from being sold to third parties. In other words, customers must explicitly opt in to the collection, use, and disclosure of this type of personal information.

Under PIPEDA, businesses must also ensure that the personal information they collect is as accurate, complete, and up to date as is necessary for the purposes for which it will be used. The information must also be stored in a secure fashion by, for example, protecting electronic records with encryption and audit trails. In addition, upon written request, companies must provide consumers with access to the personal information stored by the organization so that any errors in the information can be corrected.

Although PIPEDA is a federal statute, it also applies to personal information collected by organizations regulated by the provinces unless the province in question already has "substantially similar" legislation. Québec, British Columbia, and Alberta currently have such laws.

In summary, with few exemptions, all organizations in Canada are covered by one privacy law or another. With few exemptions, the personal data collected on Canadian citizens are subject to basic fair information principles. (See Appendix 1 for a discussion of the major privacy protection laws in Canada.)

Do these laws work? The honest answer is "Sometimes." They are crammed full of exemptions and qualifications that the average person would find difficult to understand. Our privacy commissioners are typically strapped for resources, which prevents them from engaging in constant and proactive educational and enforcement efforts and from keeping up with rapidly evolving technology. Furthermore, the federal privacy commissioner does not have the power to order organizations to comply with the law. But even those provincial commissioners who do have order-making powers tend to act primarily as ombudspersons, receiving and investigating complaints, quietly and confidentially, from ordinary citizens and working with public and private organizations behind the scenes. Not surprisingly, resolving complaints can be time consuming.

Many of our commissioners have strong international reputations and public profiles and are continually in the national and local media. They have had some high-profile successes. In 2009, for instance, federal Privacy Commissioner Jennifer Stoddart took on Facebook and forced it to change some of its policies.[9] In 2012, BC's information and privacy commissioner successfully changed the operation of automatic licence plate recognition cameras in Victoria, British Columbia.[10] Sometimes, privacy commissioners try to act collectively, as they did to challenge the government's "lawful access" proposals (discussed in Trends 3 and 7). They are also beginning to cooperate in enforcement actions on an international scale.[11]

Despite the successes of legal challenges, however, all commentators would agree that law is not enough—or at least that it can only operate if it is embedded within a society that has a fundamental respect for privacy. Privacy laws inherently require that organizations be accountable for the personal data they process and that citizens care about their privacy.

A second important factor, then, is the measures that organizations themselves take to advance the case for privacy. There is much voluntary or self-regulatory activity that organizations can, and do, undertake. Within the private sector, it is now commonplace to assert that privacy is good business practice. The reasoning goes something like this: Businesses need customers to trust them. The appropriate management of personal information is key to gaining and maintaining trust. So when a website states, "Your privacy is important to us," the business that owns the site is making that commitment so that its customers will see it as trustworthy. Some businesses even place a privacy "Good Housekeeping Seal of Approval" on their websites. But organizations that make commitments about protecting your privacy need to be made to live up to them.

There is now a significant community of "privacy professionals" who help organizations to comply with the various privacy laws and work to enhance the privacy reputation of organizations. The Canadian chapter of the International Association of Privacy Professionals (IAPP), for example, comprises consultants, auditors, lawyers, international compliance officers, and technologists, all of whom have a professional stake in the issue and who create and share best practices about appropriate "privacy management" and "risk assessment."[12]

Of course, privacy is only important at some times and in some contexts, and, quite often, it comes into headlong conflict with a variety of organizational and technological imperatives that promote surveillance. But lack of attention to privacy can, and does, harm business interests. Huge data breaches, for example, do nothing to help corporate reputations or stock prices. Neither does an adverse finding, or a fine, from a regulator. So private sector organizations have financial incentives to take privacy seriously.

Although the incentives are somewhat different in the public sector, government agencies, too, are keen to avoid the negative publicity associated with data breaches and take steps to avoid such infractions. For instance, many federal and provincial agencies are required to produce privacy impact assessments (PIAS) to try to ensure that privacy is protected when a new policy is implemented. PIAS are meant to provide agencies with a consistent framework to evaluate departmental policies and procedures in terms of their impact on privacy rights and interests. More often than not, however, they are no more than routine checklists that serve to legitimate new programs rather than to subject them to rigorous scrutiny.

Another way to protect privacy is to build it into the system of information collection and use. From the stories told here, you might assume that technology is the root of the problem—and particularly out-of-control technology that proceeds at its own pace, outstripping social analysis and legal remedies. And that *is* a big part of the story. But technology can be shaped to be either privacy protective or privacy invasive.

Privacy by Design (PbD) has now become conventional wisdom in the entire community of privacy professionals. Ontario's information and privacy commissioner, Ann Cavoukian, has promoted the idea most vigorously. PbD relies on seven principles:

(1) be proactive rather than reactive
(2) make privacy the default
(3) embed privacy into the design of information systems
(4) create a positive-sum rather than zero-sum solution
(5) protect information throughout its life cycle
(6) make your information practices visible and transparent
(7) show respect for your users.[13]

The starting point of PbD is that many organizations do not actually *need* personally identifiable data to fulfill some of their basic functions. In other words, we can have security *and* privacy with proper and proactive design. A good example is a video-surveillance system that encrypts the images by default and only allows those images to be decrypted when a crime has been committed and the police obtain a warrant. Systems like this can be expensive, and their development does conflict with a natural organizational impulse to want as much information as possible. All the same, there is now plenty of evidence that technology can be shaped to be protective rather than invasive and that privacy can be established as the default. Technology can be part of the solution.

Other privacy-enhancing technologies (PETs) are freely available to ordinary citizens. Some are basic and low-tech, and are implemented without a second thought: most of us do not want prying passersby to peer into our homes, so we close our curtains to the outside street. But the equivalent of "curtains" against prying eyes is now available online: encryption and anonymous remailer programs for our email, privacy buttons installed in most Internet browsers that prevent cookies from being logged, spam filters, and Do Not Track (DNT) systems that prevent third-party advertisers from following your browsing behaviour. You do not have to be particularly tech savvy to use these devices. Over the years, they have become more widespread and user friendly. (See Appendix 3 for a list of commonly available online tools for protecting your privacy.)

These examples illustrate that individual citizens can take steps to protect their own privacy and to hold organizations accountable. We are often asked for excessive and irrelevant personal data by government agencies and by businesses. Canadian privacy laws say that the information collected must be relevant or proportionate to the organization's needs. The simple act of asking an organization why it requires your personal information can have an important educational effect on that organization and its employees. In 2012, for example, a prospective tenant in Alberta complained when his landlord asked him to provide his Social Insurance Number on a rental application form. The Alberta commissioner forbade the practice on the grounds that the SIN had no connection to determining whether the individual was an appropriate tenant.[14]

Similarly, in the private sector, Canadians can choose to buy goods and services only from businesses that respect their privacy rights and interests. When consumers believe that a business has violated rights that are protected by law, they can report this alleged violation to their relevant provincial or federal privacy commissioner. And they can also take their business elsewhere.

Research suggests that individuals do resist surveillance. Sociologist Gary Marx has explored the many inventive ways that individuals have found to avoid or thwart surveillance efforts, among them obscuring their identities, distorting their data, and refusing to comply.[15] More radical privacy activism takes this resistance one step further when ordinary people watch and record those individuals and organizations that watch us—someone using his or her smartphone to record an abusive police practice, for instance. Mapping out the locations of surveillance cameras in a city and posting them online is a similar example.

Beyond individual resistance, there is always scope for collective action through civil society organizations.[16] Privacy advocacy organizations adopt several different strategies: they use online and offline media to publicize problems and raise issues, they lodge complaints to privacy commissioners, they engage in important research projects, they promote educational efforts, and they file access-to-information requests. They have meagre resources, but they can and do inform, embarrass, educate, and apply appropriate leverage when surveillance measures get out of hand. The Stop Online Spying campaign against the government's "lawful access" proposals, described in Trends 3 and 7, is a case in point. The success of these efforts points to the important role that public education can and does play in promoting better privacy policy.

Our children also need to be educated about the importance of privacy. The Canadian NGO MediaSmarts has been developing and delivering award-winning privacy education to Canadian young people since 1996. MediaSmarts works with schools and libraries across the country teaching young people to critically evaluate the impact of surveillance in their schools, at the mall, and on social media. The organization also helps young people to understand the important role that privacy plays in democratic citizenship. We can be proud that MediaSmart's approach has been emulated by digital literacy organizations in Europe and the United States.

Let us not also forget that some surveillance is just plain stupid, self-serving, pointless, futile, and ripe for sarcasm and lampooning. Humour has played, and continues to play, a crucial role in pointing out the oddities of our surveillance culture. In 2003 and 2006, the NGO Privacy International awarded Stupid Security Awards to the most egregious examples of absurd security measures.[17] These examples are easy to lampoon because they are visible.

Most surveillance, though, is now routine and embedded, and less and less visible even as it grows more and more commonplace. Surveillance is generally a technique of social power and control that relies on the easy visibility of the one being watched and the relative invisibility of the one doing the watching. It is also designed to enhance the influence of the watcher over the person or group being watched. Regardless of whether the exercise of such power is legitimate or benign, it inevitably challenges liberal democratic norms founded on citizen autonomy.

The conventional way to address such tensions is through openness, public debate, and oversight. The absence of such regulating measures invites abuse and corruption, as those in the privileged watcher position take inappropriate advantage of the less powerful and, consequently, have even more incentive to hide their activities. This poses a special risk when surveillance is embedded in everyday objects or buildings: such practices are rarely visible from the outside and are usually bundled up with the more legitimate activities on which they depend. Openness and transparency, then, are critical to making those who carry out surveillance democratically accountable.

We have described a variety of approaches and tools: law, self-regulation, privacy-enhancing technologies, consumer education, individual resistance, and collective activism. Each can be made to work in particular contexts. They are all necessary, and none alone is sufficient. But do they all add up to a political strategy? Is there a politics of privacy, or of "antisurveillance"?[18] Canadians undeniably care about their privacy, and politicians who forget this can find themselves up against a wall of criticism. As described in Trend 7, this is exactly what happened when the federal government tried to pass Bill C-30, its online surveillance bill.

Being Canadian in the twenty-first century means experiencing mass surveillance; our lives are transparent to many organizations. This makes a difference, not only because our privacy can be compromised but also because our opportunities and aspirations may be constrained. Profoundly, pervasively, surveillance touches us all: it is not limited to "suspects" or people with "something to hide." Nine-year-old Farah's story (in Trend 1) demonstrates that in our ordinary lives with family and friends, surveillance is a constant reality, for better or for worse. The personal is political.

The politics of personal data is focused on making surveillance processes transparent. This happens at many levels and with varied players. Of course, we should be more aware ourselves of the surveillance to which we are subject, whether we deal with data or disclose our own personal information. But to ask ordinary Canadians to discover how they are surveilled and to take appropriate action is laughably inadequate to the current reality. The onus is on those doing surveillance to recognize their responsibilities to those whose data they handle and to make their practices transparent to those affected by them. As the ones manipulating and reconfiguring our personal data, whether it be for profit or policing, they should be accountable to us. Canadian law requires no less, but, in practice, the law is lax and has loopholes.

This book is a wake-up call. We need to be vigilant about the trends we have detailed, aware of our complicity in them, and prepared to speak up for all who are negatively affected by surveillance today—for it is clear that, while we are all affected, some groups and individuals have a particularly raw deal. Large organizations that process personal data must be held to account for their activities. None of the trends is inevitable. Surveillance is reversible. Privacy is not dead.

## Notes

1   See Polly Sprenger, "Sun on Privacy: 'Get Over It,'" *Wired,* 26 January 1999, http://www.wired.com/ politics/law/news/1999/01/17538.

2   *R. v. Tessling,* [2004] 3 S.C.R. 432, para. 21.

3   Ibid., para. 25.

4   See ibid., para. 23, citing Alan F. Westin, *Privacy and Freedom* (New York: Atheneum, 1967), 7.

5   *R. v. A.M.,* [2008] 1 S.C.R. 569, 2008 SCC 19.

6   See, for example, Albert Kramberger, "Hydro's New Smart Meters Sparks Opposition in West Island," *Gazette* (Montréal), 15 April 2013, http://westislandgazette.com/news/story/2013/04/15/ hydros-new-smart-meters-sparks-opposition-in-west-island/, and the website of the BC-based Coalition to Stop "Smart" Meters, http://www.stopsmartmetersbc.ca/html/.

7   The principles of the CSA Model Code for the Protection of Personal Information were in turn based on earlier documents from the Organisation for Economic Co-operation and Development (OECD). See OECD, Directorate for Science, Technology and Industry, *Guidelines Governing the Protection of Privacy and Transborder Flows of Personal Data* (Paris: OECD, 1980).

8   *Englander v. Telus Communications Inc.*, [2005] 2 F.C.R. 572, 2004 FCA 387.

9   Office of the Privacy Commissioner of Canada, "Backgrounder: Facebook Investigations Finding Details," 4 April 2012, http://www.priv.gc.ca/media/nr-c/2012/bg_120404_e.asp.

10  Elizabeth Denham, Information and Privacy Commissioner for BC, *Use of Automated License Plate Recognition Technology by the Victoria Police Department,* Investigation Report F12-04, 15 November 2012, http://www.oipc.bc.ca/report/investigation-reports.aspx. See also Rob Shaw, "Privacy Commissioner Orders Victoria Police to Change Automated Licence Plate Recognition," *Times Colonist* (Victoria), 15 November 2012, http://www.timescolonist.com/news/privacy-commissioner-orders-victoria-police-to-change-automated-licence-plate-recognition-1.24535.

11  On the efforts of the Global Privacy Enforcement Network, see the organization's website, https://www.privacyenforcement.net/.

12  On the work of the International Association of Privacy Professionals in Canada, see the IASPP Canada website, https://www.privacyassociation.org/community/iapp_canada.

13  See Privacy by Design, "7 Foundational Principles," 2013, http://www.privacybydesign.ca/index. php/about-pbd/7-foundational-principles/.

14  Alberta, Office of the Information and Privacy Commissioner, Order P2012-11, 15 November 2012, "G.M.A. Properties Inc. / Alliance Realty Inc.," http://www.oipc.ab.ca/downloads/ documentloader.ashx?id=3125.

15  Gary T. Marx, "A Tack in the Shoe: Resisting and Neutralizing the New Surveillance," *Journal of Social Issues* 59, no. 2 (2003): 369–90.

16  Notable among these organizations are the BC Civil Liberties Association, the BC Freedom of Information and Privacy Association, the Canadian Civil Liberties Association, the Canadian Internet Public Policy Clinic, the International Civil Liberties Monitoring Group, Ligue des

droits et libertés, OpenMedia.ca, and the Public Interest Advocacy Coalition. See Appendix 4 for a full listing.

17   See, for example, John Leyden, "Gongs on Offer for Stupid Security Measures," *The Register,* 22 August 2006, http://www.theregister.co.uk/2006/08/22/stupid_security_awards/; "Stupid Security Awards 2006," *DaniWeb,* http://www.daniweb.com/hardware-and-software/networking/news/218098/stupid-security-awards-2006.

18   See Colin J. Bennett, *The Privacy Advocates: Resisting the Spread of Surveillance* (Cambridge, MA: MIT Press, 2008).

# Surveillance and Privacy Law: FAQs

In this appendix, we answer common questions about government, business, and individual surveillance, with reference to some of the laws that protect privacy rights. Laws can be very complex, can vary across provinces and territories, and can change over time. As a result, this discussion can only serve as a general and preliminary guide.

**How is the personal information I give out to businesses protected?**

When a business collects and uses your personal information, you are entitled by law to ask why it needs that information: a business is allowed to collect only information that is essential to its basic purposes. You have the right to see the information that a company holds about you in order to ensure that it is correct, and you may also withdraw your consent. As a general rule, before a business collects sensitive personal information from you (for example, health or financial information), it must explicitly request and receive your consent to do so. Businesses must also keep that information secure. In addition, they must appoint an individual to be accountable for information-collection practices and must provide his or her contact information. For more about your rights under the main federal law that governs business information collection practices, the Personal Information

Protection and Electronic Documents Act, see the guide to PIPEDA at http://www.priv.gc.ca/information/02_05_d_08_e.asp.

If you feel that your personal information has been mishandled by a business, you can file a complaint with the Privacy Commissioner of Canada: http://www.priv.gc.ca/complaint-plainte/pipeda_e.asp.

In British Columbia, Alberta, and Québec, the provincial privacy commissioners also have jurisdiction to investigate complaints about businesses under provincial private sector privacy statutes:

- Office of the Information and Privacy Commissioner for British Columbia
  http://www.oipc.bc.ca/
- Office of the Information and Privacy Commissioner of Alberta
  http://www.oipc.ab.ca/pages/home/default.aspx
- Information and Privacy Commissioner, Québec / Commission d'accès à l'information du Québec
  http://www.cai.gouv.qc.ca/

In the other provinces, PIPEDA applies, and so you would need to address your complaint to the Federal Privacy Commissioner.

**How is the personal information that I give out to governments protected?**

Both Canadian and all provincial and territorial governments restrict how your personal information can be collected and shared by all levels of government, and some provinces, such as Ontario, have specific protection for health-related information. (See Information and Privacy Commissioner, Ontario, at http://www.ipc.on.ca.)

These laws generally require government agencies to have accessible and understandable policies related to the collection and use of personal information and to collect only information necessary for the provision of services as authorized by law. Privacy legislation restricts the extent to which these agencies can share information. Laws that protect privacy typically allow a person to inquire about what information an organization has collected and stored about him or her, to review it, and to request changes when the information is not accurate.

If you feel that your personal information has been collected, stored, or shared improperly by a provincial government agency, each province has a privacy commissioner or ombudsperson who receives complaints and can act to resolve your complaint. For a list of these individuals and provincial government agencies responsible for privacy, see http://www.priv.gc.ca/resource/prov/index_e.asp.

If you feel that a federal government agency has mishandled your personal information, you can file a complaint with the Privacy Commissioner of Canada. For instructions and related forms, see http://www.priv.gc.ca/complaint-plainte/pa_e.asp.

## Can I sue if another individual violates my privacy?

Four provinces (British Columbia, Saskatchewan, Manitoba, and Newfoundland and Labrador) have laws that make invasion of privacy a tort—that is, a wrongful act that can give rise to a civil lawsuit.* The tort typically consists of a lawsuit brought by an individual who has been subjected to audio or video surveillance or impersonation, or whose personal documents have been read or used.

In *Jones v. Tsige* (2012 ONCA 32), the Ontario Court of Appeal also affirmed the existence of a common-law (i.e., judge-made law) tort of invasion of privacy; as a result, individuals in Ontario can also bring a lawsuit if they feel that their privacy has been unlawfully intruded upon. The cause of action for intrusion upon seclusion must have three key elements:

- the defendant's conduct must have been intentional (this includes reckless conduct);
- the invasion of privacy must have occurred without lawful jurisdiction
- a reasonable person would regard the invasion as highly offensive and as causing distress, humiliation, or anguish

---

• The legislation in British Columbia is the Privacy Act, RSBC 1996, c. 373; in Saskatchewan, it is the Privacy Act, RSS 1978, c. P-24; in Manitoba, it is the Privacy Act, CCSM c. P125; and in Newfoundland and Labrador, it is the Privacy Act, RSNL 1990, c. P-22.

**Am I required to identify myself to the police?**

In general, while it is perfectly acceptable for police officers to engage you in conversation and to ask questions of you, you are under no general obligation to provide them with information. There are, however, specific times when you must identify yourself to police. In *Moore v. R.* ([1979] 1 SCR 195), the Supreme Court upheld a conviction, holding that a refusal to identify oneself to a police officer who was trying to issue a ticket for a traffic offence was obstruction. When a police officer suspects you of a specific offence, in all likelihood you have an obligation to provide your name and identifying details.

**How much information do I have to provide to police?**

If you are a suspect, are detained for questioning, or are put under arrest, several common-law (i.e., judge-made law) and constitutional law (i.e., the Charter of Rights and Freedoms) protections are available to you. You are not required to answer any questions, and as soon as you are detained, you must be informed of your right to consult a lawyer. Everyone has the right to remain silent and cannot be compelled to speak to police during an investigation. However, the police are allowed to question an individual after he or she has consulted a lawyer, even when the person asserts his or her right to silence. In addition, the police may observe a person under arrest or detention and may use statements made to cellmates.

**When can I be searched by police?**

Under section 8 of the Canadian Charter of Rights and Freedoms, "Everyone has the right to be secure against unreasonable search or seizure." Typically, it is assumed that the police need to get a warrant to search you or your property. Any time you have a *reasonable expectation of privacy*, the police are required to get judicial authorization from an independent judge or justice of the peace to be permitted to violate your privacy. This means that the police must present reasonable and probable grounds to an impartial decision maker to get permission to search you, your possessions, or your home. Reasonable and probable grounds amounts to a reasonable belief that an offence has been committed and that some relevant evidence will be found through the search. It is not enough for the police to merely have a suspicion, as determined in *Hunter et al. v. Southam Inc.* ([1984] 2 S.C.R. 145).

## Can I be searched when I am arrested or detained?

Police officers are allowed to search a person immediately after arrest. The logic behind this is that the police need to ensure that the arrested person does not possess any weapons or other dangerous materials. As well, the police have an opportunity to collect evidence that might be destroyed if they take time to get a warrant.

In *R. v. Caslake* ([1998] 1 S.C.R. 51), the right to search after arrest was limited to searches that were directly related to the incident leading to the arrest. Searches that were simply an administrative formality and not related to the actual circumstances of arrest were ruled to be in violation of section 8. In *R. v. Stillman* (1997 SCC 32), the Supreme Court determined that the power to conduct a search "incident to arrest" did not include the collection of samples of bodily evidence from an arrested person.

If a person is simply detained rather than arrested, the police's powers to search are much more limited. In *R. v. Mann* (2004 SCC 52), the Supreme Court ruled that when the police have reasonable grounds that connect a person to a particular crime, they can detain the individual and, as part of that detention, can subject the person to a simple pat-down search to ensure the safety of the police officers, and not for any other reason.

## Can I be strip searched?

The police do have the power to conduct strip searches. In *R. v. Golden* (2001 SCC 83), the Supreme Court ruled that in addition to the reasonable and probable grounds for making an arrest, the police need reasonable and probable grounds to conclude that, as part of a search incident to arrest, a strip search is necessary.

Strip searches are considered to be the most invasive form of search. As such, they should always be conducted in a private location such as a police station. Only in true emergency circumstances should a strip search be carried out at the scene of arrest.

## When can my home be searched?

A home is considered to be a place where you enjoy the highest degree of privacy. Police cannot normally enter, let alone search, a home without a warrant. They are, however, allowed to enter a home without a warrant in certain limited circumstances. In emergency circumstances, police can enter a home to arrest a suspect if waiting for a warrant would risk the destruction of evidence or the safety of people involved in the situation. If a 911 call is made from a location, the police are allowed to make searches related to the 911 call only and may enter without a warrant to do so.

## When can the police search my car?

In *R. v. Caslake* ([1998] 1 S.C.R. 51), the police determined that individuals in cars enjoy a lower expectation of privacy than they would in their homes. As a result, cars can be searched incident to a person's arrest (assuming the person was in or near the car at the time of the arrest). When the police stop a person for a driving-related reason, the search of the vehicle must be related to the traffic stop, as determined in *R. v. Mellenthin* ([1992] 3 SCR 615).

In *Dedman v. The Queen* ([1985] 2 SCR 2), the Supreme Court affirmed that the police have a duty to ensure the safety of those travelling on public roads and therefore have the power to make random traffic stops to determine whether a driver has been drinking or is otherwise in violation of the law. This means that the police need very little reason to pull over a driver and initiate a search in order to detect possible traffic-related offences.

## Can my phone or computer be searched?

In *R. v. Fearon* (2013 ONCA 106), the Ontario Court of Appeal ruled that it is acceptable for police to make a cursory search of a cellphone incident to arrest, providing that it is not locked or otherwise password protected. Beyond a cursory search, or in cases where the phone is locked, a warrant is required.

With regard to search warrants, a laptop or smartphone is considered to be a separate place, distinct from the place where it is located. Therefore, if a warrant is issued for a home or car, and a computer or smartphone is discovered, the contents of the electronic device are not searchable without a separate warrant.

## Can the police search through my garbage?

In *R. v. Patrick* (2009 SCC 17), the Supreme Court allowed the police to use evidence obtained through the search of garbage placed near the edge of the defendant's property for disposal through the city's garbage collection. The court ruled that an individual has little expectation for privacy with respect to the garbage placed out for collection.

## When are the police allowed to use sniffer dogs?

In *R. v. Kang-Brown* (2008 SCC 18), the Supreme Court allowed the use of sniffer dogs in a bus terminal for random searches where there was a reasonable suspicion of illegal activity. This is a lower standard than is required to obtain a search warrant from a judge. There is a higher expectation of privacy for children in a school, however, and random searches are not acceptable there, as determined in *R. v. A.M.* (2008 SCC 19).

## When can police take DNA evidence, and how long can they keep it?

DNA evidence can be collected by the police for use during an investigation, but the police must obtain a warrant to do so.* Additionally, there is a long and growing list of offences where DNA evidence is required to be collected or can be collected after conviction at the discretion of the judge.

In some cases, stored DNA evidence must be destroyed, and, in other cases, it may be destroyed at the discretion of the commissioner of the RCMP. Evidence must be destroyed immediately if the order that allowed for its collection is set aside or if the person from whom it was collected is acquitted of all the charges for which the order to collect the evidence was granted. DNA evidence must be destroyed within one year if the person from whom it was collected is discharged absolutely and within three years if the person from whom it was collected is discharged conditionally, unless there is another

---

* Criminal Code, RSC 1985, c. C-46, s. 487.05, http://www.canlii.org/en/ca/laws/stat/rsc-1985-c-c-46/latest/rsc-1985-c-c-46.html.

order that allows for the collection or retention of DNA evidence from that person.* A refusal to destroy stored DNA evidence can be reviewed by a judge.

* DNA Identification Act, SC 1998, c. 37, s. 9(2), http://www.canlii.org/en/ca/laws/stat/sc-1998-c-37/latest/sc-1998-c-37.html.

# Surveillance Movies

Surveillance has often been the topic of popular films. The movies listed below, appropriate for older teens and beyond, can be useful in introducing the topic to high school or university students.

***The Bourne Ultimatum*** (2007) A super soldier who has lost his memory struggles to evade the watchful surveillance of the CIA agency that created him.

***Brazil*** (1985) After a man living in a dystopian future is wrongfully identified as a terrorist because of a glitch in the state surveillance system, a bureaucrat tries to correct the mistake and ends up being pursued as an enemy of the state.

***The Conversation*** (1974) Directed by Francis Ford Coppola, this classic follows a surveillance expert obsessed with his own privacy as he struggles to protect the couple he has placed under surveillance.

***Eagle Eye*** (2008) Two strangers are brought together when the technology they use on a daily basis is used to track and control them. After their family members are threatened, they agree to commit a series of acts that may culminate in murder.

*Gattaca* (1997) A dystopian look at a genetically engineered future, in which citizens are classified and tracked on the basis of their genetic code. The main character, who has been relegated from birth to the underclass because of his inferior genetic makeup, trades places with a genetically enhanced man so that he can take his place on a mission to space.

*Das Leben der Anderen* (*The Lives of Others*, 2006) Set in East Berlin in 1984, this film follows the lives of a writer, his lover, and the secret police officer who bugs the man's apartment. An excellent look at the workings of surveillance in the Communist Bloc, both for its insights into the exercise of power and its empathetic reading of those who believed in the Orwellian vision of control through total knowledge.

*Minority Report* (2002) Based on a short story by Phillip K. Dick, this film presents a future in which the police can stop crime before it happens. After a police officer is charged with a murder about to happen, the film explores the impact of surveillance on the ability of people to make choices and take responsibility for their actions.

*Rear Window* (1954) This classic Hitchcock tale examines the relationship between surveillance, voyeurism, and privacy by following the life of a newspaper reporter who is housebound while he recovers from an injury.

*Red Road* (2006) A CCTV operator in Glasgow becomes obsessed with following a man who appears on her screen.

*A Scanner Darkly* (2006) Based on another Phillip K. Dick short story, this film explores the use of surveillance in a dystopian future in which the state has lost the war on drugs.

# How to Protect Your Privacy Online: FAQs

In this appendix, we answer some frequently asked questions about protecting your privacy online. Because Internet technologies constantly change, it is not possible to provide a comprehensive guide on this topic, but the answers below provide practical starting points.

**Do websites collect personal information about me?**

Most do. Certain websites make their policies very clear and collect information about you for a variety of commercial purposes, such as customizing the pages you view or deciding which advertisements to direct your way. Many websites bury their policies in hard-to-find and long-winded terms and conditions, while others collect your information without providing an opportunity for you to consent to or opt out of the collection.

**What kinds of information do websites collect that I should be concerned about?**

Websites may collect your name, physical address, phone number, credit card details, social insurance number, passwords, IP address, personal files and folders, real-time activities, whereabouts, tastes, and preferences. Some of this information is supplied by you when you register for a service, but some may be gathered without your consent or awareness.

**Can I guarantee the protection of my personal information online?**

No. The best you can do is to constantly update yourself on measures (discussed below) that reduce the risk of your privacy being violated.

**Am I safe from an invasion of online privacy if I store personal information only on my computer and do not post any information online?**

Not necessarily. If you have not configured your computer's security settings, it may be possible for information to be accessed by a third party or even uploaded to a public location without your consent. This can happen when you open email attachments or install software. Also, certain music players, calendar apps, or photo managers sort your files for you on your computer but also gather information from your computer that they store or sell to other parties.

**How do cookies work, and should I be concerned about them?**

Cookies are small strings of computer code that store information about you on your computer so that you can be identified when you return to a website. The most common way to tell whether you are being tracked by cookies is if, when you return to a website, details such as your personal preferences and profile information appear without you identifying yourself. On websites that you visit often, certain cookies make online browsing experiences more convenient by remembering information about you (such as your name and password) so that you do not have to enter it every time you return to the website. E-shopping websites, search engines, and video-sharing websites use cookies to customize your search results and to select advertisements that will, presumably, appeal to you. Similarly, certain email providers customize the advertisements that appear on your screen based on the content of your personal emails. Disabling cookies in your browser will prevent such websites from placing them on your computer if that is your preference.

### How can I reduce tracking of my online activity?

- Manage your cookies. Although certain websites only allow you to enter if you have enabled cookies, you should think carefully about a website before you grant this permission. All Internet browsers allow you to disable cookies. And some now have a "private browsing button," which prevents cookies from being stored in the first place.
- Remove other tracking technologies from your browsing sessions with the use of third-party software. The Office of the Privacy Commissioner of Canada advocates the use of "Do Not Track," a technology that allows people to opt out of much (but not all) online tracking.
- Use a number of different email accounts. Your primary account should contain your real name and be reserved for communication with individuals you know or groups with member-only affiliation. If you participate in news groups, chat rooms, or other public forums, then you should use a secondary account with a pseudonym. Names or email addresses that you type in public spaces are often gathered and targeted by spammers.
- Use search engines that do not collect your personal information, such as StartPage.

### What is "phishing" and how can I minimize it?

Phishing occurs when a fraudster impersonates a legitimate organization and requests personal information. The request can appear in a pop-up message, on a counterfeit website, or in an email. For example, a fraudster could ask you to provide answers to common password challenge questions. What is your date of birth? What is your mother's name? What is your pet's name? Some phishing scams encourage you to click on a link; when you do, malware (malicious software) that gives the fraudster access to sensitive information, such as your passwords or private banking details, is automatically installed on your computer.

To minimize the threat of phishing attacks:

- Avoid opening emails that appear suspicious (generally found in Spam or Junk Mail folders).
- Never click on links in suspicious emails or on suspicious websites.
- Keep your Internet browser up to date, since this will give you access to the most recent privacy options.
- Make sure your Internet connection is secure or scrambled. To identify this, look for "https" (as opposed to "http") in the address bar. The symbol of a closed lock or unbroken key (usually in the address bar or in the bottom corner of the screen) also indicates that the web page is secure.
- Familiarize yourself with your Internet browser's add-on software. There are many options available that help to encrypt the websites that you visit and reduce your exposure to phishing attacks.

**How can I protect my privacy on social media websites?**

Social media websites have become a regular part of our everyday lives. Many people update their tastes, preferences, and locations in real time and disclose their political, religious, and social views on these websites. If this information is publicly accessible, you increase the risk that others, such as employers or identity thieves, may collect your personal details.

To better protect yourself on social media websites:

- Use the privacy settings to limit who can see your personal information.
- Routinely check the privacy policy of your social media website for any updates and maintain your privacy settings accordingly. This is very important because many social media websites frequently update their privacy policies without informing their users of any changes.
- Think carefully about how you might regret—even years later— posting a photograph or comment. There are numerous cases in

which employers, in making hiring decisions, have relied on the details of a prospective employee's self-publicized private-public life on social media websites. Do not post something that could come back and haunt you.

- If you are posting a photo or comments that refer to someone else, check with the person before you post it. Do not assume that content that is seemingly trivial to you will not be embarrassing or offensive to them. This will also encourage others to treat you in the same way.
- If someone has posted information about you that you are uncomfortable with, ask him or her to remove it. While this information might still be stored by the social media website after it is deleted, taking it down will reduce the risk of more people easily accessing it.

**What Internet connections can I trust and how do I keep my connection safe?**

Your safest Internet connection is usually your home connection. This is generally because there are fewer people using it. Here are some ways to make your online experience safer:

- Update your network key (i.e., your password for connecting to the network) often. Use combinations of random letters, punctuation, symbols, and numbers.
- Use strong firewall hardware and software to reduce your vulnerability to system crackers.
- Disable your Internet connection when you are not using it. System crackers search for unattended Internet connections in order to gain access to consumers' credit card details and other sensitive information.
- Think about the websites that you visit at work as opposed to at home. Employer monitoring, for example, often lets employers record and see all Internet content sent within and from a specific workplace computer. Even if you delete a file on your work computer, your manager may still be able to see it from the back end.

### How do I protect my child online?

- Become well informed about the issues your child faces online. Visit MediaSmarts.ca to learn more about online privacy, offensive content, cyberbullying, and identity theft.
- Talk to your child about the kinds of problems he might encounter and the types of websites he should visit. Although parental control software lets you block content that you deem inappropriate, either directly in your Internet browser or through your Internet provider, use this software carefully. The best way to protect your child online is to talk to him, make your expectations clear, and trust him to come to you when he makes mistakes.
- The most important thing is to establish a relationship of trust between you and your child. Relying on surveillance rather than communication can backfire. Actions like using parental control software, insisting that your child friend you on Facebook, or demanding that she give you the passwords to her social media accounts and cellphone, make it harder for her, especially as she approaches her teen years, to trust that she can come to you when she has a problem.
- Even though the vast majority of children talk online only to people they know, it never hurts to have the "stranger talk" at an early age. Teach a young child precautionary behaviour such as using a nickname; never disclosing phone numbers, addresses, or specific locations; never uploading photographs; and never agreeing to meet someone without your consent or supervision.
- Encourage your child to share his opinions in ways that are constructive and that promote creativity. Remind him that teachers and future employers may see what he posts.
- Let your child know that she can come to you if she encounters comments that are racist, homophobic, or misogynistic; that promote hate speech; and so on.
- Talk to preteens and teens about the consequences of sexting, that is, sending sexually explicit messages or nude or partially nude photos of themselves or others over a phone or the Internet. Once such a message or image is sent, the child can easily lose control over who can see it.

- Encourage your child to come to you for help if someone else has posted content about him that is hurtful, embarrassing, or offensive. Help your child to strategize solutions, such as confronting the person face to face and asking the person to remove the content. If the situation is serious, ask your child if he would like you to discuss the issue with the parents of the other child or with the school principal.

**Can Canadian law help me protect my information from online corporations?**

Yes, it can. Please see Appendix 1 for more information.

**Who can assist me if my privacy is being violated online?**

If you suspect that specific personal information (such as financial accounts) has been compromised, contact the relevant institution (such as your bank or credit-rating company) immediately to protect yourself from identity theft. The Office of the Privacy Commissioner of Canada can also help in these situations:

- If you suspect that your personal information is being used, collected, or disclosed improperly
- If you are having trouble getting an organization to correct inaccurate information about you
- If you have asked an organization for a record of the personal information it has about you and the organization is not giving you access to that information

# Canadian NGOs Concerned with Surveillance, Privacy, and Civil Liberties

**British Columbia Civil Liberties Association**

- Website: bccla.org
- Location: Vancouver
- Founded: 1962
- Stated mission: The oldest civil liberties group in Canada, BCCLA's mandate is to preserve, defend, maintain, and extend civil liberties and human rights in Canada.
- Activities: Advocacy in action, public policy, community education, and justice programs

**British Columbia Freedom of Information and Privacy Association**

- Website: fipa.bc.ca
- Location: Vancouver
- Founded: 1991
- Stated mission: FIPA's goals are to promote and defend freedom of information and privacy rights in Canada and to empower citizens by increasing their right of access to government-held information, by promoting and defending the principle of

universal and affordable access to the basic information channels of our time, by limiting the surveillance activities of the state, and by increasing our right of access to our own personal information and our ability to control the collection, use, and sharing of our personal information, wherever it is stored.
- Activities: Serves a wide variety of individuals and organizations through programs of public education, public assistance, research, and law reform

## Canadian Civil Liberties Association

- Website: ccla.org
- Location: Toronto
- Founded: 1964
- Stated mission: To promote respect for and observance of fundamental human rights and civil liberties, and to defend and foster recognition of these rights and liberties
- Activities: CCLA's work is focused on the following thematic areas: fundamental freedoms, public safety, national security, and equality. CCLA has developed a unique model of advocacy that supports five core activities: public education, citizens' engagement, monitoring, research, and litigation.

## Canadian Internet Policy and Public Interest Clinic

- Website: cippic.ca
- Location: Ottawa
- Founded: 2003
- Stated mission: CIPPIC has a dual mission: (a) to fill voids in public policy debates on technology law issues, ensure balance in policy and law-making processes, and provide legal assistance to under-represented organizations and individuals on matters involving the intersection of law and technology, and (b) to provide a high quality and rewarding clinical legal education experience to students of law.

- Activities: Researching issues and drafting reports and submissions to government, commenting on proposed legislative reforms, providing legal advice to individuals and organizations, and developing online resources for the public on legal issues arising from new technologies

## International Civil Liberties Monitoring Group

- Website: iclmg.ca
- Location: Ottawa
- Founded: 2001
- Stated mission: To defend the civil liberties and human rights set out in the Canadian Charter of Rights and Freedoms, federal and provincial laws, and international human rights instruments
- Activities: Monitoring the evolution and application of Canada's security and antiterrorist agenda, promoting public awareness of the implications of the laws and other anti-terrorist measures, lobbying and carrying out advocacy work, and supporting international efforts to address the impact of security laws in Canada and/or countries with which Canada harmonizes its security policies internationally

## La Ligue des droits et libertés

- Website: liguedesdroits.ca
- Location: Ottawa
- Founded: 1963
- Stated mission: To promote and defend the universality, indivisibility, and interdependence of rights recognized in the International Bill of Human Rights
- Activities: Working with government or other agencies, both nationally and internationally, to denounce situations of violations of human rights; conducting outreach and training to publicize as widely as possible the rights issues that may relate to all aspects of life in society

## OpenMedia.ca

- Website: openmedia.ca
- Location: Vancouver
- Founded: 2008
- Stated mission: To empower people to participate in Internet governance through fresh and engaging citizens' campaigns. OpenMedia.ca is a network of organizations that work together to promote the principles of access, choice, diversity, innovation, and openness.
- Activities: Works to engage, educate, and empower citizens to defend and advance their communication interests, values, and rights. OpenMedia.ca engages citizens through online campaigns and participatory events that resonate with everyday people and by encouraging civic involvement in media and communications policy in Canada; it educates through events and online resources; and it empowers with online tools and open processes that enable citizens to advance their vision for open media.

## Public Interest Advocacy Centre

- Website: piac.ca
- Location: Ottawa
- Founded: 1976
- Stated Mission: PIAC is a nonprofit organization that provides legal and research services on behalf of consumers—and, in particular, vulnerable consumers—concerning the provision of important public services.
- Activities: Legal research, consumer advocacy, education, and lobbying

## Privacy and Access Council of Canada

- Website: pacc-ccap.ca
- Location: Calgary
- Founded: 2002

- Stated mission: To advance and promote awareness of access to information, protection of privacy, and information governance
- Activities: Advocacy, outreach, education, training, and public engagement. PACC-CCAP administers a professional certification program pursuant to defined national standards of competence, professionalism, and proficiency.

**Rocky Mountain Civil Liberties Association**

- Website: rmcla.ca
- Location: Calgary
- Founded: 2009
- Stated mission: To promote respect for and observance of fundamental human rights and civil liberties, and to defend and ensure these protections
- Activities: Protection of freedom of expression (through changes to the Alberta Human Rights Act), advancement of education on human rights and pregnancy discrimination, and advancement of issues related to access to justice

**Vancouver Public Space Network**

- Website: vancouverpublicspace.wordpress.com
- Location: Vancouver
- Founded: 2006
- Stated mission: To champion the importance of public space to the overall livability of the city
- Activities: Advocacy, education, and outreach pertaining to Vancouver's public realm. Vancouver Public Space Network seeks to provide a blend of focused research and design work, creative community engagement, and a celebratory, solutions-based approach.

# Further Reading

**Nonfiction**

Ball, Kirstie, David Lyon, and Kevin Haggerty, eds. *The Routledge Handbook of Surveillance Studies*. London and New York: Routledge, 2012.

> This large collection of essays provides a comprehensive overview of the field of surveillance studies. With fifty contributions written by major figures in the field, it will help to define the study of surveillance for years to come.

Bennett, Colin J. *The Privacy Advocates: Resisting the Spread of Surveillance*. Cambridge, MA: MIT Press, 2008.

> Bennett studies the large network of "privacy advocates" in the context of the broader politics of surveillance and privacy. He details the diverse roles that such individuals can play, from advocate to researcher to consultant, and outlines the many challenges that they face in trying to challenge the expansion of surveillance.

Cole, Simon A. *Suspect Identities: A History of Fingerprinting and Criminal Identification*. Cambridge, MA: Harvard University Press, 2001.

> Cole provides a thoughtful account of the historical emergence and contemporary uses of fingerprinting. This book includes early

difficulties in persuading authorities to recognize the individualizing potential of fingerprints, the colonial uses of fingerprinting, and more recent questions about accuracy. The concluding chapter looks at how DNA analysis fits into this history of individualizing identification.

Funder, Anna. *Stasiland: True Stories from Behind the Berlin Wall*. London: Granta, 2003.
> This moving memoir dwells on the troubling legacies of the surveillance conducted by the Stasi. Opening the secret archives shed light on the state's surveillance practices and created opportunities for people to garner often unsettling insights into who among their friends, family, and colleagues was informing on them.

Gilliom, John. *Overseers of the Poor: Surveillance, Resistance, and the Limits of Privacy*. Chicago: University of Chicago Press, 2001.
> An often unsettling study of how poor Appalachian women in the United States are monitored in minute detail by a sophisticated social welfare computer system, this work focuses on everyday coping and resistance by those on social assistance.

Gilliom, John, and Torin Monahan. *SuperVision: An Introduction to the Surveillance Society*. Chicago: University of Chicago Press, 2012.
> This compact volume is designed as a general introduction to the study of surveillance. In addition to discussing overt mechanisms of surveillance, such as CCTV cameras and airport security measures, the authors explore the surveillance capabilities of technologies that now infuse our daily lives—cellphones, credit cards, the Internet, GPS, and so on—and examine the larger ethical and political implications of these technologies.

Hier, Sean P. *Panoptic Dreams: Streetscape Video Surveillance in Canada*. Vancouver: University of British Columbia Press, 2010.
> This is the most thorough examination of the introduction of surveillance cameras in Canada. The author presents a detailed analysis of the politics surrounding the installation of these cameras in various Canadian cities and municipalities. Questions are raised about the effectiveness of cameras as a crime-fighting tool.

Laidler, Keith. *Surveillance Unlimited: How We've Become the Most Watched People on Earth*. Cambridge, UK: Icon, 2008.

> This volume focuses on the situation in Britain, outlining such monitoring tools as state-driven forms of new identification, radio frequency identification (RFID), and surveillance cameras. Laidler considers how citizens concerned about such developments might respond politically and pragmatically.

Lyon, David. *Surveillance Studies: An Overview*. Cambridge, UK: Polity Press, 2007.

> Lyon details the diverse range of inquiries currently underway that could be collected under the umbrella of "surveillance studies." Readers can trace Lyon's unfolding thought on this topic by reading his books *The Electronic Eye* (1994) and *Surveillance Society* (2001).

Marx, Gary T. *Undercover: Police Surveillance in America*. Berkeley: University of California Press, 1988.

> This acclaimed study of undercover police practices deals with the practicalities and ethics of these practices. The concluding chapter, titled "The New Surveillance," is an inevitable point of reference because it anticipated the rise of new forms of electronic surveillance.

Mayer-Schönberger, Viktor. *Delete: The Virtue of Forgetting in the Digital Age*. Princeton: Princeton University Press, 2009.

> The digital revolution has meant that reams of information that, in other periods, would have disappeared into the mists of history are now maintained on diverse electronic systems for perpetuity. This has consequences for social memory, but it also has political implications since it is increasingly difficult for people to expect that their past actions and statements might be forgotten.

Nippert-Eng, Christena. *Islands of Privacy*. Chicago: University of Chicago Press, 2010.

> The author reports on her interviews of Chicago residents about their views on privacy and secrecy. The main lessons are that privacy remains central to human endeavours and that people will go to great lengths to protect their privacy.

Norris, Clive, and Gary Armstrong. *The Maximum Surveillance Society: The Rise of CCTV*. Oxford: Berg, 1999.

> This volume is one of the first and best analyses of surveillance cameras in England. The authors gained excellent insights by spending extended time in a surveillance control room, observing and recording the various (and often questionable) forms of deviance that the operators both watched and ignored.

O'Harrow, Robert, Jr. *No Place to Hide*. New York: Free Press, 2005.

> O'Harrow, a *Washington Post* reporter, does an admirable job of personalizing the scope of the information collected for commercial purposes. This book offers particularly unsettling details about the often cynical ways in which major information firms go out of their way to undermine privacy.

Solove, Daniel J. *Nothing to Hide: The False Tradeoff Between Privacy and Security*. New Haven: Yale University Press, 2012.

> The author explains what it means to protect privacy and whether it is truly necessary to sacrifice privacy for security. He explains how the law protects privacy, examines concerns with new technologies and the failings of our current system, and offers specific remedies.

Turow, Joseph. *The Daily You: How the Advertising Industry Is Defining Your Identity and Your Worth*. New Haven: Yale University Press, 2012.

> Turow examines how online advertisers track Internet users across websites in order to provide advertisements that they hope will shape consumer behaviour. He raises questions about the political implications of how this practice ultimately reduces the range of information to which consumer-citizens are exposed.

**Fiction**

Asimov, Isaac. *The Foundation Trilogy* (1951–53).

> This is Asimov's classic treatment of the power of prediction. Protagonist Hari Seldon seeks to avoid an intergalactic dark age by applying the science of psycho-history, a branch of mathematics that

can predict the future by monitoring and analyzing the behaviour of a mass of people equal to the population of the galaxy.

Dick, Philip K. *A Scanner Darkly* (1977).
Dick provides a cogent critique of the interplay between anonymity, technology, and law enforcement in a dystopic future where an undercover cop wears a "scramble suit" to hide his identity while he hunts for the source of a dangerous new drug.

Eggers, Dave. *The Circle* (2013).
Twenty-something Mae goes to work for the Circle, a Silicon Valley mashup of online search companies, social media, and other Internet corporations, in which the goal is total transparency, both globally and 24/7. Eggers creates a digital dystopia that touches on the increasing corporate ownership of privacy, with telling Orwellian slogans like "Secrets Are Lies" and "Privacy Is Theft."

Gibson, William. *Neuromancer* (1984).
Gibson tells the story of a washed-up computer hacker hired by a mysterious employer to pull off the ultimate hack. Part of the *Sprawl* trilogy (*Neuromancer, Count Zero,* and *Mona Lisa Overdrive*), this seminal cyberpunk classic, which popularized the term *cyberspace,* examines online communities and spaces and artificial intelligence.

Huxley, Aldous. *Brave New World* (1932).
Huxley's brilliant critique of the consumer society describes a dystopian future in which natural reproduction has been done away with and consumer-citizens are manipulated by the state through the use of hallucinogens and behavioural conditioning. Unlike Orwell's totalitarian Big Brother, the government of the year 634 AF (After Ford) controls its subjects through consumer surveillance and the destruction of individuality.

Orwell, George. *Nineteen Eighty-Four* (1949).
Orwell's classic is still a popular point of reference for discussions of surveillance. Other novels have addressed the prospect of coercive state surveillance, but in introducing the notion of "Big Brother," this book has resonated like no other.

# Contributors

**Colin Bennett** is a professor in the Department of Political Science at the University of Victoria. His research has focused on the comparative analysis of surveillance technologies and privacy protection policies at the domestic and international levels. In addition to numerous scholarly and newspaper articles, he has published six books, including *The Privacy Advocates: Resisting the Spread of Surveillance* (MIT Press, 2008), as well as policy reports on privacy protection for Canadian and international agencies. He is currently a coinvestigator with the The New Transparency: Surveillance and Social Sorting.

**Andrew Clement** is a professor in the Faculty of Information at the University of Toronto, where he coordinates the Information Policy Research Program and is a cofounder of the Identity, Privacy and Security Institute. With a PhD in computer science, he has had long-standing research interests in the social implications of information and communication technologies and human-centred, participatory information systems development. Among his recent surveillance research projects is the ixmaps.ca Internet mapping tool, which helps to make more visible warrantless wiretapping activities by the US National Security Agency. Clement is a coinvestigator in The New Transparency: Surveillance and Social Sorting.

**Arthur Cockfield** is a professor at Queen's University Faculty of Law, where he was appointed as a Queen's National Scholar. Prior to joining Queen's, he worked as a lawyer in Toronto and as a law professor in San Diego. He is a senior research fellow at Monash University in Melbourne, Australia, and was Fulbright Visiting Chair in Policy Studies at the University of Texas at Austin in spring 2013. Cockfield's research focuses on tax law, privacy law, and law and technology theory.

**Aaron Doyle** is an associate professor in the Department of Sociology and Anthropology at Carleton University. His research focuses on how institutions like the mass media, the criminal justice system, and insurance organizations deal with risk through surveillance and other means, and on the security and insecurity that results. He is author, coauthor, or coeditor of a number of articles and seven books on these topics, including, most recently,

*Eyes Everywhere: The Global Growth of Camera Surveillance* (Routledge, 2012), coedited with Randy Lippert and David Lyon.

**Kevin D. Haggerty** is editor of the *Canadian Journal of Sociology* and professor of sociology and criminology at the University of Alberta. His recent work is in the area of surveillance, governance, policing, and risk. Together with coauthor Aaron Doyle, he is currently writing a book titled *65 Ways to Screw Up in Graduate School,* which conveys a series of professional lessons for the next generation of graduate students.

**Stéphane Leman-Langlois** is an associate professor of criminology at Laval University. He currently holds the Canada Research Chair on Surveillance and the Social Construction of Risk, which runs the Virtual Surveillance Lab (vsl), a 3D test environment for the study of the behavioural impacts of surveillance. His latest books include *Technocrime: Policing and Surveillance* (Routledge, 2012), *Sphères de surveillance* (Presses de l'Université de Montréal, 2011), *Terrorisme et antiterrorisme au Canada* (Presses de l'Université de Montréal, 2009), and *Technocrime: Technology, Crime and Social Control* (Willan Publishing, 2008).

**David Lyon** is director of the Surveillance Studies Centre, Queen's Research Chair in Surveillance Studies, and professor in the Department of Sociology and the Faculty of Law at Queen's University. Since 2008, he has led The New Transparency: Surveillance and Social Sorting research team that produced the present volume. Some of his recent books are *Liquid Surveillance* (cowritten with Zygmunt Bauman; Polity Press, 2013), *The Routledge Handbook of Surveillance Studies* (coedited with Kirstie Ball and Kevin Haggerty; Routledge, 2012), *Identifying Citizens: ID Cards as Surveillance* (Polity Press, 2009), and *Surveillance Studies: An Overview* (Polity Press, 2007). He is a cofounder of the journal *Surveillance and Society* and the Surveillance Studies Network.

**Benjamin J. Muller** is an associate professor of political science at King's University College and faculty member in the Centre for American Studies at Western University. He is the author of a number of articles and chapters in the fields of critical security studies, surveillance studies, and international political sociology, with a specific focus on borders, borderlands, security, and biometric technologies. His publications include *Security, Risk, and the Biometric State: Governing Borders and Bodies* (Routledge, 2010) and *Rethinking*

*Hizballah: Legitimacy, Authority, Violence* (cowritten with Samer N. Abboud; Ashgate, 2012).

**David Murakami Wood** is Canada Research Chair (Tier II) in Surveillance Studies at Queen's University. He is a widely published specialist in the sociology and geography of surveillance and security in cities from a global comparative perspective, with a particular focus on Japan, Brazil, Canada, and the United Kingdom. He is cofounder and editor-in-chief of the journal *Surveillance and Society* and a cofounder of the Surveillance Studies Network.

**Laureen Snider** is a professor of sociology (emerita) at Queen's University, specializing in corporate crime, surveillance, and legal reform. Recent publications include *The Surveillance-Industrial Complex: A Political Economy of Surveillance* (coedited with Kirstie Ball; Routledge, 2013); "The 'Great Unwatched' and the 'Lightly Touched'" (cowritten with Adam Molnar), chapter 8 in *The Surveillance-Industrial Complex* (Routledge, 2013); "The Technological Advantages of Stock Market Traders," chapter 8 in *How They Got Away with It: White Collar Criminals and the Financial Meltdown* (Columbia University Press, 2013); "The Conundrum of Financial Regulation," in *Annual Review of Law and Social Science* (2011); and "Examining the Ruggie Report: Can Voluntary Guidelines Tame Global Capitalism?" (cowritten with Steven Bittle), in *Critical Criminology* (2013).

**Valerie Steeves** is an associate professor in the Department of Criminology at the University of Ottawa. She has spoken and written extensively on privacy. She is currently the principal investigator of the eGirls Project (funded by the Social Sciences and Humanities Research Council of Canada), which studies the performance of gender on social media, and the lead researcher for the Young Canadians in a Wired World research project (funded by the Office of the Privacy Commissioner of Canada).

# Index

Abdulmtallab, Umar Farouk, 156
abuse of power, 59, 177–9
Acxiom, 19–20, 106
activists: 48, 66; behaviour of, 48–9; police
    surveillance of, 122
adolescents. *See* youth
advertising 23, 25, 27, 31, 78, 79, 98, 141, 174, 175,
    190, 207, 208, 224: iAds, 90, 98; influence
    of, 175; personalized, 78
airports,
Alberta: Court of Appeal, 72, 199
Alberta Freedom of Information and Protection
    of Privacy Act, 72
algorithms, 7, 47, 50, 63, 77, 114, 159, 162, 174, 177
ALPR. *See* automated license plate recognition
Amazon, 61, 79, 100
analysis: of consumer behaviour, 108–9; of DNA,
    222; of geolocational data, 89, 95
Android, 90, 98, 99, 140
anonymization, 76, 84, 85n4
ANPR. *See* automated licence number
    recognition
antiterrorism, 31, 36, 39, 155, 217, 228. *See also*
    counterterrorism, September 11, *and*
    terrorism
Apple, 61: geolocation, 89, 90, 98; iAds, 90,
    98; iPhone, 89–91; Ping, 81; police
    surveillance and, 178; and PRISM, 112;
    privacy policy, 81
application: Banjo, 95; location-based, 90–1,
    94–102, 140; McDonalds, 98–9; online,
    74, 140, 168; Foursquare, 90, 95, 97; Girls
    Around Me, 95; Toddler Tag, 95;
    Twoogle Geo Search, 94
Association for Unmanned Vehicle Systems
    International (AUVSI), 123
AT&T, 60, 142, 143
authoritarian regimes, 66, 142
automated licence plate recognition (ALPR), 28,
    72, 100–1, 133
automated licence number recognition (ANPR),
    28, 100
Automated Virtual Agent for Truth Assessments
    in Real-Time (AVATAR), 151–2, 164

AUVSI. *See* Association for Unmanned Vehicle
    Systems International
«availability heuristic», 43
AVATAR. *See* Automated Virtual Agent for Truth
    Assessments in Real-Time

Banjo, 95
Barbie, 26, 172
BC Services Card, 138
behaviour, 167: and risk tolerance, 40, 41, 76;
    of activists, 48–9; consumer, 79, 224; of
    gamers, 24–5; influence of surveillance
    on, 32, 79, 84, 101; observation of, 156–7;
    online, 22, 27, 63, 66, 77, 84, 144, 190, 212
Bell, 142
Big Brother, Inc. (campaign), 66–7
Big Brother (metaphor), 15, 55, 68, 225
biometrics, 151–66: at the border, 151–2, 155–7;
    and facial features, 122; and fingerprints,
    27, 117, 138; and indentification, 27, 102,
    117, 118, 138–40; iris, 20, 27, 102, 138, 152,
    153, 159, 162; and locating people, 89, 102;
    limits of, 161–2; at school, 27, 154, 160–1;
    technology, 20, 34, 51, 67, 135, 152–4. *See
    also* hand vascular pattern recognition
BitTorrent, 142
BlackBerry, 106
"black box", 101
blurring of private-public sectors, 55–69
books about surveillance: fiction, 224–5;
    nonfiction 221–3
body. *See* biometrics
body scanner, 5, 12, 67, 118, 138, 162
Bonds, Stacy, 177–8
boomerang, 143–4
border(s), 6, 9, 29, 105, 115, 119, 164: agencies,
    67, 116, 154; agreements, 125; biometrics
    at, 151–2, 155–7; Canadian, 106–9, 116–8,
    144; crossing of, 115, 135, 138, 152, 159, 160;
    protocols, 152; Canada-US, 5, 14, 29, 47, 57,
    112, 123, 125, 138, 152, 165
British Columbia Civil Liberties Association,
    33, 215
British Columbia Freedom of Information and
    Privacy Association, 215–6

profiling, 4, 6, 9, 10, 30, 91, 94, 106, 114, 157, 159, 164, 171, 175, 177

programs (government): NEXUS, 29, 159; PRISM, 112; REAL-ID initiative, 140; secret surveillance, US, 112–3; Secure Flight, 63, 117; Smart Border, 47, 138

protection: of children, 40, 41, 119, 144, 171–3, 191, 212–3; against criminals, 35, 82; and Internet connections, 210–2; of passengers, 63, 117; of personal information, 8, 35, 72, 110, 117, 137, 145, 184, 186, 187, 198, 208; and privacy impact assessments, 157, 188

pseudonym, 81, 209

public: interests of the, 11, 33, 83, 100, 218; opinion, 51, 176; surveillance by, 167–80

Public Safety Canada, 106: minister of, 46, 59, 71

Québec Charter of Human Rights and Freedoms, 8

radio frequency identification tags (RFID), 5, 26n, 88, 89, 92, 101, 105, 108, 109, 117, 135, 139, 147n12

RCMP. *See* Royal Canadian Mounted Police

Real Time Location System (RTLS), 136

recognition: facial, 7, 29, 77, 94, 102, 117, 129, 138, 140; automated licence plate (ALPR), 28, 72, 100–1, 133; automated licence number (ANPR), 28, 100

refugees, 63, 120, 165

re-identification, 76

remotely piloted vehicle (RPV), 123

RFID. *See* radio frequency identification tags

rights: privacy, 75, 77, 137, 184, 189, 190, 197, 200, 215; civil. *See* civil liberties; organizations in defense of, 215–9

riots, Vancouver, 140, 176–7

risk: credit, 64, 83; financial, 12, 39, 43, 46, 47; management of, 5, 12, 39–40, 46, 47, 48, 50, 51, 160, 163; and phishing, 209–10; psychology of, 43; public perception of, 43, 45; and security, 5, 11, 12, 14, 39–51, 116, 156, 157, 160, 163; statistics, 12, 40, 41, 44, 45, 46, 47

risk-oriented society, 40, 42, 45–50

Rocky Mountain Civil Liberties Association, 219

Rogers, 142

routing, 97, 142, 143; "boomerang", 143

Royal Canadian Mounted Police (RCMP), 6, 29, 48, 61, 62, 63, 72, 106, 116, 119, 123, 155, 185, 203

RPV. *See* remotely piloted vehicle

SARS. *See* Severe Acute Respiratory Syndrome

satellites, 88, 110

scanners: back-scatter X-ray, 118; body, 5, 12, 67, 118, 138, 162

schools, 12, 26, 28n, 41, 65, 154, 160–1, 169, 191

Secure Flight, 63, 117

security: airport, 6, 8–9, 12, 28, 29, 30, 105, 116, 118, 155–60, 164; border, 5, 6, 9, 29, 67, 105, 106, 116–8, 125, 138–9, 154–60, 162, 164, 165; at mega-events, 68, 116, 121–3; national, 5, 9, 10, 20, 22, 60; and risk, 5, 11, 12, 14, 39–51, 116, 156, 157, 160, 163; and societal norms, 125, 191; in urban space, 12, 67, 115, 122, 133; and visibility, 159, 160. *See also* organizations

self-censorship, 32

September 11th (9/11) attacks, 12, 13, 20, 28, 39, 40, 44, 45, 47, 50, 66, 67, 118, 138, 155, 157, 163: and airport security, 12, 28, 155; and antiterrorism, 138, 155; and biometrics, 155, 157; repercussions of, 28, 50, 66, 118; and national security, 12–3, 20, 40, 118, 138, 163. *See also* terrorism

services: cloud-computing, 60, 61, 145; commercial, 11, 57, 141; government, 57, 135, 163; location-based, 89, 94, 95, 97, 101; remote computing, 60

Severe Acute Respiratory Syndrome (SARS), 136–7

Smart Border Declaration and Action Plan, 138

Snowden, Edward, 60, 112

social media, 8, 9; and categorization, 4, 6, 95, 174, 175. *See also* sorting, social; critics of, 59, 174, 191; and criminal justice, 176; and citizen surveillance, 168–81; Facebook, Facebook, 3, 7, 9, 11, 20, 22, 24, 25, 45, 55, 77, 79, 80, 94, 95, 97, 98, 107, 112, 129, 140, 168, 169, 170, 172–6, 187, 212; Flickr, 80; Google+, 80, 97; and institutional surveillance, 171, 174–81; Instagram, 80, 174; and law enforcement, 77; online surveillance, 9, 77, 168, 170–80. *See also* Stop Online Spying; Plenty of Fish, 80; and privacy protection, 8, 9, 107, 171–3, 210–1; and self-censorship, 32; Twitter, 45, 48, 51, 60, 94,

107, 168; user-generated content, 79; and youth, 171–3, 191; Zynga, 80.

social networking site (SNS), 79–81, 95, 98, 170

society: Big Brother (metaphor), 15, 55, 68, 225; and censoring the Internet, 142; "dread factor", 43; hate campaign, 177; public-private collaboration, 57–8; self-censorship, 32; transparency, 4, 34, 37, 125, 146, 177, 184, 192. *See also* citizens

software, 6, 27, 29, 56, 58, 66, 77, 101, 107, 111, 140, 208, 209, 210, 211, 212

sorting: of people, 97, 135; social, 4, 6, 7, 10, 12, 47, 50

Special Purpose Embodied Conversational Intelligence with Environmental Sensors (SPECIES), 151–2

stocks, 62, 63, 188

StartPage, 209

Stop Online Spying (coalition), 59, 145, 191

Stoddart, Jennifer, 106, 113, 187

Stupid Security Awards, 191

subscribers, access to data of, 13, 72–4, 144

Sun Microsystems, 3, 4, 183

Sun-TV, 45

Supreme Court of Canada, 185

surveillance: border-crossing, 14, 105, 116–8, 120, 152, 160; of citizens, 55, 59, 60, 63, 66, 101, 112, 145; definition of, 6; everyday, 14, 21, 67, 89, 125, 129–46; hierarchical nature of, 47–8; infrastructure, 7, 10, 36, 119; institutional, 63, 113, 171, 174–81; location-based, 14, 87–102; mass, 4, 21, 112, 192; online, 13, 134, 145, 170–80, 190–2, 212. *See also* Stop Online Spying; secretive (in US), 112–3

surveillance cameras. *See* video surveillance cameras

Tapscott, Dan, 4

technology: and authentication, 153–5, 161; biometrics, 20, 34, 51, 67, 135, 152–4; "black boxes", 101; Google Glass, 90, 102; neutrality of, 152; privacy-enhancing technologies (PETS), 155, 189, 192; satellites, 88, 110; and mega-events, 68, 116, 121–3; vehicle navigation services, 88. *See also* algorithms, data, *and* devices

TekSavvy, 60

telecommunciation systems, 112, 114, 144

telephones, 58, 74, 87, 111, 114, 172: cellphone, 75, 87–91, 93, 97, 129, 134, 140; smartphones, 20, 22, 27, 28, 51, 102, 132, 134, 140, 168, 190, 202; tracking, 27, 88, 101, 112, 136, 140

Telus, 142, 186

terrorism, 31, 36, 40, 43, 46, 50, 61, 64, 112, 122, 157, 163. *See also* counterterrorism, September 11, *and* antiterrorism

Toddler Tag, 95

Toronto, 178: automated tolls on highway 407, 100; SARS outbreak, 136; surveillance cameras, 48–9, 122, 130

tracking: of children, 11, 90; of devices, 24, 84, 88–91, 101–2, 133, 140, 142, 164, 190; global, 108, 112, 117; of people, 3, 6, 32, 42, 89, 101, 102, 117, 136–7

transactions, 28, 50, 61, 62, 68, 80, 82, 105, 125, 134, 135, 160

TransLink, 92–3

transparency, 4, 34, 37, 125, 146, 177, 184, 192

Transport Canada, 118, 154

Transportation Security Administration (TSA), 63, 118

travel, 5, 27, 29, 31, 44, 50, 56, 159. *See also* airports *and* mobility

Twitter, 45, 48, 51, 60, 94, 107, 168. *See also* social media

Twoogle Geo Search, 94

UAV. *See* unmanned aerial (or air) vehicle

UGC. *See* user-generated content

undocumented migrants, 115, 119–20

unmanned aerial (or air) vehicle (UAV), 122–6

United Kingdom: and crime-fighting, 32, 115; surveillance cameras in, 32, 34, 133; use of drones, 123. *See also* England *and* Britain

United Nations (UN), 119, 120, 121

United States (US): agreements with Canada, 11, 117–8, 165; monitoring of personal information, 8, 60, 105, 117; orbital space, 110; passports, 5, 14, 138; perception of risk, 43, 45; secret surveillance, 112–3; use of biometrics, 118, 155, 162, 165; use of drones, 123

University of Arizona, 151

US Customs and Border Protection, 123

user-generated content (UGC), 79–81